Jihad Beyond Islam

Jihad Beyond Islam

Gabriele Marranci

Oxford • New York

First published in 2006 by
Berg
Editorial offices:
1st Floor, Angel Court, 81 St Clements Street, Oxford, OX4 1AW, UK
175 Fifth Avenue, New York, NY 10010, USA

Berg is the imprint of Oxford International Publishers Ltd.

Library of Congress Cataloguing-in-Publication Data
Marranci, Gabriele.
  Jihad beyond Islam / Gabriele Marranci.
     p. cm.
  Includes bibliographical references and index.
  ISBN-13: 978-1-84520-158-6 (pbk.)
  ISBN-10: 1-84520-158-2 (pbk.)
  ISBN-13: 978-1-84520-157-9 (hardback)
  ISBN-10: 1-84520-157-4 (hardback)
  1. Jihad. I. Title.

  BP182.M37 2006
  297.7'2—dc22   2006001701

British Library Cataloguing-in-Publication Data
A catalogue record for this book is available from the British Library.

ISBN-13 978 1 84520 157 9 (Cloth)
ISBN-10 1 84520 157 4 (Cloth)

ISBN-13 978 1 84520 158 6 (Paper)
ISBN-10 1 84520 158 2 (Paper)

Typeset by Avocet Typeset, Chilton, Aylesbury, Bucks
Printed in the United Kingdom by Biddles Ltd, King's Lynn

www.bergpublishers.com

In memory of the victims of terrorist attacks as well as the innocent victims of the 'war on terror'.

Contents

Acknowledgements

This book would have never been written without the help and contribution of many people. I would like to thank all my respondents and Muslim friends for the time they spent in answering my questions and for their great hospitality. I would like to express my gratitude to Professor Kay Milton without whom my theory of identity would have never been developed. My colleagues in Divinity and Religious Studies at the University of Aberdeen have been a constant source of inspiration and provided me with a fantastic environment for my teaching and research. In particular, my special thanks go to Dr Martin Mills, Professor John Swinton and Professor John Webster. Not only did they support me, but they also appreciated my strong Indian coffee while discussing the difficult topics. Some of my undergraduate and postgraduate students have discussed my theory, argument and ideas that form this book. Others have read some chapters or the entire book, providing new insights and interesting comments; among them Mr Juan Caraballo-Resto, Mr Mark Paul Highfield and Mr Dominic Peluso deserve my special thanks. I am very grateful to Mr Mike Harris for proofreading my English and improving the text. Three anonymous readers have contributed to this book with their constructive suggestions, for which I am very grateful. I also thank Berg for believing in this project and transforming my manuscript into a book. In particular I express my gratitude to Kathryn Earle, Tristan Palmer and in particular Hannah Shakespeare, who took care, with great professionalism, of all my concerns during the different stages of production. However, there is one person to whom I owe my deepest debt of gratitude, Olivia. Her emotional and intellectual support and her patience during the different phases of my endless fieldwork and writing-up process were fundamental and essential to the pages that follow.

CHAPTER 1

Introduction

21 July 2005: I am walking back to my hotel in a post-7/7 London, when I see an unusual deployment of police and firefighters. I start to think that London could be under attack again. The closed gates of the Underground and the patrolling armed officers confirm the worst-case scenario. Approaching an Italian restaurant, I can see the waiters, customers and occasional passers-by gathering around a TV. I join them to watch a worried Mr Blair speaking to the nation. The message is clear: we are under attack, and although everything is under control, we have to stay where we are. Walking along the street, I see tourists still unaware of the attack, children playing, old ladies waiting for improbable buses. This time no life has been shattered, no other blood added to the 7/7 carnage. 'Life has to go on,' said the Prime Minister; 'life has to go on,' say the people I meet, yet the sirens of the emergency services remind me that life will not be the same. Many questions cross my mind, the most persistent of which is 'Why?' Why are these people taking their lives and killing innocent people in the name of Islam? Why are they conducting *their* jihad? What does jihad mean today?

To answer these questions, the mass media, politicians and often academics (see for instance Hoffman 1995; Hunter 1988; Huntington 1996; Kramer 1996; Lewis 2003; Pipes 1983; Roy 1994) have focused, among other things, on the political issues, on the alleged 'Clash of Civilizations',[1] on the failure of multiculturalism, the invasion of Iraq, the alienation of Muslims, the social ghettoization of young South Asians, and the radical preachers and imams. All these factors might be the tiles of a complex mosaic, but still do not explain why the mosaic itself exists; why certain individuals, who profess themselves to be Muslim, have decided to kill themselves and innocent people in the name of jihad. In this book, I am not interested in discussing the 'tiles', although I shall consider them, but 'the mosaic'. This means shifting our analysis from interpreting the 'aims' of terrorists' actions to the dynamics of radicalization. Why do some Muslims understand jihad as murder while the majority reject such a view?

Before discussing this issue, let me emphasize a fundamental premise, without which any anthropological analysis produces flawed results: no text, even the most holy, could speak without the human mind reading, understanding and interpreting it.[2] This simple, self-evident (but in the case of religion often undermined) observation has an important consequence, which other anthropologists working on Islam have emphasized. For instance, Donnan (2002: 1) has observed 'what one knows about Islam, one knows, inevitably and inescapably, with reference to the ways in which the other people come to know about Islam.' The attempts to scrutinize the Qur'an to find the Holy Grail of extremism or to describe violent and radical Muslim worshippers as 'traitors' of a 'real' Islam might be useful for political diatribes, but certainly not for understanding why so-called Islamic terrorists exist.[3] The available studies on jihad tend to undermine the role that personal identities have on it, and rather focus on the historical and political elements of jihad. This has facilitated antithetical forms of essentialism.[4] Something which is not new in the study of Islam.

Said's book *Orientalism* (1978) has played an involuntary role in this essentialization process. Said's complex critique of Western scholarship on the 'Orient' and Islam, in particular when focusing on literature and art, has too often been reduced to a Manichaean division. On the one hand, there are the *Orientalists*, the scholars who being in love with colonialism would retain a bias against Islam, on the other the anti-Orientalists, who would claim to represent Islam by respecting the *real* meaning (Milton-Edwards 2002). If we observe the social and political discussion available on contemporary jihad, we can see that this has produced two 'schools of thought', whose members, through their reciprocal denigrating cliché, have been termed neo-Orientalists and Apologists. So, following such a Manichaean division (cf. Sadowski 1993; Tuastad 2003), those suggesting that Islam leads to extremism have been classified as neo-Orientalists by those who deny that extremists are *real* Muslims; the neo-Orientalist has claimed that this latter position was nothing other than apologetic.[5] Notwithstanding their irreconcilable positions and arguments, both the 'neo-Orientalist' and 'apologist' share an essentialistic view of Islam. Let me say that I reject this distinction as useless for social scientific research for it is produced by political interests dealing with the Middle East crisis and, in particular, the Palestinian–Israeli conflict.

An example of what neo-Orientalists would call an apologetic approach to jihad is Noorani's book *Islam and Jihad: Prejudice Versus Reality* (2002). Noorani has argued, 'the so-called Islamic fundamentalist is an *impostor*. He has *misused* a noble faith as a political weapon. Of course, Islam does have a political vision; but it is *far removed from the Islam* which very many Muslims and most non-Muslims imagine it to be' (Noorani 2002: ix, emphasis added). Noorani speaks of Islam as a physical entity possessing consciousness and an authoritative voice, against which the Islamic tone-deaf Muslim (the *impostor*) may be easily spotted. In other words, Noorani has not suggested that extremists are a minority among the Muslims with unorthodox interpretations of jihad, but rather that they are *Muslims without Islam*. The issue is that the *impostors* consider themselves the best Muslims. The impasse is created by the fact that both Noorani and his 'impostors' share the idea that Islam is one. So that only one interpretation is acceptable. Noorani's argument on jihad is theological. Indeed, his argument reminds us that the majority of Muslims love peace and that terrorist actions shock them no less than us, but Noorani in his discussion does not tell us *why* a minority of these Muslims wish to immolate themselves by *their* idea of jihad.

Noorani is not the only scholar who has tried to suggest a distinction between Muslims and Islam. For instance, Esposito (1992; 2002) has argued, '[Islam], like Judaism and Christianity, rejects terrorism' (2002: ix), and has suggested that some people manipulate Islam as a political tool in order to change their societies or oppose 'imperialism'. Esposito has observed, 'many in the Muslim world, like their counterparts in the West, opt for easy anti-imperialist slogans and demonization. At its worst, both sides have engaged in a process of "mutual satanization"' (1992: 172). In his books, Esposito has introduced short histories of Islam (see also Akbar 2002 and Piscatori 1983 and 1991), which, however, have remained rather detached from the rest of his argument. So, the impression is that he is arguing something very similar to Noorani, that Muslim extremists are unable to understand the *real* history of Islam as other religious extremists cannot understand theirs: 'Although the communities in these areas [Sudan, Lebanon, Kosovo, Yugoslavia, and Azerbaijan] may be broadly identified as Christian and Muslim, it is nonetheless true, as with Northern Ireland's Catholic and Protestant communities, that local disputes and civil wars have more to do with political issues ... and socio-economic issues than with religion' (Esposito 1999: 181). Esposito has not emphasized the theological misunderstanding of the extremists, as Noorani has done, but rather the general irresistible temptation that human beings have to manipulate their religion for the sake of political and nationalistic goals. While for Noorani radical interpretations of jihad are treason against Islam, for Esposito they represent the supremacy of political over religious values. Taken to its extreme, this interpretation of extremism leads to Hafez's argument.

In *Why Muslims rebel* (2003), Hafez has suggested that the political oppression of Muslims has caused their rebellions. After rejecting socio-economic and psychological explanations, Hafez has argued:

Muslims rebel because of an ill-fated combination of institutional exclusion, on the one hand, and on the other, reactive and indiscriminate repression that threatens the organizational resources and personal lives of Islamists. Exclusionary and repressive political environments force Islamists to undergo a near universal process of radicalization, which has been witnessed by so many rebellious movements. This process involves the rise of exclusive mobilization structures to ensure against internal defections and external repression, and the diffusion of antisystem ideological frames to justify radical change and motivate collective violence. (2003: 22)

His analysis ends in blaming external repressive and exclusionist factors, but the reader who may wish to understand why these 'rebels' transform Islam into a political ideology of rebellion would again be left without an answer. Hafez has left unwritten any discussion about Islam or Muslims. Yet we know that the suicide bombers who are striking in our Western and non-Western cities use a religious language, affirm religious identities, and see the world through specific religious interpretations. Could we, as Hafez has brilliantly done, leave religion aside?

The scholars who have been nicknamed neo-Orientalists[6] have strongly argued against this possibility. Islam, according to them, is the reason why we have suicide bombers. As Noorani, so authors such as Pipes, Hunter Lewis and Kramer have based their arguments on a monolithic understanding of Islam. Islam, according to these authors, has prevented Muslims enjoying modernization and left Muslims in the dark times of Middle Age. So Pipes, Lewis and Kramer have suggested that to understand tragic events such as 9/11, March 11 and the recent 7/7 attacks we need to go back to medieval interpretations and to thinkers such as Ibn Taymiyya.[7] These extreme essentialistic viewpoints have facilitated odd arguments, such as the claim that Muslims are conducting jihad because they wish to transform non-Muslims into *Dhimmi*.[8] Although certain extremist leaders, such as Osama bin Laden, have used expressions which came from the 'dark age' of the Crusaders and Islamic chevaliers, it would be extremely naïve to believe that behind such Islamic retro-chic styles there could exist medieval minds. We know very well that the context enforces new meanings on ancient expressions. Bin Laden and his acolytes adorn themselves with a mystic aura of the past, but they speak to the present, to contemporary Muslims, not to Ottoman ghosts. In Chapter 8 of this book, we shall discuss the reasons why scholars such as Bat Ye'or, Pipes, Lewis, Kramer and Huntington prefer to believe in the extremists' masquerade rather than trying to get behind it.

Halliday, while reviewing Pipes's book *In the Path of God: Islam and Political Power*, has argued:

this book, for all its range, is deeply flawed because it overstates it
up with that fallacy that besets so many writers about Islam, not lea
faithful themselves. This fallacy is essentialism – the idea, for which the e
is rare indeed, that the behaviour of Muslims through all centuries and coun
can be explained primarily by reference uniquely to their belief system. (1984
583)

In another article, Halliday has strongly criticized the 'neo-Orientalist' and
'apologetic' positions, because these debates have only 'generated much hot
air' (1997: 401). Halliday, rejecting the use of the traditional polemic labels,
has suggested a more accurate description of these opposing academic viewpoints as 'essentialists' versus 'contingencists'. So, essentialists are 'those
who argued that the Islamic world was dominated by a set of relatively
enduring and unchanging processes and meaning, to be understood through
the texts of Islam and the language it generated' (1997: 400–1). By contrast,
Halliday has defined the 'contingencists' as those who reject any universalistic framework and prefer to focus on the 'contingent' realities that exist in
each Islamic country or socio-political situation (as Esposito).

Of course, the dichotomy between these two approaches exists because of
the methodology each side has employed. Hodgson (1993) has suggested
that a third way may be developed, combining the essentialists' and the contingencists' paradigms and concluded that the main feature of any Muslim
philosophy is to achieve the Islamic ideal. By contrast, Halliday has argued
that the study of Islamic societies involves observing Muslims' peculiarities
and differences so that the student can develop different representations of
the Muslim world. Nevertheless, both these 'third ways' have not convinced
the scholarly community. Salla, among others, has argued,

> I think that both Hodgson's and Halliday's attempts to find the 'middle ground'
> or 'a third position' are unconvincing. As far as Hodgson is concerned, his
> notion of the 'cultural unit of Islam', is not, as Leonard Binder [1988] the
> middle ground position of 'pragmatic orientalism', but a notion that is firmly
> located in the essentialist-contingencist debate in terms of an essentialist cate-
> gorisation that is sensitive to cultural variation. It is therefore a variant of schol-
> arly approaches that Said recommends in *Orientalism* – what Binder suggests are
> instances of 'good orientalism'. On the other hand, Halliday dichotomies about
> reality and what is actually out there – the real (Muslim) world. Such a
> dichotomy is a critical part of the methodological debate and therefore fails to
> produce a distinctive third position. (1997: 731)

Unfortunately, Salla has not provided any new methodological frameworks,
but suggested a pragmatic (yet analytically useless) political programme.

l thesis has never been very successful, but
ıg the political and ideological arguments,
ıture attempts to escape the vicious circle
·sus 'contingencists' diatribe.

some past or recent anthropological studies
itique of anthropology of Islam, see Varisco
l (1968) is surely one of the most quoted and
. Although Geertz knew that essentialist
approacries w... ___ risks (Geertz 1973), he ended in presenting an
analysis of Islam (observed in Indonesia and Morocco) in which texts and
myths explain Muslims' behaviour,

> If they are religious men, those everyday terms will in some way be influenced
> by their religious convictions, for it is in the nature of faith, even the most
> unworldly and least ethical, to claim effective sovereignty over human behav-
> iour. The internal fusion of world view and ethos is, or so I am arguing, the heart
> of the religious perspective, and the job of the sacred symbol is to bring about
> that fusion. (1968: 110)

Geertz has argued that the actions of scripturalists (i.e. fundamentalists) derive
from 'the Koran, the Hadith, and the Sharia, together with the standard com-
mentaries upon them as the only acceptable bases of religious authority'
(Geertz 1968: 65). At the centre of his study is neither Islam as a religion nor
Muslims as believers, rather the system of symbols which, according to him,
shapes human behaviour. There are many flawed and weak points in Geertz's
study of Islam which other scholars have noticed and discussed (el-Zein 1977,
Varisco 2005), but the most evident is the lack of real Muslim voices, his
informants are never mentioned, their words never reported.

Notwithstanding the essentialist approach that he has employed, the
author of *Islam Observed* has at least admitted that his interpretation was
only one among the many possible (see also Geertz 1973). Yet another influential anthropologist, Gellner, was not so ready to admit the same, and even
less that Islam could have more than one interpretation. Gellner's theory
has been very influential within British social anthropology until today (see
Shankland 2003).[9] In a few words, Gellner has reduced Muslims to being
products of their religion, and since he has argued, 'fundamentalism is at its
strongest in Islam' (1992: 4), he concluded that *real* Muslims could not be
other than Muslim extremists. The reasons for Gellner's argument can be
found in his most celebrated book, *Muslim Society*,

> What are the ideological cards which are dealt by Islam? The crucial ones are: a
> scriptural faith, a *completed* one (the final edition, so to speak) is available, and

there is no room for further accretion or for new prophets; also, there is no warrant for clergy, and hence for religious differentiation; and, third, there is no need to differentiate between Church and State, between what is God's and what is Caesar's, since it began as a religion of rapidly successful conquerors who soon *were* the state ... The consequences of all this is that the trans-social standard which judges the social is a Book, and not a Church. (1981: 100–1)

Gellner has presented Islam as something historically unique, though the characteristics he has described are certainly not unique to Islam; furthermore, he has overlooked the role that Muslim clergy play within the disparate Muslim traditions. It is true that Muslims do not have a centralized and hierarchical church, but it is equally true that the Qur'an cannot interpret itself. Socio-political and cultural dynamics mark the relationships between single Muslim believers and 'the Book'.

According to Fuss, essentialism is 'an ontology which stands outside the sphere of cultural influence and historical changes' (1989: 3). A clear example of Fuss's definition can be found in Shankland's work (2003), which ideologically compares Sunni and Alevi traditions in Turkey. His essentialism becomes particularly visible when he has discussed gender and Islam, 'My explanation assumes that there is something *within Islamic faith* which assumes the axiomatic inferiority, or at least separation, of women from men (and therefore the power to run society)' (2003: 316, emphasis added). While Gellner has at least developed sophisticated socio-philosophical essentialism, which, however, condemned his study to a frantic Eurocentrism, Shankland has presented an essentialist account that even lacks the sophistication of his mentor. It would be easy to reject Shankland's work as polemic, ideological and irrelevant; yet my criticism *does not* deal with his representation of Muslim worshippers as an oppressive, barbaric and fanatical force (maybe his respondents were), rather I reject his assumption that the 'Islamic faith' *in itself* may cause misogynist behaviour beyond the mind interpreting the text. Paradoxically, Shankland's representation of Islam as an *ontological essence* perfectly fits the ideology of those 'strong Muslim believers' he was condemning. Essentialist positions have discussed Islam but ignored Muslims, and in particular their identities. Identity, I shall suggest, is an emotional commitment through which people experience their autobiographical selves. This could explain why those Muslims who do not practise, or even respect the basic rules of Islam (such as drinking alcohol) still define themselves as Muslim. Simply, because they *feel* to be Muslim.

To observe how Muslims form their identities is very important if we want to understand the current uneasiness within Western Muslim communities. Tensions between Muslims and their Western governments and societies are

certainly not a novelty. The so-called Rushdie affair perhaps represents the
first event that attracted considerable scholarly attention to the European
Muslims' mood. The Rushdie affair also represented the first visible turning
point in the relationship between Muslims and the majority of the non-
Muslim population. It is certain that the affair became *the symbol* of the long-
standing concerns that Muslims and non-Muslims had about each other's
cultures and lifestyles. Some of my Muslim respondents considered that the
affair was the first evidence of that 'attack against Islam' they still perceive
today. By contrast, the famous book-burning demonstration (organized in
Bradford on 14 January 1989) convinced many non-Muslims that Islam
could be a threat to Western democracies and lifestyles. I am aware that the
majority of Muslims who performed that burning ritual could not foresee
the consequences of their actions, and their lack of knowledge regarding
European history left them surprised when journalists compared their
actions to Nazi behaviour (Werbner 2002).[10]

Kepel (1997), in his book *Muslims in the West*, has devoted an entire chapter
to this 'affair,' describing in detail the different phases. What the reader can
grasp from this account is that, apart from its international political implications, the affair became a catalyst for Muslims' deep frustrations. As Lewis
and Schnapper (1994) have emphasized, the image of the Prophet (which,
according to some Muslims, Rushdie's book would have denigrated) has a
particular emotional value for Muslims, in particular when they are of South
Asian origin. Asad has suggested that *The Satanic Verses* has followed the 'long
tradition of Christian anti-Muslim polemics' (1990: 252). However, my
Muslim respondents seemed to react not against the 'Christian anti-Muslim
polemic', but rather against the different treatment of the three monotheistic
religions: European anti-blasphemy laws protect Christians and Jews but not
Muslims. They felt themselves to be the children of a lesser God.

Many political discussions have focused on the Rushdie affair, yet in
which way did anthropologists interpret the first noticeable Western Muslim
'rebellion'? Werbner has argued that a 'clash of aesthetics' caused Muslims
to protest. She has argued that Muslims and non-Muslims have 'two distinct aesthetics, and two distinct moralities or world views. So, the con-
frontation was between *equal* aesthetic communities, each defending its own
high culture' (2002: 110). Werbner's interpretation, which is based on a culturalist post-modern viewpoint, has highlighted the degree of mutual
incomprehension between contemporary Western Muslims and non-
Muslims. On the one hand, the events of 9/11 have increasingly convinced
some non-Muslims that Islam, as a faith, is incompatible with 'democracy'
and 'civilization', on the other, some Muslims strongly believe that the West
has rejected and attacked Islam, not only as religion but also as an identity.

that represents mosques as the 'lions' den' in which Muslims plan their jihads. After presenting the everyday life of an ordinary mosque, we follow the experience of a migrant Muslim man when a suspicious itinerant imam tries to manipulate the emotional context of migration so as to result in my respondent's emotional reaction. Then I present the different discourses of jihad I encountered among migrant Muslims; from the idea of jihad as a spiritual struggle, to controversial, often unorthodox understandings of it. I show how these different 'interpretations' are in reality caused by the rumour, increasingly spreading among Muslims, that Islam is currently under attack.

In Chapter 5, after a short summary of the most important events and tragedies in the Muslim world that have facilitated the development of this rumour, I observe the role that the mass media, in particular Arab satellite TV, have in this process. We observe two Muslim migrant families watching television news concerning the war in Afghanistan and Iraq. By contrast, Chapter 6 observes how Western-born Muslims discuss jihad. After discussing and criticizing the approaches that describe Western-born Muslims as possessing 'in-between' identities, I observe how their societies (which are the host societies of their parents) constantly affirm their loyalty (Haddad 2004). This is often expressed through the recurrent question 'are you British (Italian, French, American and so on) or Muslims?'

In Chapter 7, we see that migrant Muslim women and their daughters are not passive subjects, as some scholars still argue, but active members not only within their families but also among their extended female networks. Their experience of migration is shown to be different from that of their male relatives. Muslim women use their memories and Islamic myths to adapt to the new, often not very welcoming, Western environments. Among the most popular Islamic stories and myths are those of the Muslim women martyrs, who offered their lives to defend Islam and the Prophets but also exhorted their male relatives to show their Islamic honour by performing jihad. Western-born Muslim girls know the traditional stories, but also have new models: the Palestinian Muslim women martyrs.

Muslim women are increasingly attending Islamic circles provided for them by Muslim associations and mosques. They are becoming the 'strong believers' among the members of their families. We observe how some Muslim women tend to compare 'real' Muslim men with their sons, husbands, brothers and fathers. Of course, because of the difficulties Muslim migrant men face, their masculinity is often a shadow of the Islamic archetype. In this chapter, I suggest that if some Muslim men show the characteristics of an honour and shame syndrome, some Muslim women also develop similar dynamics, which can facilitate the rhetoric of jihad within their families.

Today, many commentators link jihad and Muslim extremism to Muslim anti-Semitism. In Chapter 8, I discuss the issue of defining anti-Semitism and whether Muslim anti-Semitism might be similar, as some scholars have suggested, to the Nazi ideal. Throughout the chapter, it will become clear that, although Muslim communities in the West show a strong resentment against Israel and Jewish people, there are ideological and political reasons behind the allegations that Muslim anti-Semitism is similar to that of the Nazis. I suggest that to understand the rise of anti-Semitism among some young Muslims we need to understand a different concept: Westernophobia.

Notes

1. For my criticism of this concept, see Marranci 2004a.
2. Although some of my Muslim respondents have found this argument theologically wrong, the first word that Muhammad received from Allah was *iqra*, 'read!', which also means 'understand' 'discern', which, of course, implies a mind.
3. See Arjomand 1984; Bruce 2000; Choueiri 1997; Cooley 2000; Esposito 1999, 2002; Hafez 2003; Hoffman 1995; Hunter 1988; Huntington 1996; Kepel 2004; Noorani 2002; Pipes 1983; Piscatori 1983; Roy 1994.
4. It is important to remember that the main victims of the so-called Islamic terrorism have been Muslims.
5. Even when the allegation does not survive the burden of proof, as in the case of scholars such as Esposito or Piscatori.
6. Just to mention the most quoted: Bat Ye'or 1978, 1984, 1991, 2002; Bruce 2000; Hall 1985; Hoffman 1995; Hunter 1988; Huntington 1996; Kramer 1996; Lewis 1993, 2000, 2003; Patai 1973; Pipes 1983; Roy 1994.
7. Ibn Taymiyya (1263–1328) was the most important figure in the future Hanbali School of Islamic thought. His texts and conservative religious philosophy is at the centre of the Wahhab school which is the official school of Islamic thought in Saudi Arabia. I suggest the reader who is interested in more details concerning the relationship between the Saudi family and Wahhabism read Chapter 5 in Kepel 2004.
8. This is a medieval legal concept applicable to non-Muslims who lived under Islamic rule. Bat Ye'or (1978, 1984, 1991, 2002) has revitalized this classic Islamic concept by applying it to our contemporary problems with radical Muslims.
9. For an exhaustive criticism of Gellner's thought, Hall and Jarvie 1996, Mabry 1998 and recently Varisco 2005. For an attempt to reply to such critiques, see Shankland 2003, Chapter 8.
10. It is interesting to note that the people comparing this book-burning activity to the Nazi event have failed to observe that the Muslim demonstration might better resemble the traditional ritual burning of heretical books by the Inquisition.
11. See for instance, Alsayyad and Castells 2002; Gerholm and Lithman 1988; Haddad 2002; Kepel 1997; Khan 2000; Lewis and Schnapper 1994; Nielsen

1992; Nonneman, Niblock and Szajkowski 1997; and Werbner 2002.

12. See for instance, Amersfoort 1998; Mandel 1996; Metcalf 1996; Nielsen 1992; Rex 1998; and Roald 2002.

13. See for instance, the five volumes edited by Martin E. Marty and Scott Appleby (1991, 1993a, 1993b, 1994, 1995).

14. Just to mention some studies among many: Duquin 2000; Erikson 1968; Kitayama, Markus and Liberman 1995; Markus and Kitayama 1991; Rosaldo 1984. Yet it is interesting to note that in Rapport and Overing's *Social and Cultural Anthropology: The Key Concepts* (2000) among the key concepts discussed, *emotions, identity and self* are missing.

CHAPTER 2

Jihad: From the Qur'an to the Islamic State

Other authors have devoted time and ink trying to explain the meaning and historical developments of this Islamic concept (cf. Kolocotronis 1990; Manirujjamana 1999; Noorani 2002; Peters 1985; Pruthi 2002 and, in particular, Heck 2004). Yet my respondents referred to historical events, and I think that a brief discussion of jihad in the Qur'an, the Sunna and Islamic scholarly texts would help the reader to follow my respondents' discussions. Let me start from an ancient, but still relevant, diatribe which, although expressed in different terms, still animates the Muslim as well as non-Muslim debate: is jihad a holy war? Although the majority of Muslims emphatically reject such an axiom, we must recognize that historically a straightforward answer does not exist. During their histories, the Islamic states had to face a difficult decision: to interpret the Qur'anic teaching so that any imperialistic aspirations had to be renounced, or to venture into philosophical and theological sophisms and combine their earthly desires with Allah's injunctions. Since power and territorial control are difficult to renounce, Islamic leaders have a privileged political interpretation of jihad over the spiritual elements of Islam. Jihad cannot be understood outside the historical contexts and events. Nevertheless, it is important to explain where jihad is discussed in the recognized spiritual texts of Islam.

Muslims have two main sources of religious knowledge: the Qur'an (recitation), which is considered to be Allah's[1] revelation to his Prophet Muhammad, and the *hadiths* (reports or narratives), the record of Muhammad's sayings and actions. Both these sources mention jihad. The Qur'an has 114 *suras* (chapters) formed by 6,234 *ayas* (verses).[2] Of all these suras, only twenty-eight have some reference to jihad (the word jihad is mentioned about forty-one times). The term jihad is derived from the Arabic root *jhd*, 'to strive'. The same *jhd* serves as the root for other verbs emphasizing effort and struggle to achieve perfection in difficult tasks. Unsurprisingly, *ijtihad,* meaning 'to strive for understanding and interpreting the Qur'anic law', has the same *jhd* root as jihad. Today, an increasing number of people are aware of the correct Arab meaning through newspapers and non-academic sources, but unfortunately an increasing number of scholarly publications prefer the traditional medieval translation 'holy war'. Whether or not jihad is a holy war depends, as I have emphasized in the Introduction, on the person interpreting the concept. At a purely linguistic level we should recognize that holy war in Arabic would sound like *harb-al muqaddasah* rather than jihad. Neither in the Qur'an nor in the hadiths can we find such an expression. This does not mean that in the Qur'an a discussion of war is absent.

The Qur'an is a spiritual book but it is also a practical one. Muslims see it as a personal guide to Allah's path as well as a guide to establishing the Islamic *ummah* (community of believers). As a know-how guide to life, we can find different topics discussed in the Qur'an, and among them, indeed, is war. Pre-Islamic Arabic societies had developed a sophisticated martial terminology, such as *sira'at* (combat), *ma'arakat* (battle), *harb* (war) and *qital* (killing) which the Qur'an has inherited. For a society such as the pre-Islamic Arabian, war was part of everyday life; but in the Qur'an the specific term harb is rarely used and qital is used only thirty-four times but not always with reference in killing one's enemies. For instance, qital is often found in verses that impose on human beings a respect for life in general. So, in Sura 4:29 we can read 'Nor kill (or destroy) yourselves: for verily Allah hath been to you most Merciful!',[3] in Sura 5:32 'If any one slew a person - unless it be for murder or spreading mischief in the land – it would be as if he slew the whole people', and again in Sura. 6:151 'Take not life, which Allah hath made sacred, except by way of justice and law'. Therefore, qital seems to be used in a way that rejects arbitrary killing.

All Muslims agree that the Qur'an allows Muslims to fight in two main circumstances: self-defence and to maintain their right to worship. Yet each Muslim can decide when self-defence is needed or when the worship of Allah is jeopardized. Again, personal interpretation is far more relevant in understanding jihad than the literal text. Indeed, when we approach the Arabic version of the Qur'an it is not difficult to recognize, as far as war is concerned, a chivalrous attitude: forbidding useless violence, preserving civilians, and expressly dictating strict codes of conduct and engagement. I am not surprised that the majority of Muslims say that Islam is peace loving, since the Qur'an gives them supportive evidence on preserving civilians. One of my respondents told me that even in the case of war, Muslims have to restrict their aim to 'justice' because 'Those who believe fight in the cause of Allah, and those who reject Faith, fight in the cause of the Evil' (Sura 4:76). Yet we must observe again that concepts such as 'justice' are open not only to interpretation but also to personal emotional values.

Jihad, despite the variegated meaning it may acquire among Muslims, certainly represents a sense of totalizing effort. In the Qur'an there are many examples in which such effort (e.g. economic, psychological and physical) has been required by the new-born Muslim community (see Sura 2:218, 4:95, 22:78, 25:53). So, jihad has a different meaning from qital or harb. Yet in much popular literature as well as in some academic studies, I have noticed that many Qur'anic verses allegedly reporting good examples of the violent meaning of jihad are in reality mentioning qital. For instance, one of the most worn Qur'anic verses quoted to support the violent concept of jihad is Sura 2:191 'And slay [qtulu] them wherever ye catch them'. Often the second part of the verse and its historical context is omitted by both Islamic extremists and anti-Islamic rhetoricians: 'and turn them out *from where they have turned you out*; for tumult and oppression are worse than slaughter'. The Qur'an is a text and like any other text entitles Muslims and non-Muslims to interpret it. But to confuse qtulu with jihad (see Kelsay and Johnson 1991: 50 and Johnson 1997: 61) has nothing to do with interpretation and everything to do with ignorance or misreading.

Since, according to Muslims, the Qur'an is Allah's direct words, they recognize it as the most holy and unchangeable Islamic source. Indeed, Muslims believe that the Qur'an has been preserved from being mixed with the Prophet's sayings. Yet Muhammad was the Prophet of Islam, guided directly by Allah, and leader of the ummah; his actions, juridical decisions and explanations could decrypt some of the difficult passages Muslims find in the Qur'an. Muhammad's followers started to memorize and report the Prophet's actions and sayings. At his death, in June 632, the ummah was left without the earthly presence of the Prophet, without its ruler, its supreme judge, its Qur'anic interpreter and, most visibly, its source of unity. Although Muhammad had prepared his community for his death, and the Qur'an itself had emphasized 'Muhammad is no more than a messenger: many were the messengers that passed away before him. If he died or were slain, will ye then turn back on your heels?' (Sura 3:144), the ummah felt disoriented and tribal interests started to prevail. Although no Muslim would openly have tried to manipulate or change the Qur'an (something that indeed would have been harshly punished), the oral tradition of hadiths, which had replaced the physical presence of the Prophet, became the battlefield in which to affirm one's own version of Islam. Hadiths started multiplying uncontrollably: the first Muslims were tempted to resolve their disputes by proudly saying 'I saw the Prophet doing such and such,' or 'I heard the Prophet saying such and such,' as well as 'somebody told me that the Prophet said ...' Twenty years after the death of Muhammad, Muslims had succeeded in publishing an organized and agreed official copy of the

Qur'an, but seemed completely incapable of preventing the creation of hadiths. Soon it became clear that a reliability system to test the hadiths was urgently required.

Muslim scholars turned toward the Qur'an to find the best system to categorize the hadiths, and they found their solution in the Qur'anic requirement that Muslims must look for knowledge and ask the people who may know best (Sura 29:20). Therefore, *isnad* (the chain of authorities) appeared to be a suitable system for disentangling trustworthy hadiths from fake ones. This system had another, less 'divine', advantage: it had been used among the Arab tribes for centuries to validate their tribal traditions (*sunna*). Al-Bukhari [4] and Muslim al-Hajjaj[5] compiled the two most famous collections of trustworthy hadiths, traditionally called *sahih* (literally, it means sound). The hadiths that could not be considered as sahih, but were still considered trustworthy, became known as *hasan* (good). On a decreasing scale, we can find the *da'if* (weak) and finally the *saqim* (meaning infirm or sick) hadiths.

Goldziher (1971) was one of the first (non-Muslim) European scholars to study the hadiths. Said's suggestion (1978) that Orientalism may have affected Goldziher's views on Islam has irremediably overshadowed Goldziher's work. Nevertheless, I think that some of the findings of Goldziher's study should be reconsidered. He has argued that, after the death of Muhammad, the several Muslim factions, struggling for religious and political control of the ummah, fabricated some hadiths and imposed their own Islamic views. Certainly, many hadiths, as Muslims recognize, have been fabricated or substantially modified; but, as Burton (1994: xii) has observed, 'If hypocrisy lies precisely in the adoption of the external demeanour of the pious and the counterfeit testifies to the existence of the genuine coin, pseudo-hadiths imitate real hadiths, otherwise the exercise is pointless.' In other words, even the 'pseudo-hadiths' followed the model of the real ones and became part of the Islamic tradition.

Muslims perceived al-Bukhari's and al-Hjjaj's impeccable religious life and faith as a warranty of their genuine commitment to report Muhammad's exact words and actions. If today we might have some scepticism about the scientific efficacy of isnad, Burton (1994: xvii) has been right in arguing that for a Muslim the respect of 'every detail, however minute, might literally make the difference between eternal life or death'. I think that some of Goldziher's criticism should be taken into consideration, yet we must remember that Muslims consider the hadiths to be a vital source of religious knowledge, second only to the Qur'an.

The hadiths, however, have an advantage over the Qur'an. They are easily understandable, anecdotal and are considered to be the product of human beings reporting the actions of another (although respected and honoured) human being. This has some important implications. For instance, while Muslims avoid misquoting the Qur'an, this is not the case with the hadiths. It is the story, the anecdote that really matters. So, hadiths are still easily created, modified and forged even today. Attending Friday *khutbas* (sermons) in different mosques, I have observed imams who have modified al-Bukhari's hadiths or even transformed Zen and Hassidic stories into new 'hadiths'.

Although Jihad constitutes only 0.4 per cent of the whole Qur'an, we may find many hadiths (sahih, hasan, but in particular da'if and saqim) which mention it. In contrast to what we have discussed about the Qur'an, in some of these hadiths jihad, harb and qital can be found together in the text. In al-Bukhari's and in al-Muslim's collections, jihad never seems to justify aggression. Nevertheless, a famous, but according to some Muslim scholars controversial, hadith seems to suggest two contradictory aspects of jihad: one spiritual (striving) and the other overtly military (fighting). Al-Qari, who defined the hadith as saqim, reported it,

al-Khatib al-Baghdadi relates in his 'History' on the authority of Jabir: The Prophet came back from one of his campaigns saying: 'You have come forth in the best way of coming forth: you have come from the smaller jihad to the greater jihad.' They said: 'And what is the greater jihad?' He replied: 'The striving (mujahadat) of Allah's servants against their idle desires.' (1986 [1406]: 127)

Although in the Arabic text we cannot be sure that the word 'jihad' refers back to 'campaign', the majority of Muslim scholars accept such a correlation and recognise two jihads: the striving and the fighting for Islam (Cook 2005). From different perspectives in the following chapters many of my respondents will refer to the 'doctrine of jihad'.

Therefore al-Bukhari and al-Muslim's collections are not able to clarify, once and for all, the meaning of jihad. In al-Bukhari the concept of jihad is surely open ended, yet his fifty-second book (i.e. chapter) simply titled 'Jihad', has been constantly translated as 'Fighting for the cause of Allah'.[6] Below, I shall report three of the most quoted al-Bukhari' hadiths,

Narrated Abu Huraira: A man came to Allah's Apostle and said, 'Instruct me as to such a deed as equals Jihad (in reward)'. He replied, 'I do not find such a deed'. Then he added, 'Can you, while the Muslim fighter is in the battle-field, enter your mosque to perform prayers without cease and fast and never break your fast?' The man said, 'But who can do that?' Abu-Huraira added, 'The Mujahid (i.e. Muslim fighter) is rewarded even for the footsteps of his horse while it wanders bout (for grazing) tied in a long rope'. (al-Bukhari, Vol. 4, Book 52, hadith N 44 in Khan 1995)

Narrated 'Abdullah bin Abi Aufa: Allah's Apostle said, 'Know that Paradise is under the shades of swords'. (al-Bukhari Vol. 4, Book 52, hadith N 73 in Khan 1995)

Narrated 'A'isha: the mother of the faithful believers: The Prophet was asked by his wives about the Jihad and he replied, 'The best Jihad (for you) is (the performance of) Hajj'. (al-Bukhari , Vol. 4, Book 52, hadith N 128 in Khan 1995)

As an imam whom I have interviewed on this topic observed, these hadiths, as the others concerning jihad in al-Bukhari's book, emphasize *istidsha* (martyrdom) rather than murder. The imam observed 'According to Muslim theology, the highest act of love that a person could offer to Allah is his or her own martyrdom'.[7] The imam emphasized that Allah would reward the brave believer with an immediate access to *al-janna* (The Garden, i.e. the Paradise) and its mental and spiritual bodily pleasures. The term martyr, *shahid* (from the Arabic root *shd* meaning 'testify'), shares its root with *shahada*,[8] the Muslim profession of faith. By pronouncing it, Muslims testify their submission to Allah, by dying for it, Muslims fulfil their testimony. Indeed, which action might better testify a complete submission to Allah's will than martyrdom? Which action could ever require stronger jihad than one's own death for a spiritual ideal? The imam's interpretation of jihad (and probably the most common among the great majority of Muslims) means to offer one's own Muslim life to Islam rather than immolating non-Muslims by it.

However, Muslims have not shaped their contemporary idea of jihad only through the Qur'an and the Prophet's Sunna. The Islamic juridical traditions (*fiqh*), the history of the ummah (community of believers) and the formation of the Ottoman Empire have played a fundamental role in shifting the meaning of jihad towards holy war (Heck 2004). Increasingly divided, the Muslim jurists have been unable to develop a unitary Islamic juridical tradition. The same internal disagreements that had created a plethora of questionable hadiths, produced contrasting schools of Islamic thought and philosophy. Of course, each of these juridical schools presented their interpretation of *shari'a* (from the root *sh'* meaning 'marking out' and often translated as 'Divine Law') as the most Islamic. Known as *madhhabs* (movements or ideologies) they were named after their founders. Only four of them have survived: the Hanafi, Maliki, Shafi and Hanbali schools. The Shi'a Muslims developed a distinct school which I shall discuss latter.

As we have seen, the hadith criticized by Ali al-Qari, but accepted by the majority of Muslims, argues that there are two kinds of jihad. Later, the Islamic scholars named them as *al-jihad al-akbar* (the greater jihad) and *al-jihad al-asghar* (the lesser jihad). Then another sub-categorization took place and al-jihad al-akbar was divided into *jihad al-qalb* (jihad of the heart), *jihad al-kalima* (jihad of the tongue) and *jihad bi-al-yad* (jihad of the hand). Al-jihad al-asghar maintained its military connotation and was categorized as *jihad bi-al-saif* (jihad of the sword). Islamic scholars have described jihad as progressive achievement. So, the 'jihad of the heart' represents the struggle of the personal *naf* (soul) against worldly temptations in order to achieve spiritual purity. When Muslims reach this level, they may conduct 'the jihad of the tongue' by preaching Islam. Yet preaching is not enough, and good Muslims should perform the 'jihad of the hand' by showing the power of Islam through good deeds. Only when Islam is threatened and as a last resort, may Muslims conduct the jihad of the sword. It is important to be reminded that the Qur'an does not mention any of these categories. They are philosophical and theological products that tried to combine different scholarly opinions on jihad in a unified system acceptable among the increasingly divided Muslim communities.

Yet war limited to self-defence was hardly the dream of any medieval king. So, the contradiction between the eighth-century military expansion of Islam and the Islamic injunctions against unjust, unprovoked wars became visible (Heck 2004). Muslim scholars were required by their rulers to resolve such a contradiction to allow expansionistic wars. Despite a famous hadith narrating how the Prophet had emphasized 'The best jihad is to speak a word of truth to a tyrant',[9] we can easily understand how many Muslim scholars preferred to favour their rulers' earthly desires rather than their theological beliefs. I agree with Heck when he observes 'The umayyad logic of state had profound and lasting effects on the Islamic conception of *jihad*: *jihad* as the tool of a state oriented towards expansion and became itself conceived as a tool in the service of territorial expansion, rather than a religious struggle at the level of devotion to God's cause' (2004: 108).

Hence, Muslim scholars observed that Allah had revealed the Qur'an at different stages of Muhammad's life, and subsequently at different stages of the history of the Islamic ummah. Two verses (Sura 2:106 and Sura 16:101) seem to suggest that Allah might have replaced and modified some previous Qur'anic revelations specifically revealed to address the particular needs of the newly formed Muslim community. So some revelations written in the Qur'an may refer only to unique historical events. Based on the authority of these two verses, Muslim jurists and theologians developed what was known as *al-nasikh-ua-al-mansukh* (literally 'the abrogating and the abrogated') or simply the 'doctrine of abrogation'. *Nasikh* indicates the verse which, abrogating, replaced the *mansukh*, the abrogated. However, the Qur'an does not indicate which verses Allah might have replaced or changed. Since there is no divine indication of which verses Muslims need to abrogate and replace, al-nasikh-ua-al-mansukh became another fertile ground for disagreement among Muslims. Many verses in the Qur'an forbid aggression, a few others if isolated from their context, sound aggressive against non-Muslims. A selective use of al-nasikh-ua-al-mansukh could provide the moral shield that Muslim leaders (and today's extremists) need to religiously justify their warlike goals.

Therefore, Ibn Hazm al-Andalusi (1986) could argue that the 'peaceful' verses of the Qur'an had to be considered as abrogated and replaced by the 'verses of the sword'. In contrast, Imam Sobhy as-Saleh (1983) had refused such a radical theory. Evidently, discussion about jihad moved from the Qur'an and the hadiths to scholarly diatribes. One of the arguments used by contemporary radical Muslims says that the 'peaceful' verses of the Qur'an have been replaced by the 'verses of the sword' because the Muslim community had succeeded in overcoming its weakness and had won its important battles against polytheistic Arab tribes. The community, now strong, no longer needed the protection of the Jewish or Christian tribes it had enjoyed. Muslims had achieved enough economic, political and, most importantly, military power to commence their real divine task: Islamicize the entire world. Of course, many Muslims reject this opportunistic understanding of al-nasikh-ua-al-mansukh. For instance, an imam in Scotland observed, 'if we have to agree with this extremist argument we would have to accept the paradox of a hypocritical God'. Yet we know that what might sound hypocritical to the imam in Scotland could make perfect sense to somebody in London.

The Islamic state was becoming a superpower and needed to expand. Before developing organized military campaigns on a large scale, Muslim Arabs had conducted *razzia*. A pre-Islamic term, razzia indicated a quick raid against non-Muslim territories aimed not at conquering lands, but rather to provide essential resources (Lewis 1988). The practice of razzia had, however, another advantage that was more political and less economic. Although through razzia Muslims did not take direct control of the plundered non-Muslim territories, indubitably these rapid and persistent incursions facilitated the decision of the constantly plundered tribes to join the growing Muslim community. Indeed, Muslim tribes were not only spared from razzia but could enjoy the resources derived from this traditional practice.

Centuries later, a newly formed Islamic state, which economically and politically was increasingly mimicking the Byzantine Empire, the superpower of those times, could not rely upon razzia (Lewis 1993). The practice of al-nasikh-ua-al-mansukh allowed the newborn Muslim states, and then the Ottoman Empire, to achieve their imperialistic goals without abjuring their Islamic commitments. The extensive use of al-nasikh-ua-al-mansukh, in particular during the eighth century and the first part of the Middle Ages, is indeed undeniable (Heck 2004; Watt 1968), although philosophers, such as al-Ghazali,[10] openly criticized it and rejected its use. Yet to transform the concept of jihad as a productive expansionistic tool, another element was needed, a new geopolitical vision of the world.

The Qur'an emphasizes a universalistic and all-encompassing revelation with a holistic vision of the world.[11] Instead of highlighting divisions, the Qur'an tends to emphasize similarities. But Muslim scholars started to develop a dualistic representation of the world. If Islam was the most perfectly revealed religion, the Islamic state had to be the most civilized of all. As in any imperialistic and colonialist design, civilising the uncivilized was seen as a religious duty. Therefore, the world was divided into two geopolitical entities *dar al-islam* (the abode of Islam) and the *dar al-harb* (the abode of war). If the former represented all the lands in which the shari'a had been implemented (i.e. a territory under an Islamic ruler, thus civilized), the latter indicated all the lands in which non-Muslim law ruled (i.e. the uncivilized). Of course, *jahiliyya*, the pre-Islamic ignorance characterized the lands of dar al-harb.

Why did the Islamic scholars select the term harb (war) to geopolitically identify non-Muslim lands? To understand the reason, we should follow the rationale they employed. In the Qur'an Allah ordered humankind to allow what is good and forbid what is wrong (Sura 3:104). This led the scholars to argue that, since the non-Muslim lands, which at that time were almost synonymous with Christendom, lived in a jahiliyya state (i.e. did not recognize Islam), it was the duty of Muslims to invite citizens living under jahiliyya to follow Islam. If they refused the first (kind) invitation, Muslim states were religiously required to impose what was good (Islam) and forbid what was wrong (jahiliyya lifestyles).

Certainly, there were many similarities with the medieval Christian ideology of the Crusades. Yet Islamic scholars had to face another challenge. In the Qur'an we can find evidence that Muslims should not practise forced conversions: 'Let there be no compulsion in religion' (Sura 2:256). Historically, this modern and liberal idea was the one most betrayed by Muslim rulers around the world. Indeed, the Islamic jurists interpreted this verse as if it was referring to a single non-Muslim rather than to an entire non-Muslim state. Consequently, they suggested that Islamic rulers could grant a special status to single non-Muslims living under dar al-islam. This special status was defined by a legal contract (*dhimma*), which allowed non-Muslims the right of residence and economic transactions within the Islamic state. The dhimma recognized, among other things, the right for the *dhimmi* to practise their religion when it was not overtly polytheistic (Lewis 1988).

Extending its domain, the Islamic world increased not only in the number of dhimmi, but also in the number of non-Muslim countries sharing its borders.

Unsurprisingly, in a state in which a diffuse level of education was achieved and at least rulers could read and write, political literature was a very popular genre. The most highly rated topic was foreign policy and works theorizing the perfect Islamic state. Among the most successful and influential books that can be mentioned is Shaybani's *kitab al-siyar al-kabir* (Khadduri 2002). The title has been translated into English as a politically correct *The Islamic Law of Nations*. Yet the literal Arabic version sounds less technical and certainly more warlike: *The Book of the Great Campaigns*. Shaybani, however, argued that Muslims could not start war, they had to be attacked first. Johnson has also noticed this 'Shaybani's concept of jihad is thus fundamentally one of defensive war for faith, though his concept of defence is a broad one due to the conceptions of the *dar al-harb* as a source of perennial enmity and danger' (1997: 72). The political and juridical distinctions between defensive and offensive jihads raised another question: who was required to fight in each of them? The Islamic jurists decided that offensive jihads should be a duty shared by the community, *kifaya* (i.e. the state) and the *khalifa* was the authority that, consulting the ulemas, could call a jihad. Being the entire community, and not a single Muslim, that had to share the burden of the war, this jihad was called *jihad fard kifaya*. Yet in the case of self-defence each Muslim conducted jihad without the ruler's permission, and in this case scholars spoke of *jihad fard 'ayn*. The distinction is not just theoretical but has a practical aspect. When jihad fard kifaya was called, the Muslims who did not possess weaponry or horses were exempt from the battles (and of course from the consequent booty). The Islamic state did not provide equipment for its soldiers and poor Muslim families could certainly not afford the high costs of war campaigns. In other words, jihad fard kifaya remained in the hands of the Islamic middle class and the nobility. By contrast, each Muslim had to fight jihad fard 'ayn since in this case their personal lives and Islam were under threat.

According to a hadith, the Prophet said 'After me, there will be caliphs; and after the caliphs, *amirs*; and after *amirs*, kings; and after the kings, tyrants' (quoted in Lewis 1988: 43). The Sunni jurists argued that the khalifa (successor), as vicar of Muhammad, had the political and religious power to call for jihad fard kifaya. This, however, does not represent the opinion of all the Islamic schools. The Shi'a scholars disagreed with the Sunni on this point (and on many others, of course). To understand the Shi'a disagreement we need to understand how Shi'a Islam (Shi'a simply means party) developed and became different from Sunni Islam.

In this case, to acknowledge the chronological order of these events becomes very relevant. The division in the Muslim world started from a dispute over the first khalifa succession. Muhammad died on 8 June 632, leaving no indication of who would succeed him as leader of the ummah. Some people saw in 'Ali ibn-abi-Talib, who was Muhammad's cousin and son-in-law, a suitable candidate. Others argued that the Prophet himself had not named a successor from the line of his family because he had rejected the idea of an Islamic ruling dynasty. The Muslim community after the death of Muhammad started to crumble and tribal interests started to prevail. The Sunni became convinced that only a man respected by the Arab tribes could maintain a united ummah. Abu Bakr, one of the most loved and respected *sahaba* (companions) of the Prophet was recognized as such a man. He became the first khalifa, so that the practice that the khalifa succession had to be guided by political interests rather than by kinship was established among the Sunni.

According to the Sunni tradition, Abu Bakr was a great, just and true khalifa. When approaching his death, Abu Bakr consulted the other influential members of the ummah and then wrote down the name of his successor, 'Umar ibn-al-Khattab (also known as 'Umar I). After Abu Bakr, no other khalifa had the privilege of dying in his bed from natural causes. 'Umar I was a great commander and started the military expansion of the Islamic world; for this reason, he received the honorific title of *amir al-mu'minin* (the Commander of the faithful). But his military skills did not spare him from the anger of a woman who, having some unresolved disputes with him, killed him in 644 CE. Although 'Umar ibn-al-Khattab had no time to name his successor, he had organized a committee, which, in the event of his unexpected death, had to appoint the next khalifa. The committee elected Uthman ibn Afan, a member of the Umayyad dynasty. As khalifa, Uthman was not as successful as his predecessors had been. Tensions, divisions and disaffection spread rapidly among the Muslims, so that some organized an insurgent force and killed him. Finally, in 665 CE, the Muslims of Medina acclaimed the cousin of the Prophet, 'Ali ibn-abi-Talib, as the new khalifa. For the first time a member of the Prophet's family came into power.

'Ali's supporters (Shi'a) believed that the political power of the Islamic state should remain within the ranks of the Prophet's family. Another faction (Sunni) argued that Islam rejected any hereditary power, and they refused to recognize 'Ali as the *khalifat rasul allah*. Consequently, Muslims experienced what Islam had clearly forbidden: civil wars. 'A'isha, the Prophet's widow and daughter of Abu Bakr, led the army to the 'Battle of the Camel', so called because she stirred on her fighters from her camel. 'Ali won the battle but had to face another challenge, this time led by

Muawiyah, the nephew of Uthman. Not only had Muawiyah refused to recognize 'Ali as khalifa, but he also accused him of failing to punish the killers
of Uthman (his uncle). In other words, Muawiyah was suggesting that 'Ali
himself might have been involved in Uthman's assassination. Muawiyah was
a powerful man and controlled what today we call Syria. In 657, 'Ali
decided to take back the region under his control; at Siffin 'Ali's army and
Muawiyah's clashed. The battle was visibly favourable to 'Ali when
Muawiyah played his last card: the Qur'an. Muawiyah's army raised the
Qur'an and Muawiyah officially asked for guidance on its precepts. The
arbitration proved to be inconclusive, but had an unexpected effect on 'Ali:
it challenged his leadership and power. Since Muawiyah succeeded in maintaining his control over Syria, some of 'Ali's supporters remained unsatisfied
and accused 'Ali of being unable to fulfil the duties as a khalifa, and they
organized a new party that spilt from 'Ali's faction. The new party was
known as the Kharijites (from *kharaja*, exit) and was a particularly extreme
and violent Shi'a faction (Esposito 2002). In 661 CE, one of the Kharijites
ended 'Ali's reign by killing him five years after 'Ali had been acclaimed
khalifa in Medina.

This assassination became a central part of the Sh'ia theological interpretation of Islam. Shi'a Muslims interpreted the martyrdom of their leaders as
evidence that the world was, and would remain until the Day of Judgement,
intrinsically unjust. The subsequent martyrdom of Hussein ('Ali's son)
during the battle of Karbala against the Umayyad forces seemed to confirm
Shi'a eschatology. Shi'a and Sunni developed different cultural and theological aspects. Among these there is the Shi'a concept of the imamate
which substituted the figure of the elected Sunni khalifa. The Shi'a imam
should be a member of Muhammad's family although he does not retain
political power, as the khalifa does, he is the simply the highest spiritual
leader, the most faithful and (though he is not a prophet himself) infallible.
In 687 CE, a new theological idea developed among Shi'a Muslims, the so-
called 'hidden imam'. According to this belief, the imam Muhammad ibn-
al-Hanafiyya had not died but concealed his physical presence from human
beings. Before the Day of Judgement, he would leave his hidden place to
become the *mahadi*, the Messiah,[12] establishing Allah's justice on Earth.
According to the Shi'a school, nobody could become a rightful leader other
than the hidden imam. Yet Shi'a Muslims still needed rulers. To avoid
anarchy, they acknowledged that certain imams could act as agents of the
hidden imam and be under his guidance. Nonetheless, the vicars' actions
would be 'unjust' by definition. For this reason, according to Shi'a
Muslims, the only jihad that their leaders may invoke is a defensive jihad.
The exaltation of martyrdom among the Shi'a facilitated the odd tradition

of the so-called suicide bombers, who first acted in Lebanon under the banner of Hezbollah. Yet Hezbollah's activity was understood as a fight against the occupation and was never aimed at civilians, but rather targeted military installations (see the 1983 attack on the US Marines in Lebanon).

In other words, any concept of jihad could not exist outside six different variables: time, space, social context, interpretation and, last but not least, personal identity.

Conclusion

Jihad, even from a historical viewpoint, shows a complex relationship between personal faith and political vision. The jihad that we have discussed here is derived from our idea of history as formed by 'bookmarks' along space-time dimensions. This represents the intellectual phylogenies of jihad in the Islamic world. Although historical accounts are relevant to the understanding of how concepts develop and propagate, we have to recognize that no concept could maintain exactly the same meaning in different historical times, nor are they employed in the same way as they were. Yes, it is true that people like bin Laden may use the medieval rhetoric of jihad, but this rhetoric has more to do with Hollywood than the language of Shaybani. History deals with macro levels, we can only observe history from the viewpoint of the political elite. We can only speculate from documents, poems, novels and other written sources what ordinary Muslims during those times thought about jihad, since history tends to silence the individual in favour of the state and its leaders.

The concept of jihad and the idea of suicide bombers are today becoming entangled in the imagination of both Muslims and non-Muslims. As we have seen in this historical excursus, they are an absolute novelty in any Islamic traditions. The collapse of the Ottoman Empire and the end of the caliphate also signalled the collapse of unified political Islamic doctrine and the fragmentation of the former centralized power. In such a political-religious vacuum, who would become responsible to call for a jihad fard kifaya or decide that Islam might be under threat? If emotions and personal identities have played a relevant role during the classical history of Islam, today they have even a greater relevance in Muslims' understanding of contemporary jihad. In other words, jihad is what Muslims (or non-Muslims) say it is. There is no solution or escape from this tautology. The other way out would be to affirm that jihad is what God says it is. Yet, even by accepting Muslim theology, we have to observe that Allah revealed the Qur'an in the form of a book. Books exist because people can read them and the very act of reading is just the first step of interpretation. But here we have another tautology, interpretation is only possible through identity and we interpret texts (as well as the world in general) starting from our identities. Therefore, to avoid surfing from tautology to tautology, we need to address the key issue: the mother of all interpretations of jihad – whether political, theological, opportunistic, esoteric or materialistic – is personal identity.

Notes

1. Is Allah the God of both Christians and Jews? Muslims as well as non-Muslims have answered in two different ways. One position, which is the most widely shared among liberal Muslims, Christians and Jews, suggests that Allah is exactly the same God that Christians and Jews worship. A second position, advocated by some Muslim as well as Christian extremists, argues that Allah, although being the same God worshipped by the Jews, is not the same God of Christians since Christians believe in the Trinity (this is, for instance, bin Laden's argument).

2. The number reported here does not include the 112 unnumbered *bismilla* (in the name of Allah) occurring at the beginning of each sura.

3. Throughout this book, all the quotations from the Qur'an are from Yusuf Ali (1983).

4. Al-Bukhari (810–70 CE) purposely travelled through the Islamic state in search of hadiths to collect. After a careful critical analysis, he organized them thematically. For Sunni Muslims, the importance of his hadith collection is second only to the importance of the Qur'an.

5. Muslim B. al-Hjjaj (817–75 CE) has also compiled a book of hadiths which is as respected as al-Bukhari's.

6. I refer here to the translation by Muhammad M. Khan, which is also available on line, http://www.usc.edu/dept/MSA/fundamentals/hadithsunnah/bukhari.

7. The imam also referred to Sura 22:58, 47:4, 2:154.

8. The shahada, which phonetically sounds *ashhada an la-illa-llah,wa ashhadu anna muhammadar-rasulillah*, and means 'I testify that there is no God but God and Muhammad is the Prophet of God'.

9. It is interesting to note that even in this hadith jihad is linked to martyrdom. Indeed, opposing tyrants could easily lead to death.

10. Al-Ghazali was one of the greatest Islamic jurists, theologians and mystical thinkers. He lived in the northern part of Iran and studied Islamic theology and philosophy in different schools of thought. He was also involved in Sufi practices from an early age. His ideas and writings became so successful that he was appointed head of the Nizamiyyah College at Baghdad in AH 484/109 CE.

11. Maybe I should say 'of the universe' since in several suras the Qur'an speaks of 'worlds' instead of one world and Muslims believe that other planets could indeed have intelligent forms of life.

12. For many Sunni Muslims the Messiah is Jesus, who Muslims recognize as a prophet but not as God's son.

CHAPTER 3

I am What I Feel to Be

September 11: A day like many others until two planes crashed into New York's Twin Towers killing thousands of innocent people. The suicide bombers saw themselves as *mujahidin*. We may try to explain this tragic event either with rational or irrational theories. Yet the keyword that can help us to make sense of an unthinkable and inhuman action is a simple one: emotion. The hijackers, despite all the pathological or eschatological, theological or political, rational or irrational, philosophical or practical reasons they might have had for their actions, wanted only one thing, to induce emotions.[1] To do so, they did not just use a knife, a plane or their own lives, but a concept and word that has 'emotional' implications for Muslims and non-Muslims: jihad. They killed themselves, and thousands of others, while exclaiming 'Allah Akbar'. They martyred themselves and murdered innocent people because they *felt* they were Muslim. They destroyed two American symbols because they *felt* they were Muslim. That feeling of being Muslim is what they would have called their 'Muslim identity'. My argument is that without reconsidering what human identity might be, we cannot discuss the meaning that jihad might have for my respondents. We need to go deep down into the roots of identity formation to see how the environment in which people live has the power to shape what they are and how they might think and act. In the previous chapter I have described the events that have shaped the different historical understandings of jihad. Indeed, some Muslims, as we shall see, may refer to those ideologies, rhetorical languages and histories. Yet still a question remains: why? You do something (whatever it might be) because you feel you are something, your 'I'.

I have been fascinated with the idea of identity since the first time I started to question myself on what this 'I' might be. During my last year at high school in Florence, on sunny spring weekends, I used to visit San Miniato al Monte, a stunning medieval Dominican monastery. Periodically, the Dominican monks of this monastery would hold interfaith forums inviting other religious speakers for public lectures. One Sunday, while I was admiring from there the beautiful landscape that Florence offers, someone came towards me, stopping at my left side: a Buddhist monk. The beautiful landscape opened the topic of our conversation. Suddenly, in the middle of it, he asked, 'What are you?' I naturally answered, 'I am a student.' A few seconds of silence divided my answer from his next, unexpected, question: 'do you need the "I"?' An old friar arrived, asking the young Buddhist to follow him. The young Buddhist left with a nice smile, his question was never answered. This chapter deals with that 'I', which the Buddhist monk left me struggling with for a long time; the same 'I' that brought the 9/11 hijackers to take their and others' lives on behalf of a concept of 'jihad'. In this chapter, I will discuss what people call 'identity'.

To focus on 'identity' is certainly not a novelty for a study on Muslims living in the West. You can rarely read a few lines in a newspaper or an academic article concerning Muslims in the West without coming across the word 'identity'. Yet the meticulous reader may have observed that 'identity' is often mentioned but its specific use is seldom explained even in academic works;[2] the impression is that the word 'identity' is self-explanatory. Nevertheless, try to ask yourself what identity might be and your mind will whirl across abstractions. For this reason somebody with a good sense of humour has stated 'trying to define yourself is like trying to bite your own teeth'.[3]

In social science, identity has been studied mainly from an 'outside' perspective. In other words, scholars have mainly analysed what we do every day when we interact and use each other's identities in an instrumental way (i.e. to know how to behave). For instance, when a non-Muslim invites a Muslim friend to their house for dinner, they need to know in what ways their guest differs from them (e.g. by not eating pork or drinking alcohol). Of course, identity in such a context becomes a matter of differentiation and it has facilitated the interpretation of people's actions as boundary markers. But because differentiation marks identity in the social world, should we assume that the individual experiences his or her identity as social differentiation? It is my contention that this has been, for a long time, a misrepresentation of how personal identity might operate. Unsurprisingly, one of the most quoted books in reference to what some call 'cultural identity' is Fiederik Barth's *Ethnic Groups and Boundaries* (1969). Barth's intention was not to develop a theory of identity, but rather to analyse the formation of ethnic groups. Yet the success of his study ensured that the model has also been often misused to define Muslim identities per se, particularly in the case of so-called 'second generations'. But if *personal* identity is not defined by people's social actions, in what way is identity formed? Why have some of my respondents, as we shall see in the following chapters, made links between 'identity' and 'jihad'?

To explain these points, we need to reconsider the concept of identity, and to do so we need to observe a very basic reality that often we forget: in order to feel our identities there is a need to have a *conscious* brain. For a long time the relevance of our bodies in the formation of identity has been neglected because culture and society have been arbitrarily abstracted from nature.[4] It is our brain, or better, its complex neurological system that, as we shall see, enables us to attain consciousness and consequently achieve a long-standing sense of selfhood. Yet because this process may be successful, we need another two elements: the external world and its inputs (be they natural, social or cultural).[5] For this reason, throughout this book I would summarize such a 'web of external inputs' in the simple word *environment*. Yet we, as human beings, have continuous input–output relationships with our surroundings. As we shall see in this chapter, it is what we call emotions that have the function of interconnecting with the external environment and with the internal one and vice versa (Milton and Svasek 2005).

My argument in this chapter will unfold as follows. First, I will describe how theories of identity have started from within the field of philosophy and psychology and moved on to sociology and anthropology. Of course, the discussion does not need to be a comprehensive review of all the available theories of identity, rather I will focus on those theories that have implicitly or explicitly been used in the academic discussion of Muslim identities. Second, I shall discuss Damasio's theory of emotions (2000) and Milton's idea of 'Emotions as ecological mechanisms' (Milton and Svasek 2005). Starting from these two theories, I shall present my understanding of identity as an emotional commitment through which people experience their autobiographical selves, so that it is what we *feel* we are that determines our identities for us. Finally, I introduce Bateson's concept of *schismogenesis* (2002) and how it can affect personal identity and form what I shall define as 'acts of identity'.

'I' and 'Me'

One of the issues we have when we try to discuss 'identity' is the excessive terminology that has proliferated with the growing numbers of studies devoted to this subject. The frustration here is not with this 'excessive terminology' per se, but with the fact that from one study to another, this terminology has become 'common sense', and consequently lost its specification. 'Identity', 'self-identity', 'personal identity', 'self', 'selfhood', 'personhood', 'I', 'me', 'Me' and many other terms[6] have become synonyms referring to that phenomenon which gives human beings their sense of themselves throughout their lives. All these terms want to mark one important and everyday experience event: we tend to experience ourselves as the same 'I' though time elapses and life changes continually. To quote Heraclitus, although we cannot bathe twice in the same water of a river, the person bathing in it feels the same both times. Water flows, the 'I' remains.

'Identity' derives from the Latin *idem*, 'the same', and the *Oxford English Dictionary* defines it as,

> the sameness of a person or thing at all times or in all circumstances: the condition or fact that a person or a thing is itself and not something else; ... it underlines the continuity of the personality ... the quality or condition of being the same in substance, composition, nature, proprieties, or in particular qualities under consideration; absolute or essential sameness, oneness ...

The philosopher Locke, in the second edition of *An Essay Concerning Human Understanding* (1959), tried to answer why we humans feel we are the very same person every year (I would add, every month, day, hour, minute and second). Locke deduced that humans have a continuity of consciousness: 'since consciousness always accompanies thinking, and it is that which makes everyone to be what he calls self, and thereby distinguishes himself from all other thinking beings, in this alone consists personal identity' (Locke 1959: 449). As we shall see later, in focusing on consciousness, Locke had the right intuition.

From this unitary vision of identity, which has endured through different disciplines and theories, we have reached, in the so-called post-modern era, the opposite position: a multiple and constantly changing identity. This has also instigated a proliferation of terms attempting the difficult task of imposing a meaning on the 'thing' that we call 'self', and these definitions have changed according to the writer's exigencies (Gleason 1982; Henry 2002). During these years, the discussion about identity and self has become so entangled that somebody has suggested that we might 'throw this identity into the junk heap' (Straub 2002: 59). How did we arrive at an idea of identity that contradicts the very origin of the term? As some of my readers may have just noticed, to discuss identity in abstract academic terms can become difficult and confusing. So let me introduce Mr Hussein, a fictional character on whom, as a guinea pig, the different theories can be tested. The only thing at this stage that readers need to know is that Mr Hussein declares himself to be Muslim.

One of the milestones in the study of identity has been James's analytical distinction between the 'I' and the 'Me' (1890); in other words the distinction between the self seen as 'knower' and the self seen as 'known'.[7] James has recognized the 'I' as composed of three different, but related, aspects of the self: the 'material' (e.g. body, belongings), the 'social' (e.g. social relationships) and the 'spiritual' (e.g. the feeling of our own subjectivity). Nonetheless, James, by emphasizing the social construction of the self, started the tendency to overshadow the individual in favour of the society; 'a man', he has stated, 'has as many social selves as there are individuals who recognize him and carry an image of him in their mind' (1890: 294). We can agree with James that our Mr Hussein could have a Muslim social self, an Algerian social self, a terrorist social self (though he might not be a terrorist), since some individuals know him as Algerian, Muslim and carry an image (stereotyped) of him as a terrorist. The problem is that this overemphasis on Mr Hussein's social self has become in James the most relevant aspect of Mr Hussein's identity. The danger is that James's idea that Mr Hussein has as 'many social selves' as the number of individuals 'who recognize him and carry an image of him in their mind' could end in denying what Mr Hussein feels himself to be. Nevertheless, James established the plurality of the 'social self', he cannot be held responsible for the confusion that his argument would finally bring to the study of identity. Indeed, he never suggested a dichotomy between the 'I' and the 'Me', rather he argued for a certain unity within the self.

Nonetheless, this Jamesian argument of the 'unity of the self' would disappear in the more recent social constructivist theories of identity, in which identity would be represented as extremely variable, fragmented and somehow structured only by culture. James was a psychologist with an interest in sociology and social dynamics. His theory, however, became very successful among sociologists and later anthropologists. The shift from physiological to sociological analyses altered the balance between mental (bodily) and culturally, socially controlled, processes.

From Psychology to Sociology

James's argument that people possess different selves in their everyday lives was further developed, if not radicalized, by Cooley (1992), Mead (1934) and Goffman (1959) in what became known as 'symbolic interactionism'. They started from an issue that James had left unresolved: how could people move from one identity to another, or even understand the identities of others. Cooley, Mead and Goffman shared the idea that symbols enable individuals to modify their personal self in accordance with their social environment. In other words, the act of sharing symbols allows people to experience themselves in the roles of others. This suggests a mutual interdependence between society and the personal self (Blumer 1969 and Strauss 1959), which would be systematically theorized in Goffman's masterpiece *The Presentation of Self in Everyday Life* (1959).

Goffman suggested that interactions among individuals (actors) may be interpreted as 'performances' aimed at providing the others (the audience) with the right impressions, but inevitably these performances are shaped by the very same audience the actor is performing for. So, according to him, the individual, through exchanging and manipulating information, forms his/her identity *as a function* of interaction with others. This process is achieved through what Goffman called the 'front', 'that part of the individual's performance which regularly functions in a general and fixed fashion to define the situation for those who observe the performance' (1959: 22). In other words, Goffman suggested that the act of representing the persona or self to the other is what we call identity. Since to maintain their identities people depend upon others, they need social interaction. Any stigma that may prevent such social interaction could lead the individual to isolation and alienation. He defined individuals' efforts to present themselves to others in a certain specific way as 'impression management'. Of course, symbols are at the very centre of Goffman's theory since it is through them that people can impress others and achieve social consideration. In conclusion, culture and society shape human interaction and consequently human identity.

Therefore, following (though simplifying for the sake of space) Goffman's main idea, Mr Hussein would have formed his Muslim identity as a function of interacting with both Muslims and non-Muslims. It is this manipulation and exchange of the cultural element (in this case Islam) that defines Mr Hussein as Muslim and lets others recognize him as Muslim. Of course, depending on the observers' viewpoints, Mr Hussein might be a good, bad, fanatical or moderate Muslim. Now let us say that Hussein is a Muslim migrant in a predominantly non-Muslim host society. Hussein, as a member of a minority that is often stigmatized has problems developing social interaction and consequently he becomes increasingly alienated. Marginalized and alienated, Hussein, who wants to maintain his Muslim identity, starts to radicalize his Islamic views. Following Goffman's theory, we must say that the radicalization of Mr Hussein, and for example his extremist idea of jihad, are the results of his cultural stigmatization. In other words, Mr Hussein's radical ideas are the consequence of his incapacity to meet his audience's standard sociocultural expectations. Some of you have probably recognized this argument as one we often read in newspapers or hear on talk shows. It is a straightforward, convincing argument, which, however, tells us more about how stereotypes might be formed rather than Mr Hussein's identity. Although stigma and stereotype processes have an impact on an individual, it may be reductive to argue that they shape identity.

Starting from Goffman, McCall and Simmons (1978) have further discussed the interdependence between self and society and developed the so-called 'role-identity theory'. The core of their theory argues that 'the character and the role that an individual devises for himself as *occupant of a particular position*' within society forms what we call identity (1978: 65, emphasis added). Through this definition, McCall and Simmons have hoped to explain what Goffman had left answered: how individuals may pass from one identity to another (or, to use Goffman's terminology, from one character to another) and remain, at the same time, part of the audience. Indeed, according to McCall and Simmons, any one person occupies a range of social positions allowing the individual to have several identities taking part in more than one social role. Yet McCall and Simmons found themselves facing the same question that Locke tried to answer; many people still affirm that they *feel the same* and have the same identity although living in different social circumstances. The two authors tried to resolve the issue by arguing that people constantly try to *impose* on others the identity that they are *keen to preserve*. This is achieved through social interaction which allows individuals to establish 'uniqueness' within their group of reference.

McCall and Simmons seem to suggest that Mr Hussein has to struggle in an endless competition to acquire and maintain the best of his identities (for instance, Muslim) within his group of reference. Yet since, according to McCall's and Simmons theory, Mr Hussein *needs* to express his role identity, he finds himself forced to negotiate his role identity with other members of the group. (Burke and Reitzes 1981). As we can see, this theory tends to focus primarily on how people select and maintain their roles within society rather than how people form their personal identities. So, how might role-identity theory explain an eventual radicalization of Mr Hussein? The answer is that Mr Hussein's radical ideas might have derived from his *need* to express a strong identity within a certain group; a group of which he *needs* to be part in order to express his identity. We can observe that role-identity theory, indissolubly linking the individual to the social group, tends towards a certain tautological representation. This issue brought Stryker to develop his 'identity theory'. He understood that if scholars did not want going around biting their own teeth, one question had to be addressed: why it is so central to people's actions.

Although Stryker has focused on the right questions, his theory has ended up suggesting an even more fragmented and variable idea of identity than role identity did. Actually, Stryker's 'identity theory' has many points of contact with McCall and Simmons' role-identity theory (Thoits and Virshup 1997). Stryker, as the other student of identity we have mentioned, has argued that the self is a direct product of the society in which the individual lives. Yet the starting point of Stryker's observations has been that since societies are complex and ruled by difference, though organized, in the same way human self must be equally complex and ruled by differences, though organized, So, people, according to Stryker have complex and differentiated selves that are expressed through different identities according to the social context in which people find themselves (Stryker and Serpe 1994). Mr Hussein, in this case, has different 'selves' (Muslim, father, imam, mujahidin and so on). One of these 'selves' would become his committed identity because a number of people, who are relevant in his life, would require him to play that certain role (for instance imam) within a certain context (the mosque on Friday). This means that in another context, with another group of people, Mr Hussein might be a mujahid. Yet somebody might ask why Mr. Hussein should accept an identity that other people and the social context has ultimately dictated to him? Stryker has answered that people select their personal identities to satisfy their personal interests. In other words, the identity that in a certain context fulfils the interest of the individual would be the most likely to be activated.

'Interest' is what prevents people rejecting the identity that the social context has imposed on their personal self. But at this point, we might ask who controls whom: is it Mr Hussein who by selecting a certain identity in order to fulfil his desires, controls the group (i.e. society), or the opposite, the society which, by imposing a certain identity on Mr Hussein, controls him and his desires? There is no answer in Stryker's theory to this issue; if we accept his theory we must postulate a continuum between self, society and identity in which one element shapes the other in an endless circle. Furthermore, we must also understand society as an all-encompassing, abstract, (and ever existing) force. I have to say that observing Mr Hussein through Stryker's lens I reach the conclusion that Mr Hussein is a passive human being and driven by self-interest. Now, if there might be a Mr Hussein fitting such a description, it is difficult to agree that all humanity in any place and culture could be so passive and completely driven by self-interest. Indeed, there is a certain Pavlovian influence in Stryker's theory. If one were to reject Stryker's Pavlovian vision of personal identity, but still believe that people have identities because of societies and cultures, one would need to explain how people might renounce their individuality in exchange for social acceptance. Two scholars have attempted to resolve this sphinx-like enigma through two correlated theories: Tajfel's 'social-identity theory'[8] and Turner's 'self-categorization theory'.

Tajfel has observed two important facts: first, that self-esteem (as James had suggested) has a paramount relevance for identity formation; second, that people categorize social and non-social stimuli in order to self-identify with others and to form 'in-groups', which differentiate themselves from 'out-groups'. Differentiation allows groups to form a group identity (i.e. an in-group A feels itself to be A because it is not part of an out-group B). Therefore, Tajfel's social-identity theory (Tajfel 1979), has suggested that personal self-esteem can only be achieved through in-group membership, personal identities depend upon the social identity of the in-group and the self-esteem of each member of the group depends upon the self-esteem of the others involved within such an in-group. Mr Hussein needs self-esteem like any other human being, but he can achieve self-esteem only if he becomes part of a group, namely, his in-group. Mr Hussein's in-group (formed by Muslims) provides him with his identity (Muslim) because through his Muslim in-group he can be differentiated from the 'others', or, the non-Muslim out-group. So, Tajfel can now explain what the other authors we have discussed could not: how society and culture shape Mr Hussein's identity and self. Yet Tajfel's theory tells us that Mr Hussein (and the rest of humanity) could not experience their identity *as individuals* but only as members of an in-group. Tajfel's theory has denied the very concept of the individual. His theory has had an incredible influence on anthropologists, who in their research have ended up overemphasizing society at the cost of individuality. Tajfel, however, has not explained how 'collective identification' might be possible.

One of Tajfel's students, Turner decided to bring to perfection his mentor's theory (Tajfel and Turner 1986; Turner 1999). Turner has developed the so-called 'self-categorization theory' to address the issue of 'collective identification':

> The basic process postulated is self-categorization, leading to self-stereotyping and the depersonalization of self-perception. It is argued that where people define themselves in terms of shared social category membership, there is a perceptual accentuation of intergroup similarities and intergroup differences on relevant correlated dimensions ... where social identity becomes relatively more salient than personal identity, people see themselves less as differing individual persons and more as similar, prototypical representatives of their ingroup category. (1999: 11)

So, Turner's solution is a process called 'depersonalization', which is caused by the natural human attitude of stereotyping others. Yet Turner and Tajfel have disagreed on whether emotion plays a role in the formation of in-groups. While the former has strongly argued against the idea that people might form in-groups through emotional processes, the latter has suggested that cohesion and identification were the result of a 'depersonalization' process controlled by emotions. So, Mr Hussein's radical ideas would be the result of the necessary stereotyping process of the out-group (non-Muslims), so that being in the in-group enhances self-esteem and, hence, allows Mr Hussein to enjoy a stable identity. If the self-esteem of the in-group is challenged or endangered, Mr Hussein would risk losing his identity, which is only socially determined, and he might turn to extremist acts to preserve the in-group. In conclusion, according to Tajfel's 'social identity' and Turner's 'self-categorization theory', Mr Hussein's radicalization and activity would just be the by-product of in-group versus out-groups dynamics.

In this section, we have discussed the different theories of identity that have been widely used in social scientific researches. These theories, though different in some aspects, have shaped the mainstream idea that identity is only socially and culturally produced. Yet, though society and culture have an important role, they cannot constitute the whole truth. According to these social-centric theories, individuals, who however form their identities through society itself, themselves form society. This tautology leaves us with a dilemma: our identity would not be exactly ours; *you are not what you feel to be*. According to these theories, Mr Hussein's 'I'm Muslim' would not represent what Mr Hussein *feels* to be but what Mr Hussein was told to be or the context forced him to be. Not only is this deterministic, but it means that what determines Mr Hussein's identity is an abstract, imagined, category called group or 'society'.

During my research, I have not met the fictional character Mr Hussein but Husseins in the flesh for whom individuality was a reality and society an abstraction. While living with them, observing them, trying to understand their understanding of themselves, I have had the strong impression that their identities did not derive from passive cultural processes, that the relationship between individual and society was much more complex than these theories have suggested. Trying to understand this 'plus', we need to approach the nurture–nature discussion from a new viewpoint.

The Self and the Anthropologist

During the 1970s, a long debate started: are we products of nurture or nature? Holland (1997) has presented the discussion in terms of universalists (those who maintain the prominence of nature) versus culturalists (those who maintain the prominence of culture). The 'universalists' argued that, although in the formation of self/identity, culture might have some role, it is subordinated to universal biological and natural psychological structures. The 'culturalists' argued the opposite, making self/identity an excusive domain of culture. Culture, according to the former, shapes a person's identity as a bottle shapes the water it contains. This conceptualization of identity has received support from cultural psychologists who have tried to prove scientifically a deep correlation between culture and identity.[9] Although the main anthropological focus in studying identity has been on culture, the majority of anthropologists have avoided universalists' and culturalists' extreme viewpoints.

Anthropologists, however, have shown an interest in studying identity much later than other social scientists. There has been a certain agreement among anthropologists (see Whittaker 1992) that Hallowell was one of the first anthropologists to discuss 'self' and 'identity' in an ethnographic work (1955). Indeed, Hallowell attempted to reconcile the universal and cultural aspects. His study of the Ojibwa,[10] which could be considered one of the first structural-functionalist analyses of identity, has suggested a connection between self and social institutions. Although he has argued that self-awareness and self-reflexivity are universal features, he has also emphasized that other aspects of the self are culturally shaped and cannot be interpreted in terms of a universal perspective. More recently, another anthropologist has tried to cross the nature–nurture dyad in the study of identity. Obeyesekere (1981) has suggested that symbols play an important role in solving psychodynamic problems and difficulties that people have to deal with. He has argued that people use symbols (the cultural side) to manage the psychological effects (the universal side) they have to face. Nonetheless, the influence that social constructivism has had on anthropology[11] has promoted anthropological analyses of identity and self (often discussed as if they were interchangeable terms) as inconsistent entities. So inconsistent, 'fleeting, fragmentary, and buffeted', to use Holland's words, that 'from the extreme ephemeralist position, daily life, especially in the post-modern era, is a movement from self to self' (Holland 1997: 170).

I agree with Holland's view, since by reading many anthropological analyses concerning Muslim migrants and their children (see Chapter 6), I have found myself thinking of Welsch's words, 'to be healthy today is truly only possible in the form of schizophrenia – if not polyphrenia' (1990: 171). Yet it is not only the representation of Muslims as 'polyphrenic', but also the fact that, as Sökefeld has critically observed, 'In anthropological discourse, the question of identity is almost completely detached from the problem of the self. In the vast body of literature about ethnic identity the self is rarely mentioned, and in writings about the self, a relation between the self and identities is some time noted but remains unexplored' (1999: 419). Sökefeld has argued that because of the overemphasis on society we have just discussed, anthropologists have denied the relevance that individuality and the personal self have in the study of the 'others'. He has suggested that social anthropologists took 'Durkheim's concept of "collective representations" ... as justification for the fact that social anthropology gave little attention to

the individual, regarding the social as its only object' (1999: 428). This is
not so surprising, if we think that theories of identity, which I have summarized in the previous section, have been widely (though often implicitly)
employed as the theoretical framework for anthropological studies.

We have seen that a major role in the denial of individuality in the formation of identity has been how social scientists during the 1960s understood 'culture'. So, Sökefeld has observed that in anthropology culture has
been seen 'not as something ephemeral but ... as a "power" constituted by
a system of shared meaning that is effective in shaping social reality' (1999:
427). This, according to him, has prevented some anthropologists recog-
nizing the existence of a *stable and individualistic self*. Indeed, many anthropologists have accepted the idea that self and identity are as unstable and
fluid as the cultures that allegedly create them. Sökefeld has suggested that
a solution could be achieved by conceiving 'the self (used here as generic
term including "individual", "individuality", "person", etc.) as [a] relatively
stable point' (1999: 427).

Sökefeld's article has raised a debate in the journal in which it was published (*Current Anthropology*). Almost all the scholars who have commented
on Sökefeld's article agreed with him in principle (with the unsurprising
exception of Gellner, Mageo and Werbner).[12] Rapport was the most sympathetic to Sökefeld's criticism and has even advocated 'a human-existen-
tialist anthropology which recognizes the radical freedom of the apartness of
the individual ... Individuals carry with them their own experiential contexts, in short, and human social life is the story of a diversity of individual
worlds abutting against one another' (Rapport quoted in Sökefeld 1999:
439). Traditionally, post-modern scholars studying migrants, and in particular Muslim migrants, seem to be keen to deny what Rapport has rightly
observed. Indeed, to use a vivid comparison that Ingold has made 'in
anthropology, culture has tended to play the role that the DNA is made to
play in biology' (Ingold 1996: 114). Notwithstanding the fact that I agree
with almost the whole of Sökefeld's argument, I still perceive the traditional
division between nature and nurture. This dyad does not help develop a
clear understanding of the self and consequently identify what identity is.

Geertz has defined culture as a 'control mechanism – plans, recipes, rules,
instructions (what computer engineers call "programs") – for governing
behavior' (1973: 44). In a previous version of the same article, he also
emphasized that such a 'control mechanism' is achieved by 'the imposition
of an arbitrary framework of symbolic meaning upon reality' (1964: 39). In
other words, humans without culture could not control their behaviour and
would act as ungovernable, chaotic, shapeless, a-meaningful beings (Geertz
1964: 46). Non-humans (animals), though lacking symbols and culture,

avoid such chaos because they have natural 'control mechanisms' (i.e. instincts) that substitute culture. However, I agree with Ingold when he has observed that Geertz's conceptualization of culture tends to represent humans as 'suspended in webs of significance [and] puts humans in a kind of free-floating world in which we are ascribing significance to things "out there"' (Ingold 1996: 130). Geertz has presented humans as something different from the rest of nature, as beings resembling mythological fallen angels now trapped between the two dimensions of nature and nurture.

Recently, some anthropologists have tried to completely overcome the nature–nurture dyad and have suggested that we can interpret cultural phenomena as one of the many realities of nature. So, Milton has argued,

> any debate about the naturalness or unnaturalness of cultural phenomena is most accurately seen as a debate about human nature and human experience (often expressed as 'nature and nurture') rather than nature and culture. What confuses the issue, apart from a failure to recognise the different meanings of 'nature', is that human experience and its products are often described as 'culture', while attributes of human nature are often described as 'non-cultural'. (2002: 17)

By agreeing with Ingold who has argued, 'perception involves the whole person, in an active engagement with his or her environment' (1996: 115), Milton has reconsidered the role that emotions have in the way in which we relate to our environment. Milton's work on emotions as well as Damasio's study of consciousness (2000) are central to my understanding of identity and will be discussed in the next section.

From Consciousness to Self

As I have mentioned earlier, Damasio's book *The Feeling of What Happens* (2000) suggests one of the most recent and intriguing theories on human consciousness. Damasio is M. W. Van Allen Professor and Head of Neurology at the University of Iowa. As a neuroscientist, he has developed a particular interest in the study of emotions and consciousness. Damasio has conducted both laboratory experiments and clinical observation of people suffering brain damage affecting consciousness and emotional reactions. This has allowed him to study the relationship between emotions, consciousness and self. His theory has changed the way in which we used to think about emotions and feelings.

Damasio (1995) has argued that emotions and feelings are not exactly what we ordinarily think they might be. Emotions are *reactions* to external environmental stimuli *producing bodily changes*, such as changes in heart rate, blood pressure and neurological activities. Although many of these bodily changes remain undetected by the ordinary external observer, some produce visible alteration of, for instance, facial expressions, increase in sweating and alterations in behaviour. By contrast, what Damasio has called feelings are *mental representations* of the body-state; they are the *private experience of emotions*, inaccessible to observation, and consequentially to other fellow humans. Damasio has observed that emotions pertain to the bodily domain, while feelings to the mind. Consequently, we first have emotions and then the feelings caused by them. While emotions do not become part of our mind, since they are only reactions to external stimuli, feelings become a consistent part of the mind as the lasting memory of emotions. In other words, happiness, sadness, joy, love and other more complex 'sentiments' are not (as common sense understands them) emotions but rather feelings.

Starting from Damasio's observations, Milton has suggested that emotions 'are an ecological rather than a social phenomenon, that they are a mechanism through which an individual human being is connected to and learns from their environment' (Milton and Svasek 2005: 32). Milton does not reject the idea that emotions are generated during social interaction, but rather that they do not have a 'social ontology' (2005: 35) and the 'other' producing the emotional behaviour 'does not have to be a social or human other, it can be anything with which the individual organism engages, for emotion is part of that engagement' (2005: 35). This leads to the conclusion that through the engagement with different environments 'people learn to love, hate, fear, or be disgusted by different things, so that their body reacts differently when things are encountered' (Milton and Svasek 2005: 36). As Damasio has explained, we translate these bodily reactions (i.e. changes) into feelings. Now, it is my contention that emotions, and the process of learning through them, have an important role in the formation of human self and identity.

Damasio has argued that because emotions could have an impact on organisms, they started to develop what we shall call 'self' so that organisms could stimulate internal and external changes. According to Damasio, evolutionary processes have originated increasingly complex systems of 'selfs', the simplest of which he has called *proto-selves*. All living organisms (even a mono cellular paramecia) have *proto-selves*, an unconscious system that is 'a coherent collection of neural patterns which map, moment by moment, the state of the physical structure of the organism in its many dimensions' (2000: 154). Some organisms, however, become more complex than others and not only have proto-selves but also *consciousness*. Damasio, reminding us that consciousness *is not* monolithic, has suggested the existence of at least two kinds of consciousness: *core consciousness* and *extended consciousness*, which then form two parallel kinds of self, the *core self* and the *autobiographical self*.

Core consciousness, which is less complex than extended consciousness, occurs when the brain's representation devices create an image of how the internal state of the organism is affected by an external object and locate it in a salient spatial-temporal context. This leads to the *core self*: 'the transient protagonist of consciences, generated for any object that provokes the core-consciousness mechanism' (Damasio 2000: 175). The core self, which depends on the proto-self being modified, is continuously generated and time related because, of course, we encounter an unending number of objects in our environment. The result of core consciousness is what Damasio defines as 'the feeling of knowing'; yet, although the core self is formed through a conscious process, we hardly notice it, 'the images that dominate the mental display are those of the things of which you are now conscious' (2000: 172). It is clear that memory has a fundamental role in the formation of the sense of 'self', which, in Damasio's terminology, is represented by the *autobiographical self*. The autobiographical self is formed by two elements, the core self and 'reactivations and display of selected sets of autobiographical memories' i.e. what Damasio has defined as the *autobiographical memory* (Damasio 2000: 196). He, through convincing clinical examples, has suggested that without autobiographical memories our sense of self (i.e. our sense of past, future and historical-temporal continuity) could not be developed. At the same time, however, without the core self, derived from the core consciousness, 'we would have no knowledge whatsoever of the moment, of the memorized past, or the anticipated future that we also have committed to memory' (2000: 219). So, emotions, and the consequent feelings they induce, are the 'engine' of these complex neurological processes that we simply call the 'self', and we have seen how emotions put us in relationship with our environment.

It is becoming clear that 'self' and 'identity' are not the same, as some of the theories we have discussed seem to imply. The self (but not identity) is something that *exists*; it is the product of our complex neurological systems. Following Damasio's theory of self and consciousness, we can now resolve Friese's dilemma: 'it is neither clear whether the reflecting subject *has* self-consciousness or whether it *is* self-consciousness, nor is it clear how subjectivity thus understood can be unified, and related to diversity at the same time' (2002: 21 emphasis in the original). The 'reflecting subject', we can now affirm, *is* self-consciousness, since without consciousness we cannot have a reflecting subject. Damasio's theory of the self resolves another issue left open by sociocultural theories of identity, namely, to reconcile the

Jamesian's 'ever-changing self' with the self seen as the stable element of the persona. Damasio's theory of self explains that, although closely related, the core self and autobiographical self are two different entities. While the core self represents the Jamesian's 'ever-changing self', the autobiographical self provides the sense of stability.

Mr Hussein, before we discussed Damasio's and Milton's theories, formed and maintained his personal self/identity through social interaction, so culture and society shaped him as a Muslim. Mr Hussein changed his personal self through negotiations with his group (or society), he could make sense of himself because an out-group existed, and he was happy to 'depersonalize' to the advantage of his in-group. Mr Hussein, like all human beings, was a product of 'culture', which acting as a control mechanism could govern his behaviour; without it he could have only acted chaotically, shapelessly and a-meaningfully. (Geertz 1973: 44). From this perspective, Mr Hussein's self was 'suspended in webs of significance' (Ingold 1996: 130). Mr Hussein is a fictional character, yet starting from these views of self, we would certainly not be more real. Even before discussing Mr Hussein's self and identity, the observer has to acknowledge, and fully accept the consequences, that he is a human being, that he is made of flesh and blood, that he has a brain which is conscious, which reacts bodily to changes in his environment.

If we take into consideration these points, we can observe the 'human being' Mr Hussein. To do that, we may use Damasio's and Mitlon's theories. Since Mr Hussein is physically and mentally a healthy human being, he could interact with his environment, he could watch TV by using his eyes. Mr Hussein was watching the Arabic channel al-Jazeera when he became aware of the horrible pictures he was watching, children mutilated, women in despair, blood and death. This 'stimulus' activated a bodily response (emotion) and Mr Hussein's heart throbbed, his blood pressure increased, his face became red and his hand formed a fist. Mr Hussein felt anger (perception of emotion) and shouted 'we have to conduct jihad and kill the bloody Americans' (action). Milton and Svasek (2005) have told us that Mr Hussein's emotions are 'ecological mechanisms' through which we learn from the environment and they have a deep impact in the formation of feelings. We form our consciences only in relation to our environment; in other words the external objects forming what we call, in general terms, the environment have an impact on our neurological system and create, through different neuron maps, what Bateson (2000) has described as the abstract account of a concrete external world. So, Damasio (2000) has told us that emotions and feelings influence Mr Hussein's *proto-self* and consequently his *core self* which with Mr Hussein's *autobiographical memory* form his *autobiographical self* (what we normally just call the *self*). The emotions induced by the pictures that Mr Hussein has watched are, through the feelings of anger, now part of Mr Hussein's self. So far so good, but we still have to understand what is that thing called 'identity', symbolically represented by the English pronoun 'I.'

Rethinking Identity

As Locke had intuitively suggested about three centuries ago, human beings have a strong tendency towards a single sense of self. The philosopher Kant argued, 'I am ... conscious of my identical self, in relation to all the variety of representations given to me in an intuition, because I call all of them my representations' (Kant 1990: 138). Not surprisingly, McAdams has stressed,

> [The 'I'] puts experience together – synthesizes it, unifies it – to make it 'mine'. The fact that it *is* mine – that when I see the sunset, I am seeing it; that when you hurt my feelings, those were *my* feelings, not yours, that were hurt – provides a unity of selfhood without which human life in society as we know it would simply not exist. (1997: 57 emphasis in the original)

Damasio, from a neuroscientific rather than a philosophical perspective, has suggested something very similar: the 'I' would be a 'delicately shaped machinery of our imagination [which] stakes the probabilities of selection toward the same, historically continuous self' (2000: 225). Human beings, however, need to make sense of their autobiographical self so that they can express it. Indeed, feelings (i.e. the perception of emotions) are so personal that other human beings cannot directly experience them. Although I agree with Damasio's idea of identity, I suggest that *identity* is not just a mechanism that 'stakes the probabilities of selection' toward the same self, but rather a *process* that allows human beings *to make sense* of their autobiographical self and to express it.

An act of identity is a symbolic act. Geertz has provided the most successful and famous definition of symbols. He has interpreted symbols as an extrinsic source of information. According to him, symbols lie *outside the individual* and provide a way of looking at or understanding the world and its processes (1973). Unsurprisingly, Geertz has compared symbols to genes:

> this comparison of gene and symbols is more than a strained analogy of the familiar 'social heredity' sort. It is actually a substantial relationship, for it is

precisely because of the fact that genetically programmed processes are so highly generalized in men, as compared with lower animals, that culturally pro-grammed ones are so important; it is only because human behaviour is so loosely determined by intrinsic sources of information that extrinsic sources are so vital. (1973: 92–93)

Geertz has described symbols as extrinsic sources of information that provide humans with what in non-humans are provided by intrinsic sources (i.e. instincts). He has added another pre-programmed element, this time social and cultural, which not only would control human behaviour, as genes do, but also make the behaviour 'human' and 'normal', in other words, non-schizophrenic.

As I have said in the previous section, I disagree with Geertz, finding Milton's argument on 'ecological emotions' more convincing and certainly less dogmatic. I suggest that symbols do not lie *outside the individual* but are part of that mechanism that allows us to 'feel' the so-deeply personal and incommunicable human feelings. Turner (1967) has described symbols as 'storage units' filled with information that not only carry meaning, but also transform human attitudes and behaviour. He described symbols as a 'set of evocative devices for rousing, channelling, and domesticating powerful emotions' (1969: 42–43). Although I agree with Turner's definition, fol-lowing Damasio, we have to read 'feelings' where Turner speaks of emo-tions. In other words symbols are a storage unit filled with references to stimuli capable of provoking emotions which induce certain selected feel-ings. Damasio has told us that emotions have a direct impact on our minds:

In organisms equipped to sense emotions, that is, to have feelings, emotions also have an impact on the mind, as they occur, in the here and now. But in organisms equipped with consciousness, that is, capable of knowing they have feelings, another level of regulation is reached. Consciousness allows feelings to be known and thus promotes the impact of emotion internally, allows emotions to permeate the thought process through the agency of feelings. (Damasio 2000: 56)

So, we can argue that symbols also have a direct impact on minds, and they are used (not only among human beings but also among non-humans) to communicate at an inner level feelings which, in other ways, would be, at the level of direct experience, incommunicable.

Let us go back to our Mr Hussein. He has an autobiographical self of which he makes sense through that delicately shaped machinery of his imag-ination he communicates with the *symbolic* expression 'I am Muslim'. Finally, Mr Hussein *is what he feels to be,* regardless of how others, engaged in countless public discourses around the use of cultural markers, might perceive him. 'I am Muslim' means that Mr Hussein *feels* himself to be Muslim. Now we can observe that there exists a sort of circuit; the environment produces stimuli that produce emotions (the body-reactions), which are perceived by Mr Hussein as feelings, which affect his autobiographical self, which is experienced (makes sense) through the delicately shaped machinery of his imagination he calls his Muslim identity, which, of course, is now affected by the feelings he perceived. In other words, what I have described until now is a circuit of causalities based on information both internal and external to the individual. This system aims at maintaining equilibrium at different levels. And we know from physiological as well as psychoanalytic studies that equilibrium between self and identity is essential for a healthy life.

Human beings are not the only ones who tend to stability. Bateson (2002) has observed that any circuit tends toward stability and to counterbalance changes. So, a system, in order to function and survive, *should be self-corrective*, this is achieved by maximizing certain variables. Indeed, we can see 'identity' as exactly a self-corrective mechanism. So, Bateson's study becomes very relevant to our attempt to understand it. Bateson has suggested that stability could be maintained through circular causations, in which small changes are repeated until the *status quo ante* is re-established after each disturbance; he exemplified this process in these terms:

> Imagine a machine in which we distinguish say, four parts, which I have loosely called 'flywheel', 'governor', 'fuel', and 'cylinder'. In addition, the machine is connected to the outside world in two ways, 'energy input' and 'load', which is to be imagined as variable and perhaps weighing upon the flywheel. The machine is circular in the sense that flywheel drives governor which alters fuel supply which feeds cylinder which, in turn, drives flywheel. (2002: 97)

It is easy to see that, in such a circular system, an altering event affecting one part of the circuit reproduces itself again and again in the other parts, until it reaches the point of origin so producing a final change. Stability is maintained until a new alteration in some part of the system occurs again initiating the same process. In this hypothetical circuit, each part is in relationship with the preceding and the following, exactly as in our circuit involving Mr Hussein's identity. Bateson has observed that the type of effect which the parts have on each other could be of two orders: positive gain or no gain. In the case of positive gain, the system would inevitably accelerate, run away and, finally, break down. In the other case, Mr Hussein would experience a 'breakdown', a crisis of identity, with all the consequences that I will not discuss here, but which are easily found in psychological studies.

Bateson, during his study of the Iatmul tribe (1936) had occasion to observe cases of 'positive gain', 'various relations among groups and among various types of kin were characterized by interchanges of behaviour such as that the more A exhibited a given behaviour, the more B was likely to exhibit the same behaviour' (2002: 98). Bateson called these kinds of relationship *symmetrical changes*. However, he also noticed another pattern in which the behaviour of B although being different from that of A was *complementary* to it. According to Bateson (2000: 323), examples of simple *symmetrical changes* are armament races, athletic emulation, boxing matches; while examples of *complementary* behaviours are dominance submission, sadism–masochism, spectatorship–exhibitionism. Both symmetrical as well as complementary changes are subjected to forms of progressive escalation, which Bateson has called *schismogenesis*. By affecting the relationship between the elements of the circuit, schismogenesis (both symmetrical and complementary) has the power to break down the circular system.

Certain circumstances could trap people in schismogenetic processes that could 'break down' the delicately shaped machinery of our imagination called identity. Schismogenetic processes that affect the relationship between the autobiographical self and identity are often the result of a 'circle of panic'. Bhabha has suggested that circles of panic are caused by 'the indeterminate circulation of meaning as rumour or conspiracy, with its perverse, physical affects of panic' (1994: 200). As we have seen, emotions raise feelings that then lead to action; the circle of panic leads to a self-correcting mechanism, so the person can again experience his or her autobiographical self as meaningful. This self-correcting mechanism is what I call an *act of identity*. Because derived from strong emotional reaction to the schismogenetic events, acts of identity tend to be extreme in their essence. Although they are often expressed through rhetoric, sometimes the rhetoric becomes desperate action. In some cases, we can read suicides, particularly when involving young people, as extreme acts of identity. (Dabbagh 2005). A particular circle of panic is trapping many Muslims, and the 'rumour' declares that Islam, both as religion and source of identity, is under attack. This 'circle of panic' leads some of them to develop different degree of 'rhetoric of jihad'.

Conclusion

After a pilgrimage among the different theories of identity and self that emphasized the unique role of culture in their construction, I have observed that another interpretation could be brought to the fore. By seeing, as Milton suggested (2002; Milton and Svasek 2005), culture as an ecological part of nature, I have focused on how the environment has an impact on human beings. Emotions, some recent anthropological studies have argued (Ingold 1992, 1993 and Milton 2002; Milton and Svasek 2005), are central to the way in which we perceive our surroundings or environment. Damasio has challenged the common idea of emotions as subjective feelings and suggested that emotions are bodily responses which are perceived to provoke the feelings (2000). For these reasons, Milton has proposed that emotions are an ecological rather than a social phenomenon (Milton and Svasek 2005), though social interaction surely raises emotions. If this is the case, as I believe, what we call self and identity could not be, as the majority of social scientific theories claim, the product of social interaction, though social interaction could provoke changes in them. Damasio has provided us with a convincing theory of how we form our autobiographical self. I have accepted Damasio's viewpoint and agreed with him that identity is a 'delicately shaped machinery of our imagination [which] stakes the probabilities of selection toward the same, historically continuous self' (2000: 225).

I have explained, however, that identity is a *process* that allows human beings *to make sense* of their autobiographical self and to express it through symbols, which communicate at an inner level feelings that are in other ways directly incommunicable. I have suggested that it is what we *feel* to be that determines our identity. Mr Hussein's 'I am Muslim' is, therefore, the symbolic communication of his emotional commitment through which he experiences his autobiographical self. As we have seen, we can represent the process that forms personal identity as a circuit. Bateson has explained how 'positive gain' or progressive escalations, which he refers to as *schismogenesis*, could disrupt the circuit. Indeed, the relationship between the autobiographical self and the process (identity) that allows human beings to make sense of it could be subjected to schismogenetic events, often caused by a circle of panic to which people react, trying to self-correct their identity through 'acts of identity'.

Today an increasing number of Muslims feel that Islam, as religion and identity, is under attack. In certain circumstances, this 'rumour' traps some Muslims who react to the schismogenetic process with the rhetoric of jihad as a form of an act of identity. Jihad in this sense goes beyond Islam to become part of some people's identity processes. Of course, the general surroundings in which Muslims live (environment) could influence the degree of the schismogenetic process. So, it is fundamental to understand the dynamics through which the schismogenetic circle of panic develops and is maintained. In the next ethnographic chapters, I shall observe some of these dynamics in different contexts and their consequences in the formation of jihad beyond Islam.

Notes

1. As we shall see in this chapter, emotions here should be understood as bodily changes such as such as changes in heart rate or brain activity, some of which become visible to others because of facial expressions or agitation. Indeed, following Damasio's theory (2000) I will argue the distinction between emotions and feelings (i.e. fear, joy, love and so on). The latter are reserved for the private, mental experience of an emotion.

2. See, for instance, Alsayyad and Castells 2002; Gerholm and Lithman 1988; Haddad 2002; Haddad and Esposito 2000; Kepel 1997; Lewis and Schnapper 1994; Nielsen 1985, 1992; Nonneman, Niblock and Szajkowski 1996; Werbner 2002, just to mention some.

3. Alan Watts (1915–73), British-born US philosopher.

4. For more discussion on this point see Ingold 1992 and 1996, as well as Milton and Svaslek 2005.

5. As Ingold (1992 and 1996) has suggested, culture could be easily seen as a human-environment relationship.

6. For an interesting list see Holland 1997.

7. For a discussion of this distinction see Ashmore and Jussim 1997.

8. The name 'social identity theory' was coined by Turner and Brown (1978) to regroup the varied terminology Tajfel employed in his research and which might otherwise create some confusion.

9. See, for example, Markus and Kitayama 1991; Kitayama, Markus and Liberman 1995.

10. The Ojibwa are a native American ethnic group located in the upper Great Lakes (i.e. Lakes Superior and Huron) in both Canada and the United States.

11. See for instance Davies and Harré 1990; Harré and Van Langenhove 1991; Kondo 1990.

12. I think that it might be useful to mention all the contributors to this debate: Driessen, Ewing, Fuchs, Gellner, Haley, Mageo, Rapport, Schlee, Beek and Werbner.

13. As far as collective identities are concerned and the concept of *ummah*, see Chapter 6.

CHAPTER 4

Discussing *Jihad* with Muslim Migrant Men

Migration is probably one of the most ancient things human beings have practised since we populated planet earth. Actually, we know that migration is not just a human trait, it is also a non-human activity as well. Animals move to reach the most hospitable place in order to reproduce and survive. Yet the majority of human beings became inhabitants and few of them have remained truly nomadic. Is this the reality? This is what we might learn at school during our first approaches to human history, but today people migrate as never before, as far as foreign locations, over great distances and to different cultures. It is just not a truism that millions every year leave their home for good (which however is still a migratory act). Many of these are the people we sometimes call aliens, foreigners, migrants and refugees. They are people who have left their homes to find a new one near other people's homes. Home, a deep-rooted concept in our mind, which has been affected by our childhood experience, is becoming today a concept difficult to define. So as Rapport and Dawson have argued, a more mobile conception of home should come to the fore, 'home as something "plurilocal", something to be taken along whenever one decamps' (1998: 7), since home would be, 'a cognitive environment in which one can undertake the routine of daily life and through which one finds one's identity best mediated' and a person could feel 'homeless when such cognitive environment is eschewed' (1998: 10). It is not difficult to see that the 'cognitive environment' Rapport and Dawson are discussing is influenced by what we have referred to as emotions and feelings. For many migrants, as we shall see, Islam become this ubiquitous 'cognitive environment' we may call home.

Many Muslim migrants reaching our cities had great-grandfathers and grandparents who were levied under the rule of European 'Empires'. Others have personally collected the memory of the oppression of colonialism perpetrated by what today they call 'the West'. Others again, who never experienced nineteenth-century colonialism, have transformed the history of colonialism into a powerful metaphor to explain contemporary oppressions. (see Bhabha 1994; Ganguly 1992). Among Muslim migrants I interviewed, colonialism has not been limited to the idea of land usurpation, political oppression and lack of independence, though according to many Palestinians and Iraqis these elements are felt as part of the everyday life of their people, but also include the disruption caused by Western ideas, cultures, lifestyles (Bonnet 2004; Buruma and Margalit 2004) to that 'cognitive environment' called Islam.

Being a Muslim and living in the land of the 'colonizer' raises some questions which even the most moderate Muslim might ask themselves. Emotions run high when people find themselves trapped between the assumed right 'moral code' and the advantages of disregarding it. So, Muslims migrants living in the West could easily feel guilty about their new status and the advantages achieved through adaptation and negotiation of their learned ideas of morality and honour. It is not difficult to find in Islamic literature, newsletters, websites and sermons the condemnation of Muslim migration to non-Muslim countries, when the act is purely economic and not dictated by the need for refuge or by missionary work. Yet if *fatwas* never had real power over ordinary Muslim opinions, these seemed to have even the opposite effect since statistics tell us that from the 1991 Desert Storm operation to Bush's 2003 pre-emptive Iraqi war, Muslim migration to the West has not decreased, but considerably increased.

Increased also is the mistrust between Muslims and non-Muslims, with the last attacks in London challenging community relationships in one of the most cosmopolitan and multicultural cities in Europe. Discussing in the aftermath of these events with Muslims as well as non-Muslims, I had the impression that some non-Muslims read terrorism as axiomatically Islamic, and a similar number of non-Muslims read anti-terrorism as axiomatically anti-Islamic. In both cases one word plays a central role: jihad. Recently, I have asked my first-year students to write down what they thought jihad might be. Although I expected some students to refer to the traditional argument that jihad *means* 'holy war', I was surprised when a consistent number 'translated' the Arabic word into terrorism or the murder of innocent people. To understand how some of these students had formed their conceptions of jihad is not difficult like a sudoku puzzle: Hollywood, television, fictions, novels and bad journalism provided them with fertile ground for misconceptions. Yet I started my 'sudoku' when I asked myself how ordinary Muslim migrants form their ideas of jihad. Why do they have different opinions about it? On which occasions do they discuss jihad?

The majority of studies concerning jihad have focused on the historical meaning of the term (see Chapter 2), or the political discourses of Islamic leaders, ulemas and imams, or both (see Kepel 2002; Lewis 2003; Sanchez 2002).[1] The already amplified voices of the Islamic 'leaders' (better, 'extremists' or 'radical') have been further amplified by the mass media, so that the Muslim laymen's opinions have remained silenced. Jihad among Muslims has been neither a secret word nor a taboo, but a religious concept.[2] The word jihad could be mentioned as part of an *aya* recited during one of the daily prayers, as reference to the striving for a Muslim lifestyle in a predominantly non-Muslim place in the context of political or religious discussion. It is not the word in itself that tells us something, but the formation of rhetoric around the idea of jihad, which becomes a possible act of identity for some Muslims.

In Chapter 3, I used the fictional character Mr Hussein to present, and simplify, different theories of identity. Now, it is time to leave Mr Hussein to meet my respondents, their idea of jihad, their life-experience in non-Muslim contexts, their being Muslims sometimes trapped in what I have called 'a circle of panic'. Yet they share with Mr Hussein, and all of us, the way in which we make sense of their autobiographical self, their identities. Although I shall focus on the dynamics that brought some of my respondents to develop a rhetoric of jihad because of the circle of panic they ended in, and compare them with others who avoided it, it is important to remember that people experience the world through their emotional commitment, as Milton has correctly suggested,

> As fully conscious beings, who not only experience feelings but also know that we do, we can use them to guide our actions. We can plan to avoid sadness and fear, and to maximize happiness. This is how emotions motivate; they identify what matters to us. Whatever we find most emotionally compelling – most exciting, most interesting, most tragic, most satisfying, most awe-inspiring, most guilt-provoking, most enjoyable – becomes what matters most, what we hold most sacred. (2002: 149)

Therefore, in this chapter, I shall explain how in the case of some migrant Muslims, social rejection and guilt inducers have facilitated the circle of panic and consequently their rhetoric of jihad.

Jihad and the Mosque: The Religious Context

I still remember the strange feeling, a mixture of curiosity and fear, which grasped my friends and me when, aged between ten and thirteen years old, we used to walk near the entrance of a recently opened mosque in Florence. The mosque did not match our childish imagination – minarets and intricate oriental arabesques – but rather it was a small prayer room: a former garage turned into a busy, multi-ethnic, colourful place of worship. The coming and going of the worshippers, the incomprehensible sound of Arabic, and the loud voice of the *mu'adhdhin* (the prayer caller) calling daily prayers marked the place with an aura of mystery. Of course, parents had recommended their children to avoid the former garage and to cross the street. We had to avoid the 'Mohammedans', the 'Saracens'. In our imagination, affected by adult xenophobia, the garage was transformed into the scene of horrific crimes, magical and demonic rites as well as indescribable plots against 'us', the 'Christians'. Children's fantasies, somebody might say.

9 June 2003: A Muslim friend has phoned, 'Watch BBC 3 now; there is an episode of *Spooks* that you must see.' The authors of the fiction have set this episode in Birmingham. The local mosque looks like an ordinary place of worship; in reality Muslim children are trained to become suicide bombers ready to hit the UK. The episode increases in its shocking and violent narration; a child carrying out a suicide operation in a Birmingham school; Muslim children taught to hate the West; MI5 spies caught and beaten to death; 'bad Muslims' with long beards and turbans; 'good Muslims' showing a Western appearance and ready to collaborate with MI5. Of course, jihad was the main topic of this episode and Muslim children were made to say words like, 'if I kill an infidel, I will go straightway to paradise'.

In both my childhood fantasies as well as the childish imagination of the *Spooks'* authors, the mosque was the 'lions' den'; the place in which bearded fanatical cut-throats organize the next plot against Western civilization. In the aftermath of 9/11, incidents like the 'shoe bomber' have reinforced the idea that mosques are *'madrassas* of terror'. Indeed, journalists have overemphasized that Richard Reid, better known as the shoe bomber since he failed blow up his foot and the transatlantic aeroplane he was travelling on with explosive hidden inside one of his shoes, worshipped in Brixton mosque, in south-west London; a mosque increasingly accused of attracting radicals. On 20 January 2003, the word 'mosque' appeared again in the main banner headlines of British and international newspapers. This time police in body armour and equipped with battering rams, and supported by helicopters, special units and sniffer dogs, decided to pay a 'visit' to the North London Central Mosque in Finsbury Park, one of the most notorious and controversial places of Islamic worship because of the radical cleric Abu Hamza. Officers, some dressed in chemical protection suits, searched the premises. Briefing journalists on the operation, a Scotland Yard spokesperson said 'Police believe that these premises have played a role in the recruitment of suspected terrorists'. These few words transformed the mosque, an inanimate building, into a dangerous entity capable of changing common people into Muslim terrorists. Many non-Muslims seem to fear mosques; I have noticed this fact when students are writing their final year dissertation on an Islamic topic, asking whether I could introduce or take them to the local mosque for their research; something that other students writing on Buddhism, Sikhism or Jehovah's Witnesses have never required.

At this point, somebody may be curious to know about the activities hidden behind the closed doors of an ordinary mosque, and whether mosques should be blamed for religious intolerance and Islamic radicalism. Although mosques differ in their architecture, organization and Islamic affiliation, they share (at least those I have visited) a certain standardization in their daily activities. Usually, the members of the mosque elect a president, a committee and some trustees. The committee (rarely the president) appoints an imam to lead the prayers and guide the religious life of the mosque. Yet many mosques in the West cannot afford a full-time paid imam, and would rather opt for volunteers.

We could divide the weekly activity of mosques into three main parts: weekdays, Fridays and Sundays. During the weekdays, the five daily prayers (*salat*) are performed at dawn, after midday, mid-afternoon, at sunset and about an hour and a half after that. The attendance may vary considerably from prayer to prayer, with the last two (*salat al-maghrib*, and *salat al-'isha'*) being usually the best attended. These daily prayers are performed without any sermon and tend to be very short. Then, while Muslims who are working leave the mosque quickly, unemployed and young Muslims spend more time in the premises, indulging either in religious or everyday talk.

Friday is the most important day in the Islamic week; although the five daily prayers are performed as usual, a special congregational prayer (*yawm al-jum'a*) is organized around midday and the imam, who leads the prayers, has the responsibility of delivering the *khutba* (sermon). Most Muslims, even those who avoid congregational prayers during the rest of the week, try to attend the yawm al-jum'a, since it is an emphatic part of the Islamic tradition (Sunna). So, on Friday, if one walks near a mosque, one can see groups of Muslims chatting in their local dialect. The atmosphere is festive since it is an opportunity for Muslim migrants to meet their fellow countrymen, discuss events and exchange opinions and, of course, comment on the *khutba*. Friday is also the day in which some mosques organize the *halqat* (circles) dedicated to men and women who wish to memorize the Qur'an and learn the practice of *tajweed* (proper recitation). Almost all mosques have an internal self-organized *madrassa* (school) for the worshippers' children, which for preference meets on Sunday. In this 'Sunday school' children study the Qur'an and receive basic Islamic education. Parents collect their children at the mosque after midday, when congregational prayer is also held, though some spend the time of their children's lesson talking to each other. In the majority of mosques, madrassa volunteers and untrained Islamic teachers form the teaching staff, many of whom are the children's parents and Muslim university students.

So, on what occasions might the word jihad reverberate within the mosque's halls? Potentially, people could mention 'jihad' during any of the described activities. For instance, the imam might recite one of the ayat concerning jihad (i.e. Sura 9:73, 25:52, 66:9) during one of the daily congregational prayers or discuss jihad in one of the khutbas. A teacher might decide to explain what jihad means to his class. Muslims spending time within the mosque with their friends might discuss jihad as a conversational topic. However, the few times I heard the Arabic word 'jihad' mentioned in a mosque was in some khutba discussing the duty of Muslims to fight temptation and because of my questions to my respondents. Indeed, imams leading congregational prayers usually select the shortest *suras* among the last thirty in the Qur'an, and these do not mention jihad; khutbas rarely focus on topics that require a use of the word, and so far, I have never observed Muslim children receiving an explanation of what jihad is during their madrassa classes. Actually, this could explain why many of the Muslim children whom I asked if they could tell me what jihad was were lost or influenced by the stereotyped representation of the mass media. Surprised by my findings, which remained the same despite changing cities and mosques, I decided to ask one of the teachers why Muslim children were not told about jihad, despite the word being widely (mis)used in different contexts in which these children might come in contact with it. Abd al-Tawwab, a 23-year-old Yemeni student, who volunteered to be a teacher in Dublin mosque, replied:

The most important thing is that our children memorize the Holy Qur'an and recite it. We have a lot of problems with this task, because many of the children do not speak Arabic. Then, we have to teach them how to pray and the basic things of Islam. Although, many children know how to pray because they see their parents doing it, often they make mistakes that need to be corrected. Then we have to teach the life of the Prophet, be peace upon him, and basic elements of personal Islamic law. Jihad is not one of the most important things. But there is another reason, we do not know what their parents think about this topic [jihad]. Everybody seems to have their own opinions on jihad. It is too sensitive a topic today.

The fact that an increasingly popularly debated Islamic concept such as jihad has been ignored in the children's madrassas is certainly a negative factor. I had grasped from the few questions I had asked some Muslim children (about jihad) that they tend to form their idea of jihad from their peers, TV and the Internet. Within the majority of mosques in the West, a serious discussion of jihad is lacking, leaving space, as we shall see, for possible manipulative appeals aimed at instigating or reinforcing guilt among the migrant Muslims who know they are enjoying better lives than their 'brothers and sisters' left behind in their homelands.

Despite what the *Spooks* episode suggested, the 'jihad triggers' rarely sound 'Go and kill the infidels so you can enjoy the paradise, wine and carnal pleasure.' The process through which the circle of panic is facilitated is more complex. Usually, the main actors are what we might call 'Muslim itinerant preachers'. Although they do not need a mosque to pass on their messages, some of them, when visiting a mosque, are kindly invited, as a symbol of hospitality and respect, to give the Friday khutba. One might expect these preachers to deliver inflammatory speeches, but in my experience, this is often not the case. In fact, after attending many khutbas, I have noticed that not only are heated sermons unpleasantly aggressive, but also incredibly ineffective, since they could only arouse an audience that shares the preacher's radical views. By contrast, these preachers deliver the most successful controversial khutbas through apparently harmless rhetorical expressions, sometimes accompanied by particular studied body language, facial expressions and voice-tone patterns, aimed together at convincing the listener that Islam is endangered while Muslims are enjoying themselves. Before I provide an ethnographic example of these subliminal, controversial khutbas, it is important to know how they are traditionally delivered.

The standard khutba is divided into four parts; first, the official imam (or any person selected to be in charge of that prayer) praises Allah and recites a prayer celebrating the Prophet. Then he stands up and delivers the first section of the khutba, often discussing a specific Islamic topic, or a topical argument regarding the local community, or events in the Islamic world. At the end of this first sermon, the imam sits down and, together with the con-gregation, concentrates on a silent *du'a'* (supplication to Allah). Then, after standing up again, he presents the second part of the khutba, which may be either a shorter summary of the first speech, a translation of the khutba into the local language, or a new brief reflection on the selected topic. Finally, the imam recites two supplications, one which is a standardized prayer asking Allah for forgiveness for all believers, and a second which is made by him. It is particularly in this second supplication that emotional triggers may reach a climax. We shall follow the experience of Nasim, a 45-year-old Iraqi migrant who has spent his last twelve years in Britain as the owner of a suc-cessful takeaway.

The Invited Shaykh's Khutba

Nasim defines himself as a moderate Muslim; he rejects any form of radicalism, and 9/11 had horrified him. Although he usually does not pray five times per day, he constantly attends the Friday congregational prayers at one of the local mosques. This Friday, the president of the mosque has invited a guest to deliver the khutba. The 'shaykh', whom I had met the day before, speaks with a strong American accent, although he is of Saudi origin; but has a very *wahhabi*[3] style both in his behaviour and dress. The shaykh wears a long white one-piece tunic that drapes just above the ankles (*dishadasha*) and a red chequered head scarf folded diagonally to form a triangle and placed with the fold in front (*ghutra* or *smagh*). Despite his young age (no more than thirty years old), the shaykh, with his soft, persuasive tone, inspiring eyes and smiling face framed by a short line of beard, is certainly someone who could overawe others with his charisma.

The shaykh enters the prayer room; Nasim is seated near me. The shaykh adjusts his red ghutra and, welcoming the congregation, says his 'salaam'. He slowly sits on a chair while listening to the second *adhan* (call for prayer) being recited; then, when the last words of the mu'adhdhin echo in the mosque, he stands up. With a soft voice, looking at his congregation, he says the introductory praise of Allah and His Prophet. This introduction is emotionally neutral and is used to prepare the congregation for the main body of the sermon. In the main body of his khutba, the shaykh questions the lifestyle of contemporary Muslims and contrasts it with how Muslims used to live during the time of the Prophet. Then, after quotations from the Qur'an and some *hadiths*, he recalls how the Mongols disrupted the centre of Islamic life when they invaded Baghdad but how Islam prevailed because the people defended it. Finally, the shaykh rebukes his fellow Muslims in the congregation because of their laziness, 'You are enjoying a nice life, you are selling your soul for an earthly enjoyable life.' The shaykh increases the emotional level and mentions the 'brothers' and 'sisters'[4] suffering around the world because of abuses and injustice. He describes how children are killed in Afghanistan, the desperation of elderly Muslims in Chechnya, the horrible experience of raped Palestinian women. 'How' he asks, raising his forefinger, 'could you feel ready to meet your Creator, how could you explain to Allah that you have enjoyed your money, family and life while your brothers, sisters and their children are suffering the worst torments at the hands of kafurs.'

Now, his voice changes, his face turns grim, his eyes point toward the ceiling. The shaykh seems to address an invisible entity while saying 'They [Muslims around the world] are suffering the worst torments, but you know that such torments will be nothing compared to the eternal sufferings we will endure if we do not forbid …' A long, extenuating, pause, the shaykh's eyes slowly point back to his captivated audience, his hand moves down again with his middle finger curling, in mute cryptical language, while finally he spells '… what is wrong and only allow what is right.' Silence. Unhurriedly, the shaykh sits down. He concentrates on his silent supplication, his face has a fascinating expression of religious devotion.

During the first silent du'a', the Muslim congregation starts to feel uncomfortable while, in their supplications, they address Allah, the Creator and final Judge. Nasim, later that day recalled and discussed with me this first part of the khutba,

> You are there, you hear about Allah and his Prophet; how Muhammad lived and conducted his *ummah*. He [Muhammad] is our example, the perfect one! I mean you listen to the shaykh's words, you look at his expressions and you see a good Muslim, a person who has strong *din* (faith). His words condemn the differences between the Prophet's ummah and our lifestyle. So, after all this, you have to approach Allah directly in your du'a'. I mean, you have to ask Him something and you feel completely uncomfortable because you know your sins, you know that you are enjoying your life while other Muslims have miserable lives. So, you realize that you contribute to making their lives even more miserable. You realize that you pay the taxes to this country [UK] and they used them to bomb Muslims and attack Islam.

The first part of the shaykh's khutba has emotionally destabilized Nasim, it has made him feel uneasy about his Western lifestyle. Nasim feels guilty. The shaykh has challenged Nasim's Muslim identity. Yet this is only the first part of the shaykh's khutba. So let me flash back to the mosque.

Nasim stops his du'a', his hands are open in front of him as if holding a symbolic Qur'an, and then he passes them over his face in a simulation of washing it. A few minutes later, the shaykh speaks again surrounded by an attentive silence. The second part of his khutba is a short English version of the first. Yet the shaykh's gesticulations increase in intensity. When I concentrated on the shaykh's gestures, I observed that it was very difficult to relate the words to the hand movements. His hands seemed to deliver a different message.[5]

After the standardized supplication, the shaykh's second supplication begins. The emotional climax increases while the congregation, in a responsive form to each supplicant section, repeats the 'Ameen' (Amen). The shaykh pronounces the supplication faster and faster in Arabic; he rhetorically controls the rhythm. The words sound hypnotic while he is supplicating Allah to protect the *mujahidin* and glorify the martyrs in Afghanistan, Chechnya, Kashmir, India, Iraq and other less known places. By contrast, the shaykh asks forgiveness for the Muslims who are *qu'ood* (lazy).[6] The strings of repeated 'Ameen' become less clear since some people are crying. Nasim is crying. His hands holding the invisible Qur'an, his eyes closed and his mouth half open while repeating the rhythmical 'Ameen!' Nasim's body is near me, but his mind is lost in feelings triggered by the artificial emotional environment the shaykh has created. Nasim could no longer understand the shaykh's warlike supplication. He has to say 'Ameen!' even when the shaykh openly praises Allah for the recent successful mujahidin operation in Palestine, which also killed some children. The khutba ends, the shaykh sits down and makes another silent du'a' while some members of the congregation make other salats.

When, in our post-khutba conversation, I asked Nasim some comments about this second part of the sermon, he observed,

> I felt guilty. You pray for the people that do something, when you know that you are not doing anything. Du'a' is important because it puts you in direct contact with Allah, and it is the moment in which, if you ask something right with you heart, you know that Allah will do it for you. So, you realize that you are a hypocrite, and you know what the Qur'an says about hypocrites. The supplication was the strongest part, you feel that everybody does concentrate on asking Allah to help the people that defend Islam ...We need to do something; Islam is under attack. We sit, pray, and then we go back to our business. They [Muslims] die, and you say in your heart: 'I am among the hypocrites.'

Although the shaykh carefully avoided the word jihad, his khutba achieved its aim; he challenged the identity of his audience, he raised strong feelings, he pushed them towards the circle of panic.

Discussing the Islamic Concept of Jihad

We have observed that many mosques in the West provide religious services, but rarely become places of intellectual discussion. While at the mosque children receive some basic Islamic knowledge and learn traditional techniques for memorizing the Qur'an, the teachers usually tend to emphasize the proper recitation of the Qur'an rather than its understanding. Adults just pray, listen to the sermons, read the Qur'an and, sometimes, debate the internal political affairs of the mosque. In this religious intellectual vacuum, how do Muslim immigrants form their views on the religious concept of jihad? Often lacking any form of exegesis, from which sources do they develop their concepts of jihad? To answer these questions I present four different accounts which summarize the approaches to jihad that I have encountered during my researches.

The spiritual struggle

Faruq is a 38-year-old Egyptian who lived in Milan and worked in a bakery located not very distant from a small local prayer room. Faruq migrated to Italy ten years before our meeting at the local Friday prayer place. He spoke good Italian, looked smart, and was very polite. He used to enjoy Lebanese music as well as Western pop, and on Saturday nights he used to attend one of the most famous Milan discos. Yet he defined himself as 'good, practising Sunni Muslim, with some interest in mystical Islam'. Faruq explained jihad in these terms:

> In Islam we do not have the concept of holy war. Definitely, jihad is about spiritual things and let me say that the Qur'an is clear about that. So, according to the Prophet there are only two kinds of jihad: a greater and lesser jihad. *Jihad al-asghar* is the struggle against oppression. Yet I ask, do we need to use weapons or to kill people? Sorry, but I do not think so. The Qur'an does not teach violence but love. I want to also say something that may be surprising. Jihad is not something that only Muslims have to conduct. The Qur'an is a universal book, and we can see that some non-Muslims have conducted both jihads. Take Gandhi for example. He struggled against the occupation and oppression of his country with religious fervour. For example, I have no problem in describing his actions as jihad. The *jihad al-akbar* is something different and deals with your soul. This is the jihad that fights against the *shaitan* [the devil] and his temptations.

Faruq had formed his idea of jihad by reading some articles on the Inter-net and discussing the topic with a Senegalese *marabout*,[7] who reinforced Faruq's beliefs in the spiritual values of jihad. Indeed, Faruq's knowledge of Islam is derived from different sources. His concept of jihad perfectly suited his Muslim identity, the way in which Faruq has experienced his autobiographical self. Observing Faruq's life, we notice that he certainly was not trapped in the circle of panic affecting other Muslims today. He had a happy life in Milan, enough money to lead a comfortable life and buy presents for his family in Egypt. Faruq had Italian as well as Maghribi friends; as he used to say 'I feel at home here and I am respected as a good Muslim back in my country'. Indeed, in Egypt Faruq is seen as a successful young man of whom his parents are proud. He has never felt guilty because of his 'privileged status'. Jihad for him was just one of the many religious concepts within Islam and it was not charged with a particular meaning or rhetoric. Faruq did not need a specific act of identity to feel Muslim.

The Ultimate Jihad

I met Tahar when I was in the library of the Institut du Monde Arabe, during my fieldwork in Paris (August 1998). I was waiting for the lift to reach the café-restaurant at the top of the building when a young dark curly-haired smiling Maghribi politely asked me which floor I wanted. We were going to the same place, the nice panoramic café. Our conversation, one of the many which then followed, started when he asked whether I was a 'Spaniard' tourist. Before I could even satisfy his curiosity and correct the mistake, he told me that he had lived in Oran, Algeria, and many times had crossed the sea separating his native town from Alicante. Slaloming between his torrential words, I presented myself as an Italian anthropologist conducting research in Paris. Perhaps Tahar had an idiosyncratic inquisitiveness, but this was certainly useful to an anthropologist. Indeed, when I told him that I was studying the cultural identities of Algerians living in France, he straightforwardly said 'So, I am your man! Shall we have a coffee?'

Tahar, a 32-year-old Algerian living in Paris since 1990, worked in an Algerian music shop in Barbés, the traditional Parisian Arab neighbourhood. Tahar sold music cassettes and CDs of raï music (an Algerian pop-rock). Of course, this is a genre of music that Islamic extremists have labelled *harmful*; so *harmful* that they allegedly killed one the most famous raï singers, Hasni (Marranci 2000a, 2000b and 2003a). In one of our interviews, I asked Tahar whether killing Hasni could have been an act of 'jihad'. He replied

> I do not think that targeting Muslim singers may be a jihad. These [the terrorists] are only people who have mental problems. What they do in Algeria is horrible and against Muslims. In some rural village, they have killed pregnant Muslim women and have removed their foetus; they have killed elderly people, children and even imams. These fake mujahidin say 'jihad! jihad!' and whom do they kill? Muslims! Sorry I cannot buy it. Jihad does exist in Islam. But the target is very different. It's written in the Qur'an 'And kill them wherever you find them.'
>
> OK, you probably need some explanation. There are two jihads, one which you do every day, fighting temptations like ... well ... lust, and if you look around [pointing to a group of French girls sitting nearby] you understand what I mean, don't you [laugh]? The other is called lesser jihad, and it means to fight non-Muslim enemies without rest, for this reason the Qur'an says 'Wherever you find them kill them.' This does not mean that now [taking a knife from the table and making the gesture as pointing it toward me] I have to slit the throat of the first non-Muslim I may meet.

He went on to explain that there were some rules. Muslims could start jihad only if non-Muslims attacked first. In this case jihad meant that Muslims do not stop until they have killed their enemy or the enemy has killed the Muslims. At this point Tahar smiled when he emphasized that to be killed was even a better blessing from Allah because the Muslim in question would become a *shahid*, a martyr, and despite his previous sins would end in paradise. This was not so new to my ears, but finally Tahar disclosed his theory of jihad, 'I tell you something; I strongly believe that one day there will be an ultimate jihad and all non-Muslims will have to decide whether they want to accept Islam or be destroyed.' This last sentence left me surprised, I did not know that there was such a doctrine within any orthodox interpretation of Islam, or even jihad.

During the time I spent with Tahar, it became clear that he was certainly not a mosque-going Muslim. He did not respect the five daily prayers and sometimes his breath smelt unpleasantly of alcohol. Yet I learnt not to try to challenge his firm conviction that he had a Muslim identity. This was what Tahar *felt to be*, despite his contradictory behaviour. Tahar's rhetoric of jihad had something unorthodox about it. He learnt the concept of jihad from family, friends, and reading the most disparate material he had come across in the Institut du Monde Arabe; of course some Islamic websites[8] played a major role. I would probably not be far wrong to say that Tahar and Faruq had derived their concept of jihad from similar sources; yet we can see that their interpretations could not have been more divergent. Although Tahar's apocalyptic battle between Muslims and non-Muslims was not part of any orthodox vision of jihad, it was part of Tahar's dichotomized experience of the West and, in particular of France. During our interviews, Tahar narrated that, since his arrival in France, he had felt rejected and marginalized. Before living in his new location, Tahar had lived in a northern Paris *banlieue* (suburb) in which the majority were Maghribi and Muslim. Furthermore, he worked in a music shop in which the customers were almost exclusively Maghribi and the few contacts he had with French non-Muslims were not free from discrimination.[9] As for any other human being, Tahar's understanding of himself was derived from his primary emotional commitments. The fact that he was perceived as the 'dangerous Other' (Dewitte 1999; Khellil 1991) and often rejected because, as he half-jokingly observed more than once, 'I have the face of an Islamic terrorist', facilitated Tahar's vision of jihad as the last hope for final divine justice.

An Eye for an Eye, a Tooth for a Tooth

Yesterday (5 March 2003) a suicide bomber blew up himself in Haifa killing
the passengers of an express bus packed with Israeli high school and college
students. The Palestinian suicide bomber claimed the lives of thirteen
people, injured forty and left many shocked for life. The 'martyr' was
himself a student, a Palestinian from Hebron. He blew himself and his
victims to pieces when he ignited his explosive belt. 'Allah Akbar', the first
sentence of Muslim prayer, became his last in the conflagration of his jihad.

Today, Husayn is sitting in his preferred corner of the quiet, empty
mosque and whispering the hypnotic Arabic letters of a torn old Qur'an.
Part of Husayn's family is still living in Hebron and suffering the oppression
of the Israeli occupation. Twenty years before the Palestinian Hebron
student decided to become a shahid, Husayn had reached Britain. Now,
aged forty-seven, Husayn works in a local shop, has a Palestinian wife and
three British children. One of his children is the same age (thirteen) as Yuval
Mendelovitch, the youngest victims of this last Hamas carnage. Husayn is a
lovely father, a kind, clever and in many respects open-minded person. But
he supports the actions of Hamas. He calls them jihad.

I enter the prayer room, when, raising his eyes, Husayn sees me. He
stands up, carefully kisses the Qur'an's cover and puts it on the shelf among
the others. Husayn knows my opinions about Hamas and its jihad. It was
something that we had discussed over and over again. Yet it is the first time
that we have met after one of these atrocities or, according to him, one of
these 'successes', has taken place. Husayn welcomes me and says, 'You want
to speak about what happened in Haifa, don't you?' I did. He slowly shakes
his head in disagreement, 'You know that we have two opposite views about
these actions.' Yes, definitely we have, but I strongly wanted to understand
why such a nice person could still support such horrible actions. Husayn
retraces his steps, takes two books from the mosque's bookcase; an Arabic
copy of the Qur'an and a book of al-Bukhari's collection of hadiths. Back to
the corner, he taps his hand against the floor in a typical friendly gesture and
invites me to sit. Then he starts,

I do not have any personal opinion about jihad because the Qur'an and the
Prophet's Sunna are neither questionable nor negotiable; but I can show you
that Hamas' actions are Islamic and part of a rightful jihad. Jihad means fighting
an enemy, as you can read [pointing to an opened page of Sura 2: 90–1]. Now,
it is clear that the enemy has to attack first, and we, the Palestinians and
Muslims around the world, were the ones attacked first. Jihad is total war and
this is clear when Allah says 'Slay them wherever ye catch them.' The other part
of the text stresses that jihad should be stopped only when order has been re-

established. Order means justice and respect of Allah's will. 'Well, observe an important point here', [he points with his finger to the Arabic words] 'But fight them not at the Sacred Mosque, unless they (first) fight you there.' You see? You can even fight in the Sacred Mosque, Mecca, if they, the enemies, attack the Muslims there. So, an eye for an eye and a tooth for a tooth, as the Jews say. But there is a difference between them and us: we are defending our lives and Islam, not just our lives.

I tell him that I am still unconvinced that killing innocents is acceptable, and I still see some contradictions between Allah as a merciful and peace-loving God and the Allah as petitioner of violent, indiscriminate jihad. But what might be illogical to me, is logical to Husayn,

> OK, the problem of civilians, children and women, [he takes the *ahadith* book] … where is it? … where is it? … uhmm … Here, listen to this point,
> *When he [the Prophet], salallaahu 'alayhee wa sallam, passed by a slain woman (after one of the battles), he said: 'She was not (able) to fight' This was narrated by Ahmad and Abu Dawood.*
> So, the Prophet was saying 'She was not fighting.' You see, this means that if a woman fights against the Muslims, she could be killed, and since military service in Israel is compulsory for everybody, each of them could be seen as a fighter. Many of them [Jews] voted for Sharon and in doing so they supported the oppression of Muslims. As for children, another *hadith* explains that jihad should not be stopped because of the presence of women and children or in general what you call civilians.

Although Husayn acknowledges that Islam forbids suicide, he does not consider suicide bombers to be people taking their own lives, rather, according to him, they are just mujahidin who employ an extreme stratagem. To convince me, Husayn recalls a hadith in which the Prophet stated 'War is the name of stratagem and astuteness.' Yet when I still challenge his ideas and define suicide operations as carnage without justification, Husayn radicalizes his position and his answer becomes very emotional,

> Are you speaking of your people? I mean Italians? No! You are speaking of Muslims. Have you seen our children, baby, little girls killed? Yes, surely you have on al-Jazeera. Have you experienced the Israeli oppression? Surely, you have not. Have you seen your neighbour's only house, built with incredible sacrifice, razed to the ground by the Israeli tanks? I can mention a thousand other horrible things they have done to us. Non-Muslims fear jihad because it is something more than war. We can only act and He decides when to accept or refuse mujahidin sacrifices. If He accepts their lives, they become *shuhada*. You have to feel all this in your heart and not in your mind.

It is late and we decide to leave the prayer room. Outside, we meet Husayn's youngest daughter who flings her arms around his neck. In front of my eyes Husayn metamorphoses into the nice, smiling father I have always known. While holding his daughter, tanks and jihad seem to be so remote.

There are some common points between Tahar's conceptualization of jihad and Husayn; both of them see jihad as the last resort as well as a form of apocalyptic event. Yet while for Tahar jihad was a theoretical aspect of his religious beliefs, for Husayn jihad was, though indirectly, part of his life, part of the experience of his people. Similar also are the selection of the Qur'anic verses that they referred to in trying to justify their rhetoric of jihad. Both of them have emphasized that jihad is not aimless but eschatological. It tends towards justice, freedom and Muslim pride being re-established. Emotions play a fundamental role in the interpretation of jihad that Husayn has developed. Although distant from the battlefield, Husayn's support for jihad helps him to overcome his guilt of being in Europe, enjoying his nice house and well-paid job.

The bin Laden Syndrome

Dublin, the Winding Stair Café; two salads and one cheese sandwich, three coffees, from the windows we admired the Ha'penny Bridge shining on a beautiful day in the summer of 2002. Haroun, a Tunisian, 29 years old, Ratib, an Algerian, 33 years old, and an anthropologist, Italian, 29 years old, have just finished their salad. An elderly couple stand up and vacate the table next to us. Throughout their lunch the elderly couple, while sipping their soup, had looked at my two Maghribi guests and listened to their Arabic accents. 'Tell me anthropologist, who hates whom?' Haroun asks me sarcastically.

Ratib and I had met Haroun only three hours earlier, while we were buying some fresh *halal* meat at the mosque's shop. Haroun immediately surprised us because of his overfriendly attitude. Indeed, he was talkative. Although tormenting us with his inquisitive questions, he revealed very little about himself. Haroun had arrived in Dublin as an English student, he found a job (which he did not specify) and decided to settle in Dublin, or at least this was his story. He began by patronizing Ratib and me about Islam and the best halal meat from the mosque shop, when Haroun decided that we should have lunch together. Muslim politeness forced us to accept and together we started to walk towards the Winding Stair Café. Ratib and Haroun started a mixed Tunisian-Algerian conversation on Bush's war on terror. During the time it took to reach the café I became increasingly worried that the different opinions Ratib and Haroun had on Islam could

turn the discussion into an argument. Indeed, Haroun could not understand how a Muslim brother such as Ratib who was as Arab as him could
reject 'the truth'.

Haroun's truth: Muslims are responsible for the rotten condition of Islam
because they do not defend their religion. The CIA is paying fake Islamic
leaders and *mullah* in order to change the revolutionary message of Islam.
Haroun explained to us that Islam is the ultimate revolution, the Qur'an a
revolutionary message to be imposed. The new *dar al-harb* (mainly symbol-
ized by America) fears this revolutionary spiritual force and tries to undermine and destroy it. For this reason, Haroun concluded, Islam is under
attack. Haroun had just finished this argument when, facing me, he pointed
at the elderly couple and exclaimed,

> Tell me anthropologist, who hates whom? They [Westerners] hate us, but we
> [Muslims] do not hate them. We must fight them with jihad because they do not
> believe in Islam and reject it. This is what the Qur'an says. They [non-Muslims]
> can fight against us, but you know that Muslims will win; Allah clearly says so
> in the Qur'an.

Ratib was visibly upset, rejecting Haroun's argument, he rebuked the
Tunisian,

> It is people like you that ruin Islam and shame Muslims. Your ideas are wrong.
> I do not know if CIA agents are infiltrating our mosques and I would not be so
> surprised if they are doing so. But do you really think that they can control Islam
> without Allah allowing this? If you think so, you are the *kafirun*! Your interpre-
> tation of the Qur'an and *ahadith* is inaccurate and very simplistic.

Ratib reinforced his argument by reminding Haroun that in the Qur'an
Christian and Jews are called People of the Book and are not kafirun.
Haroun remained unimpressed and unexpectedly shifted from an aggressive
to a polite, teaching attitude; he had his well-prepared counter-argument,
which he revealed with a smile on his face,

> Yes, I know your point of view; it's exactly what hypocrites use. You read the
> Qur'an without knowing the rule behind it. The Qur'an is a complex book.
> Allah told the Prophet that he could replace some revelations with new revela-
> tions. This is called abrogation and it is clearly explained in the Qur'an. Now, if
> you look carefully at the Qur'an you can see that all the tolerant verses have been
> abrogated by the verse in *al-tawba* [The repentance], which states [speaking in
> Arabic] *'But when the forbidden months are past, then fight and slay the pagans wher-
> ever ye find them, and seize them, beleaguer them, and lie in wait for them in every
> stratagem (of war).'* [Sura 9:5]

Ratib could not stand one more word and with an excuse he left me with Haroun. When the discussion between Ratib and Haroun began, I had promised myself to remain just an observer and record the conversation. Yet before paying the bill and going back to the station with Ratib, I could not help myself and reminded Haroun that the aya he had quoted mentioned the *musharikun* (pagans) living in the Arabian peninsula at the time of the Prophet. Haroun's middle finger points, like a gun, to a group of people waiting just in front of me for their turn to pay, and whispered,

> Who are the *ahl al-kitab* [People of the Book i.e. Jews and Christians] today? Certainly not these people who just do all the wrongdoings their religions have forbidden them. Allah has abrogated all the tolerant verses. Sorry for them. In the first phases of the ummah Muslims needed the support of Christians and Jews, but when Muslims took Mecca, by Allah's Will, they became strong enough to fight their jihad. They [Christians] are kafirun [infidels] because they believe that Jesus is the Son of God. Do you think that Islam could accept this heresy forever? By the way, could you tell me how many of these people believe in God? I tell you the truth, the majority of people in the West are musharikun; they do not even worship Jesus any more, they just play at being the good Christian.

I caught up with Ratib outside the café and we rushed to the station trying to catch our train home. On the way Ratib appeared quite depressed. He told me that he could not understand how some people could turn Islam, 'that it is a hymn to love and peace' into an 'ideology of violence.'

The improvised trip to Dublin had become an interesting ethnographic experience; the fact that Ratib was not only Muslim but also North African had compelled Haroun to proudly defend his viewpoint on jihad. Haroun had an essentialist vision of Islam, according to him there was a 'true Islam' and a 'fake Islam', and he constantly compared our contemporary world to the time of the Prophet. It is not difficult to spot the schismogenetic circle of panic trapping Haroun, who believed that a reactionary and regressive force called 'the West' was threatening and disrupting the revolutionary message of Islam. There is a fundamental difference between Haroun and my friend Ratib that goes further than their understanding of jihad. Although I do not know any aspect of Haroun's life, I know something about Ratib's. Ratib came to the UK to study as a PhD student in engineering. He married an Irish woman and now has two children. He has a good job, a nice semi-detached house and many friends, both Muslim and non-Muslim. Ratib is a very religious Muslim. He prays five times a day and attends the local mosque not only on Friday, but also in late evenings at the *'isha'* prayer. Ratib believes that there is no division between Islam and everyday life; Islam for him is strongly associated with the knowledge and experience of life. During his lifetime, Ratib has not experienced any major traumas, he has defined his life as 'normal' and 'happy'. Although he believes that the war on terror is wrongly conducted and the Western approach to Muslims and Islam is misleading, Ratib does not believe that the 'West' is purposely attacking Islam as religion, but that ignorance and blind Islamophobia should be blamed for certain controversial political actions. Ratib feels unchallenged in his Muslim identity; he does not need the rhetoric of jihad in order to feel Muslim. By contrast, although Haroun used some 'theological' arguments to justify his interpretation of Jews and Christian as kafirun, what mattered to him was the question, 'who hates who?' Emotions had guided Haroun in his rhetoric of jihad, which clearly appeared to be his main act of identity. Haroun felt himself to be Muslim because of his rethoric of jihad, because he knew that following it he was not part of the musharikun, the other Muslims accepting and living among those whom 'hate him because of Islam.'

Conclusion

In this chapter we have started to observe how some of my respondents have discussed the topic of jihad. Being Arab migrants and defining their identities as Muslim are the only two things that Nasim, Faruq, Tahar, Husayn, Ratib and Haroun have in common. Their ideas of jihad appeared to be different and partially unrelated, though all of them referred to the Qur'an and Sunna. Each of them interpreted the Islamic sources according to the feelings that shape their autobiographical selves, their identities. Faruq and Ratib were not trapped within a circle of panic, since their relationship with their environment was not marked by emotions inducing feelings such as guilt. By contrast, Tahar, Husayn and Haroun have experienced their environment as emotionally negative and confrontational. They felt that 'the West' was attempting to 'colonize' Islam and consequently their personal Islamic identities. They have formed a rhetoric of jihad as a primary act of identity. Yet the circle of panic could be facilitated by emotional manipulation. We have observed how a Muslim preacher was able to trigger and induce certain emotions in parts of his audience without resorting to direct violent expressions. Not only did Nasim react to the preacher's words but also to the preacher's meta-communication (gestures, facial expressions and so forth). The preacher succeeded in making Nasim feel like 'a bad Muslim', he subjected Nasim to emotions that translated themselves into depressing feelings affecting his identity and how Nasim felt to be Muslim. In the next chapter, we shall observe how some Muslim families have reacted to the broadcasting of tragedies affecting the Muslim world. Indeed, some Muslim satellite channels have used particularly emotional language and graphic images to produce reactions in their audience. We would observe the dynamics of this process that has facilitated the spreading of the circle of panic among many Muslims.

Notes

1. I also suggest Peters 1996, Rashid 2002 and Rattu 2002.

2. Although in the aftermath of 9/11 the Muslim speaker's voice tends to be softer while pronouncing the word in public places, and recent plans brought fore-wards by the UK government to outlaw words and sentences which could be inter-preted as an invitation to conduct 'jihadi' violence, such as (according to the UK government advisors) 'jihad' and 'shahid', could jeopardize the ordinary use of terms among ordinary Muslims. Actually, if terrorism has achieved anything so far it is jeopardizing freedom of speech, although as we shall see, it is not by listening to extreme sermons that Muslims can be manipulated in order to become suicide bombers.

3. Wahhabis are the followers of the very strict teaching of Ibn 'Abd al-Wahhab, which is the official Islamic school based in Saudi Arabia.

4. Muslims call each other brothers and sisters in Islam.

5. In France, about five years before this khutba, an Algerian, who claimed he was involved in an 'Islamic Algerian resistance movement', told me that the members of his group used particular coded movements of their hands in order to communicate sensitive messages when, for instance, speaking to another member about completely unrelated things. He also added that in certain circumstances what he called the 'messenger' could even be unaware of the presence of a 'receiver' among the audience the 'messenger' was addressing. The messenger had only one task to perform: to repeat on each different occasion and in each place the coded message; many of which, the Algerian revealed, dealt with military instruc-tions and terrorist operations. The shaykh's gesticulations had the power to recall that five year old conversation to my mind. Although I could not exclude that that day a hidden message was delivered, I was sure that Nasim was not the receiver.

6. It is interesting to mention that many Muslims see *qu'ood* as the antinomy of jihad.

7. Marabout means 'a holy man', but in Senegal also indicates a religious func-tionary.

8. On the role that the Islamic website might have, see Bunt 2003.

9. For other experiences of North African Muslims in France see Lepoutre 1997.

CHAPTER 5

Sofas, Families, Tellies and Jihad

Stephan was reading the last news on the Internet when, with a horrified expression, he told me 'An airplane has crashed into one of the Twin Towers in New York, such a horrible incident!' We had not recovered from the shock while watching CNN from the screen of his PC, when another airplane struck the other tower. Osama bin Laden had kept his promises. Although the terrorist action did not hurt Stephan's family or his friends, he felt as if he had lost all of them. A mixture of depression and anger overwhelmed his mind the day after. Stephan blamed Muslims, all of them. They represented the apotheosis of the bloodthirsty terrorists, a barbaric and cruel people, unmerciful and inhuman people. It was not the attack, however, that turned Stephan into a Muslim-hater, rather the Palestinian celebrations of 9/11, which the CNN had broadcast. The footage showed some Palestinians in Lebanon, East Jerusalem and the West Bank celebrating the atrocities. Stephan concluded 'They [Muslims] just sit watching jihad and enjoy it on their sofas.' Nonetheless, some Palestinians had cheered not because of the carnage, rather for the 'divine punishment' on the most powerful of Israel's main weapon suppliers.

In recent years, academic publications attempting to analyse the role that the mass media have in both Bush's war on terror and Osama bin Laden's terrorizing strategy have flourished (cf. Greenberg and Thompson 2002; Hess and Kalb 2003; Schechter 2003). Not only was 9/11 a cruel act of terrorism, but also an unprecedented mass media event. People could watch each second of the tragedy as they would in the case of the subsequent Afghan and Iraqi wars. Millions connected to the Internet, spent nights watching satellite channels, exhausted their eyes scanning newspapers and could not help watching 24-hour all-news channels. Many of us turned into 'newsaholics', at least my Muslim friends did. September 11, however, did not mark the first minute-by-minute mass media coverage of a tragic event involving Islam. In 1991, Saddam Hussein blessed CNN by allowing an exclusive broadcast of Desert Storm's operations. To Americans belonged the bombs and comments, to Muslims belonged the indignation. Despite the fact that many Muslims[1] foresaw a new Vietnam for the multinational coalition, the Iraqi dictator suffered a humiliating defeat. This was the first and last time that the West had the monopoly of widely broadcasting war tragedies. Since 1996, al-Jazeera has guaranteed not only an unprecedented international access to Arab opinions, developing a kind of pan-Muslim-Arab forum (Al Theidi 2003; El-Nawawy and Iskander 2002), but it has also become an ambitious competitor of Western satellite channels. In the aftermath of 9/11, al-Jazeera, with its shocking reportage, has won the heart and minds of Muslims (and as we shall see not only Arabs), yet it has alienated Western governments. The main reason is that Osama bin Laden's seraphic face, soft snakelike voice and warlike messages have provided the Qatar-based satellite channel with publicity it could only have dreamt about at the beginning of the venture. With its reporting of Muslim suffering often narrated more through pictures than texts, al-Jazeera has attracted a varied Muslim audience, some of whom have basic Arabic or none at all.

We know that the mass media has an impact on opinions and ideas, and is able to provoke emotions. Muslims living in Western countries have always been a loyal audience for satellite channels because of their interest in following the many Middle East crises. Yet they often have a tense relationship with the mass media. So, since the Rushdie affair and the 1991 Gulf War, Muslims have shown an increasing mistrust in the Western mass media representation of Islam and Muslims. Many of my respondents, who came from different Muslim countries, believe that this misrepresentation is in reality an attack on Islam for the sake of political interests. They, as we shall see, argued that the Western mass media hide what the Arab satellite channels have shown openly; Muslim children, women and elderly people being killed.

Nonetheless we may observe that these Muslim channels do not just show the suffering, but professionally dramatize it while presenting the controversial Islamic 'insurgency' as legitimate 'resistance'. If we analyse the political comments, pictures and texts of some Arabic-Muslim satellite channels we notice that they aim to raise emotions to such a pitch that, according to my theory of identity, they are able to facilitate the circle of panic. Before observing some ethnographic cases, I shall discuss my respondents' version of the events that, according to them, have marked not only an unprecedented tension between Muslim and non-Muslim countries, but also what they perceive as new colonization that is aimed not just at land and oil, but Islam itself.

From Desert Storm to Operation Iraqi Freedom

The 1991 Gulf War, militarily known as 'Operation Desert Storm', started when the Iraqi dictator Saddam Hussein refused to withdraw his forces from the invaded and then annexed Arab state of Kuwait. Saddam Hussein hoped that Kuwaiti oil could revitalize the disrupted Iraqi economy, which was still suffering the consequences of the eight-year (Western sponsored) Iraq–Iran war (Freedman 1993). The war started on 16 January 1991. The UN allowed military force to be deployed and used. The USA, with the support of a large international coalition (in which some Muslim countries took part) attacked the dictator's country. Saddam asked for a ceasefire just eleven days after the first bombs hit Baghdad. Although influential Muslim states supported the military operation, many Muslims living in the West deplored it[2] since they interpreted the American intervention as an attempt to reinforce Israel's position within the Middle East. Nevertheless, it was the presence of American soldiers, invited by the Saudis and camped close to Mecca that shocked Muslims the most. Amid the uproar, there was the unknown voice of Osama bin Laden, who was the member of one of the most influential and powerful families in the Saudi Kingdom. At that time only the Russians would have defined Osama bin Laden as a terrorist. For the USA and other Western governments, bin Laden and his *mujahidin* represented the heroic freedom fighters who had liberated the Afghan people from the USSR communist yoke (Robison 2001).

Muslims have never loved Saddam the dictator, but have appreciated Saddam the defender of Arab-Muslim pride. In 1998, during my fieldwork in Paris, I did not expect that Desert Storm could still be 'storming' the feelings of my respondents. The 1991 Gulf war and the subsequent UN embargo had become the symbol of a brave resistance (some preferred the word jihad) against the new American 'Satan'. Yet Muslims knew that Saddam used Islam to reinforce his image. So, another group, which seemed faithful to the precepts of Islam, the Taliban, became the new myth in the hope of the construction of a perfect Islamic country. The Taliban's successful jihad against the Russian communist occupation (from 1979 to 1989) was fought with Islamic faith, Muslim blood, Western money and weaponry. In 1996 this radical faction of Afghan and Arab Muslim fighters took power in Kabul after an internal struggle with other mujahedin. The Taliban enforced a violent and gruesome version of the *shari'a* which disregarded basic human rights. Again Muslims became disillusioned and found themselves between the devil and the deep blue sea whether to accept and recognize the obscurantist, tribal Islamic views of the Taliban or reject the Islamic experiment for a 'real' state based on shari'a. For instance, in 2000, Iqbal, a 53-year-old Pakistani man living in Ireland, told me,

> The Taliban don't know very much about Islam and they are making some mistakes, in particular about women. But we must remember that they are conducting an experiment: a new kind of Islamic state, and you know, we mustn't concentrate on the mistakes but appreciate the good results. Afghanistan was pure hell; now it's sort of state with a certain rules and order. The people in the West have to thank the Taliban. You know, they are very active in fighting the cultivation and exportation of opium that kills our children here. Jihad in Afghanistan was successful and inspired many people; but now we need good Muslim politicians and leaders. Afghanistan could provided a new solution for all Muslims.

Indeed, the majority of my respondents have recognized that the Taliban's Islamic state had an oppressive view of shari'a, but they also emphasized that to have an Islamic state was better than having none. They believed that with time and international help the Taliban would have changed their medieval regulations.

The US also had their plans for Afghanistan. What the US government envisaged was not democracy and human rights for the Afghan people, but securing through agreements with the Taliban regime its oil-related interests (cf. Rashid 2002b). The Taliban were enjoying a friendly relationship with Washington when bin Laden started his terrorist organization and set up its anti-American training camps in the country. Osama decided to turn his back on the West. Now that he had defeated the 'Red Devil' (Russia), he aimed at the Devil in Stars and Stripes. In his monolithic view, the USA personified the evil and corrupt 'West'. This time the heated and violent khutbas and *fatwas* of bin Laden, which were unknown to the West during the mujahidin's struggle against the USSR, reached non-Muslim ears. On 23 February 1998, he issued his most famous fatwa against 'America and its allies', which other extremist ulemas readily endorsed. The fatwa touched emotional themes for many pious Muslims such as the 'American occupation' of Mecca since 1991, the cruel trade embargo against the Iraqi people, and the Israeli occupation of Palestine. Finally, bin Laden invited Muslims, wherever they lived, to act:

> We, with God's help, call on every Muslim who believes in God and wishes to be rewarded to comply with God's order to kill the Americans and plunder their money wherever and whenever they find it. We also call on Muslim ulema, leaders, youths, and soldiers to launch raids on Satan's US troops and the devil's supporters who ally with them, and to displace those who are behind them so that they may learn a lesson.[3]

Osama bin Laden had a better chance of fascinating Muslims than the grim Saddam. Some Muslims read Osama bin Laden's victory against the 'Red Devil' in Afghanistan as the evidence that Allah had blessed his jihad. Bin Laden's anti-Americanism forced the US government to list him among the most dangerous enemies of America, though the bin Laden family had economic relationships with influential American politicians such as the Bush family.

On 19 April 1995, a bomb exploded at the Alfred P. Murrah federal building in Oklahoma City killing 168 people and injuring hundreds of others. The American mass media hurriedly blamed Muslim extremists and Osama bin Laden for this atrocity. Anti-Muslim crimes increased to unprecedented levels, but the culprit was a fascist extremist group led by Timothy James McVeigh (a white American). Nonetheless, the US government knew that bin Laden, one day or another, would carry out his threat to strike against American interests. The expected attack arrived three years later, on 7 August 1998. It was directed against two US embassies in Nairobi (Kenya) and in Dar es Salaam (Tanzania). Although different Islamic terrorist groups claimed responsibility for the attack, the US government presented Osama bin Laden as the mastermind behind the plot. The US government retaliated and on 27 August 1998 a missile attack hit six sites in Afghanistan hoping to assassinate the former anti-communist hero Osama bin Laden, while other missiles hit a Sudanese factory, which the US intelligence had indicated was producing chemical weapons. Later investigation would prove that the factory had produced pharmaceutical products and the attack had resulted in the loss of several innocent Muslim workers' lives. Nobody apologized for the terrible mistake. President Clinton's attempts to assassinate Osama bin Laden remained frustrated. Bin Laden did not waste time and, playing the victim card, asked Muslims to punish the 'American terrorist actions'.

The US retaliation could only reinforce the popularity that bin Laden enjoyed among some young Muslims. According to some of my respondents he had all the necessary requirements to present himself as the paladin of the oppressed Muslims. Bin Laden had exchanged his rich and comfortable life for a uncomfortable jihadi lifestyle, his jihad against the Russians was miraculously successful, he wished to replace the corrupt Saudi power with an Islamic state and he could easily make parallels between the Americans attempting to assassinate him and the pagans who attempted to assassinate the Prophets. Furthermore, even the US government could not prove, beyond any reasonable doubt, his involvement in the terrorist actions. The Oklahoma bombing had set a precedent; the majority of my respondents were ready to suggest that bin Laden was a scapegoat, while others observed that Osama bin Laden had attacked military forces in *dar al-islam*, something that many Muslims considered an acceptable jihad.

During these years, Muslims have not only paid attention to the Middle East crisis, but also to another, less discussed, conflict. The cruel conflict in Chechnya has indeed attracted less mass media interest and attention than the Palestinian–Israeli conflict. The brutal Russian repression of the Chechen struggle for independence started in 1994 and officially ended in 1996, when the Russian forces left Chechnya (German 2000; Hafez 2004). In 1999 several bombs exploded in Moscow and in two other southern Russian cities, killing 200 people. The Russian authorities blamed Chechen Muslims and this gave them the excuse to retake control of Chechnya. While Russia presented its action as anti-terrorist operations, the reality was that the Russian military forces have been conducting an inhuman repression of all Chechens. Yet on 23 October 2002 a suicide Chechen commando group unexpectedly stormed a Moscow theatre and the Chechen war again attracted the attention that it had been missing. The terrorists, many of whom were widows, kidnapped over 800 hostages, 130 of whom would die four days later because of the lethal gas the Russian special forces employed to overwhelm and kill the rebels. If the Russian military operations in Chechnya passed unnoticed in the Western mass media, the Chechen tragedy was emphasized on Muslim satellite channels. Al-Jazeera and the radical Lebanese al-Manar overwhelmed their Muslim audience with shocking pictures. They showed the atrocities of the Russian mercenaries through the crude and tragic pictures of mutilated children and women, footage which had allegedly been taken as souvenirs by Russian soldiers showing raped women was screened, causing uproar among many Muslims.

While the Russians were fighting their last post-Soviet conflict, the Americans suffered another attack. On 13 October 2000, a suicide bomber struck the 'Cole', one of the most powerful American warships. The ship was docking in a Yemeni port when the blast killed 17 sailors and injured 33. The terrorists had planned the action to inflict not only the most extensive damage, but also produce the most spectacular attack on an American warship since the Second World War. The attack killed several American soldiers and revealed the American forces' vulnerability to suicide attacks. My respondents, both South Asians and Arabs, welcomed these attacks against US military targets and rejected the description of these 'operations' as terrorist. Bilal, a 32-year-old Pakistani living in Birmingham, explained to me that during the Soviet occupation of Afghanistan, the UK and USA advertised through Pakistan's secret service (ISI) Osama bin Laden's training camps as the bulwark of liberty, 'You know' said Bilal, 'politicians are just hypocrites. They praised Osama bin Laden for his operations against the communists, but now that his jihads move against American arrogance it becomes terrorism.'

My Palestinian respondents were the most critical of the term terrorism, which they label as 'controversial and politically manipulated'. On 28 September 2000, Sharon visited the *Al-Haram As-Sharif* (Temple Mount) and declared it 'eternal Israeli territory'. With a few words, he alienated the Muslim and Christian Palestinian population and triggered the *al-aqsa intifada*. The 1993 Oslo agreement, which reinvigorated the hope of a peaceful solution to the endless conflict, among both Palestinian and Israeli people, was finally over. The circle of violent riots and Israeli retaliation culminated in Mohammed A-Dura's death being internationally broadcast in our homes. Millions of Muslims watched the images of the Israeli-Palestinian crossfire trapping the twelve-year-old boy and his father behind a wall until deadly bullets reached the young boy's body. Muslim resentment and anger against Israel and Jews reached its climax the day after. In every mosque and Islamic centre I was visiting, I could perceive a mixture of distress, disillusion, rage and anger. Many shared the impression that Islam was under attack and that Muslims had to react. In particular, young people saw the defence of the threatened 'Muslim identity' as a priority.

An imam, whom I interviewed in Ireland at the time, felt very frustrated by the tension he could perceive among his co-religionists. Islam asks for rationality, he emphasized, while observing that many contemporary Muslims seemed to have lost this essential requirement,

> If you speak to our brothers and sisters, you find out that they use their tongues and souls (*naf*) irrationally. Muslims that describe jihad only as fighting against Americans, Muslims saying that all Westerners are 'Americans', Muslims who want to kill all non-Muslims, Muslims accepting unbelievable conspiracy theories. Some of them say that America would destroy Mecca if we did not conduct a global jihad. I think that these Muslims think as non-Muslims because they do not realize that only Allah can decide the future. There is no rationality at all in the things these people like bin Laden are saying. I fear that some Muslims may have reduced relational Islam to irrational jihad.

However, many Muslims felt guilty at the oppressed condition of their 'brothers and sisters' living in other Muslim countries and particularly in Palestine. Nonetheless, the worst was still to come.

A terrorist commando unit hijacked four commercial planes, transformed them into flying missiles, hit the twin towers of the New York World Trade Center, part of the Pentagon, but failed to target the White House, and killed about 3,000 people. It was 9/11. The mass media broadcast the tragedy in real time. Shocking images reached the eyes of astonished people.

All of us watched people jumping from the windows of the Twin Towers, all of us heard again and again the broadcast 'Oh my God! Oh my Gooood!' and the collapse of the Towers. Some non-Muslims had the impression that 'Western civilization' itself was under attack, some Muslims interpreted the attack as Allah's punishment for American actions. The rumble of the collapsing towers had not yet become silent when Osama bin Laden's name reverberated as the evil mastermind of the tragedy. Although bin Laden strongly denied direct responsibility for the terrorist attack, he claimed moral responsibility by praising the perpetrators and encouraging other 'pious' Muslims to follow the example of the nineteen 'martyrs'.

The day after the attack, CNN showed a group of Palestinians, in particular women and children, celebrating the tragedy of 9/11. Despite the Palestinian authority revealing allegations that CNN had made up the footage, those images had a devastating impact on many Muslims living in America and Europe since Islamophobia spread quickly and claimed some innocent lives. Meanwhile, the Taliban decided to protect bin Laden by arguing that the US government had not provided sufficient evidence to charge the *shaykh* under shari'a law. The Taliban's position found support among the majority of my respondents, which believed that a Muslim could not be deported from an Islamic to a non-Muslim country without the latter providing clear evidence of the alleged crime. Furthermore, some Muslims had started to blame Israel for the attack. Yet the American administration was no more careful in its political language. Bush Junior emphatically called the American commitment to stop bin Laden's organization a 'Crusade against terrorism'. Muslims saw Bush's gaffe as evidence that by 'terrorism' Bush in reality meant Islam. The Bush administration realized the mistake they had made and adopted a generic 'war on terror'. Yet my respondents thought that the word 'Crusade' better represented the intention of the hardcore Christians in the neo-Conservative movement; to get rid of the Islamic world and present Islam as an inhuman religion.

On 7 October 2001 the US and British Armies launched their attacks against Afghanistan in the attempt to topple the Taliban regime and capture, or kill, the 'Master of Terror'. The American and British governments had raised extensive international support for the Afghan military campaign among not only Western countries, but also some Muslim nations, such as General Pervez Musharraf's Pakistan. The American troops easily gained control of Kabul and other important Taliban bastions such as the city of Kunduz. Yet they failed to capture their most important target: Osama bin Laden. He had mocked the 'Satan' again and despite losing his jihad in Afghanistan, he had won the hearts and minds of many Western Muslims. Although not all of them appreciated bin Laden's actions or him as person they liked the idea that he had mocked the Western super-powers.

During the Afghan anti-Taliban war, the Western mass media emphasized that this war, which cost at least 4,000 civilian lives, could bring democracy to the Afghan people and in particular its burqa-covered women.[4] By contrast, the main Muslim mass media broadcast the other side of the coin: the suffering children, the distressed and starving refugees, the innocent victims of missed targets, the women mourning. Indeed, for many of my respondents these represented the real American gift to Afghanistan. Furthermore, rumours spread that in Afghanistan food was exchanged for conversions to Christianity. Even the most moderate Muslims I knew started to fear that 9/11 had irreversibly changed the relationship between the Islamic world and the Christian one. The feeling of being oppressed and recolonized rose among my respondents when the USA and several European countries introduced special anti-terrorism legislation. It did not take much time before the images of the extra-juridical Camp X-Ray and Camp Delta, which the USA run at the military base of Guantanamo Bay (in Cuba), convinced even the most sceptical Muslims that Muslims and Islam were being treated with contempt and oppressed. As Rashid, a 29-year-old Bangladeshi, put it 'if you are Muslim you are guilty before proof'. Independent organizations such as Amnesty International and the Red Cross criticised the international anti-terrorist policies that the Bush administration had implemented; they feared that innocent Muslims could face mistreatment. This time, Muslim and non-Muslim organizations started to campaign against the anti-terrorist legislation and the war so the Muslim community felt less isolated than before. Nonetheless, although the British government officially disagreed with the controversial US solutions, it issued a no less damaging Anti-Terrorism, Crime and Security Bill. The majority of British Muslims interpreted the new legislation as being aimed at Muslims rather than targeting terrorists. The most controversial point regarded the derogation from Article 5 of the European Convention on Human Rights (ECHR) in order to detain, without trial, non-British citizens suspected of terrorism. This legislation increased British Muslims' mistrust of their government.

The tension between Muslims and the US and UK governments could only rise to an unprecedented level when President Bush and Prime Minister Blair accused Saddam Hussein of threatening the security of the world (and in particular Israel) by possessing weapons of mass destruction deployable in forty-five minutes. Bin Laden was still freely sending his messages but he was no longer target number one. Bush Junior had to conclude what his father had started. France and Germany, supported by millions of Europeans, opposed the new Iraqi war, and the opposition to this new war,

resulted in an astonishing majority of European non-Muslims joining with
Muslims in their protests. Democracy is often a very odd machine, so
despite the majority of people in the UK opposing the war, Prime Minister
Blair joined his friend Bush in this campaign. They started their war on 20
March 2003. The war was relatively short: on 1 May 2003 the Bush administration declared the end of 'major military operations', underestimating
the local resistance and foreign mujahidin, which would result in the highest
number of civilian and military casualties since the end of the Vietnam War.

Although politicians who send soldiers to war traditionally do not trouble
themselves with the destiny of these young people, they tend to be very sensitive about their own political future. A shadow seemed to be cast over
Bush and Blair when they had to face the fact that neither the international
nor the American inspections could confirm that Saddam had weapons of
mass destruction. The war left, according to *Lancet*, 10,000 civilians dead
and many others struggling with poverty, hunger and everyday terrorism.
Allegations that American soldiers were systematically sexually abusing and
torturing Muslim prisoners in Iraq reached several Western mosques long
before the press confirmed their disgraceful actions. Then the photos of
abuse in Abu Ghraib prison confirmed what many had said to me. The tor-
mentors had specifically selected their humiliating torture in order to deni-
grate the Islamic identity of their victims. For many Western Muslims, the
American attacks against Islam now had unchallengeable evidence. Muslim
Arab satellite channels started their campaign to reinforce such an idea.
Before discussing the effects that these satellite channels might have on their
audience, let me explain how Arab channels have become what they are
today.

Discovering the Arab Muslim Satellite Channels

I met Karim (a 33-year-old Algerian migrant) in 1998; he used to pray in a
small mosque located in a suburban area of Paris. After knowing him for a
while, I discovered that Karim still saw the 1991 Iraqi war as a tragedy for
the Arab and Muslim world.[5] The humiliating defeat of what he considered
a powerful Arab country turned into the humiliation of his Muslim pride.
Karim had many reasons to dislike Saddam. Karim's Kurdish friends told
him terrible stories about the persecution of their families and how Saddam
had also oppressed the majority *Shi'a* population. When Karim used to
speak of the Iraqi dictator the preferred reiteration after saying Saddam's
name was 'bloody secularist!' Yet he still saw the Iraqi tyrant as the only one
who could protect Muslim interests in the Middle East. Karim followed
Desert Storm from the start, eager for the latest broadcast news. He could

not believe that, in his words, 'the Americans planned to invade Iraq as the Mongols did centuries ago'.[6] Karim's supposed Middle East superpower melted after just a few days. The Iraqi defeat frustrated Karim but what really upset him was that the only political comments and images Muslims could receive from Baghdad were as American as the supposed 'intelligent' bombs which were killing Iraqi Muslims. Indeed, Karim had to depend upon the CNN, being the only channel operating in bombed Baghdad. As if this was not enough, Karim could not help noticing that the Arab newspapers available at the Institut du Monde Arabe in Paris were, of course, just reporting what the CNN journalists said. In other words, Karim, as other Muslims, had no choice other than to rely on the Western viewpoint.

When I met Karim and some of his friends, they expressed their fear that the Western mass media could colonize the 'mind of too many Muslims' (see also Eickelman and Anderson 1999). In the same suburban Parisian mosque in which I had met Karim, worshippers hoped for the development of a real Muslim voice in the world of the mass media. Some of Karim's friends presented this difficult task as part of a jihad to maintain a Muslim identity. So, Hakan (a 42-year-old Turkish man) argued,

> We are between the devil and the deep blue sea; we can only select between news provided by corrupt Arab regimes or put up with the anti-Muslim Western mass media. We need something that can challenge both. I mean something that is similar in quality to Western products but having a Muslim soul. If we could have very good Arab channels, Muslims who don't speak Arabic would easily learn the language of the Qur'an, something that every good Muslim should do.

Finally, in the 1990s, some Arab channels seemed to move in the direction Karim and his friends hoped for. Soon they would achieve a totally unexpected success. Two factors have assisted this success: the increasingly affordable costs of satellite technologies, and an improvement in the quality of the Arab programmes. These are the two elements that have allowed al-Jazeera to claim eight million subscribers in Europe (*Guardian*, 25 March 2003). Although al-Jazeera has been the most successful satellite channel, it was not the first.

Wars, tragedies and economic interests often go arm in arm and this is particularly the case when we observe the causes of the mass media. The Lebanese civil war triggered the mass media race to win the hearts and minds of the Christian or Muslim Lebanese living in Canada (Kraidy 2002). In the late 1980s, the Lebanese LBC (Lebanese Broadcasting Corporation) decided to target an Arab and Muslim migrant audience. If the civil war was behind the development of a Lebanese satellite system, the reasons for starting the MBC (Middle East Broadcasting Corporation) dealt with the struggle for the political hegemony over the Muslim world. The Saudi bil-lionaire Saleh Kamel set up MBC in 1991 in London to broadcast pro-grammes of general interest; MBC achieved relative success since it was a no-subscription channel (Boyd 1999). Nevertheless, the alleged independ-ence of MBC from Saudi control ended in 1994, when the channel passed to Walid and Abdelazziz al-Ibrahim, both brothers-in-law of King Fahd.

After the Iranian revolution in 1979, the Saudi regime understood the role that the mass media could play against revolutionary Shi'a forces inside and outside the kingdom as well as against the Egyptian hegemony in the sector. Indeed, since the 1960s Egypt had the monopoly of regional broad-casting and used to depict the Saudi Kingdom as an un-Islamic reactionary regime, sometimes even calling for its downfall (cf. Hafez 2001). The involvement of the Saudi royal family in the satellite broadcasting business reached its apogee in 1994, when ART (Arab Radio and Television) and Orbit started to operate. These channels broadcast general programmes as well as television news but they carefully avoided any criticism of Saudi pol-itics. Local Arab regimes could easily control the terrestrial Arab TV sta-tions, but starting from the 1990s, satellite technology increased the possibility of pluralistic opinions. New satellite stations, which could reach Muslims in different places and particularly in Western countries, started to broadcast. Among those, al-Manar (meaning the beacon) was surely the most politicized.

The Lebanese government licensed al-Manar in 2000 and the station became the voice of the radical Shi'a party Hezbollah. Symbolically, the channel decided to start broadcasting (eight hours per day) on the same day on which the Israeli troops withdrew from South Lebanon (24 May 2000). Self-defined as 'The Channel of Arabs and Muslims',[7] al-Manar's propa-ganda is not only pro-Palestinian but also anti-Israeli and overtly anti-Semitic. Unsurprisingly, Al-Manar again increased its broadcasting time to ten hours when the *al-aqsa Intifada* began. September 11 and the subse-quent wars in Afghanistan and Iraq increased the channel's traditional attacks against the 'Nazi-Zionist Jews' and 'the 'American Devil'. The majority of these controversial materials were broadcast through video clips, some of which praised jihad and Islamic resistance. These video clips in MTV style quickly became the channel's most attractive feature. I have to admit that almost all my respondents, even people who I would never dare to define as radical, showed a certain appreciation of al-Manar and its videos.

In July 2001, I had occasion to watch Al-Manar for the first time. Farid (a 40-year-old Lebanese Shi'a) had invited me to his home for a cup of coffee. I arrived at his home, he opened his door and told me to wait for him in the lounge while he was preparing our Lebanese coffee. I started to watch the Arabic programme that Farid had on. An anchorman, speaking in Arabic, was presenting the latest news from Palestine. At the close, he praised the courage of the Palestinian *shahid* (martyrs) who sacrificed their lives while conducting jihad against the 'Zionist enemy'. After the news, there followed a video clip. The images, many of which were highly shocking, portrayed the funerals of children, women crying and crowds following the flagged coffin with photographs of the Palestinian martyrs. Heroic mujahidin songs accompanied the footage. Farid came back and smiled, 'Do you know this channel?' I shook my head to say no. 'It is al-Manar', my host went on, 'it is a satellite channel linked to Hezbollah, the Lebanese Shi'a resistance. They broadcast many religious programmes, *dua'a* [supplications] and jihad songs. It may be a bit radical but at least you know that the programs are Islamic and not *haram.*'

Notwithstanding the success that the al-Manar channel has achieved among many Muslims, my respondents increasingly reported that al-Jazeera was the best Arab satellite channel. The exclusive coverage of the 2001 Afghan war had transformed the Qatar broadcaster into the CNN of the Muslim world. Surprisingly, the audience of al-Jazeera is not restricted to Arab Muslims, but extends to a number of Muslims from non-Arabic speaking countries. Al-Jazeera broadcast its first programme in November 1996; it primarily focuses on television news and political analysis. Today we can consider al-Jazeera a pan-Arab-Muslim channel (El-Nawawy and Iskander 2002). In a Muslim audience disaffected with Western mass media, al-Jazeera has achieved an unprecedented influence. The recent success of this satellite channel is such that Jessica Hodgson, in the Guardian supplement, *The Observer*,[8] has observed, 'British Asians have taken to Al Jazeera like pre-teens to Harry Potter – some 87 per cent have access to the channel via Sky.' Hodgson's reference to 'British Asians' is not a mistake, as some people might think. Some British Asians are indeed al-Jazeera addicted. Yet we might ask, for instance, what could make al-Jazeera so interesting to a 26-year-old man of Pakistani origin. I had occasion to understand it when I went to Saad's home.

On 9 April 2003, the American troops reached Baghdad. Saad and I were listening to al-Jazeera's commentator describing the American soldiers toppling the dictator's huge statue, when unexpectedly a black American soldier covered the bronze tyrant's face with the American flag. The al-Jazeera journalist commented 'This flag shows what the new Iraq will be. Everything will smell American and this flag shows what Americans want to do to Iraqi Muslims.' Saad became upset and started to say, 'Shit! Bastards, bloody imperialists, I would know what to do with your fucking flag.' He hated Saddam as much as the American flag. Saad can understand some Arabic, and he claimed he had improved incredibly since he had started watching al-Jazeera. Saad explained that if Muslims wished to avoid Western propaganda and manipulation they had to learn Arabic. Yet young South Asians like Saad do not watch the channel just to learn Arabic, but because they can watch on al-Jazeera what the Western channels censor: videos and photos showing a very different reality about 'the war on terror'. So Saad observed, 'Al-Jazeera has shown Bin-Laden's messages without any cuts so this channel lets us to know the reality of the Afghan and Iraqi war; I mean, the dead children and women.' Saad loved another aspect of the Arabic channel, its capacity to challenge American and British hypocrisy. He provided me with this example, 'al-Jazeera recently dared to show dead British soldiers and for these reasons, they [Americans] bombed al-Jazeera's installations and killed some of its journalists.' Saad told me that Muslims could see al-Jazeera as conducting a defensive battle against hypocrisy and Western propaganda. Yet we might wonder what effects this shocking reportage might have on some Western Muslim families.

Muslim Families Watching Western 'Just Wars'

In many Muslim (and non-Muslim) homes watching television programmes represents a collective family ritual which may also involve the family's guests. Before 9/11 and the 'war on terror', films and television dramas glued Muslim families to their sofas (see also Eickelman and Anderson 1999). September 11 and the Afghan war shifted Muslim families' preference towards television news and political talk shows. As I have mentioned before, the mass media, and in particular television programmes, may provoke powerful emotional reactions in their audiences (cf. Christiansen 2004; Nisbet, Scheufele and Shanahan 2004). Channels such as al-Jazeera and al-Manar purposely employ very shocking images and provocative comments as part of their strategy (Nisbet et al 2004). During my fieldwork, I had occasion to observe the effect of such emotional triggers on some Muslim families. In this section I shall discuss two different examples.

Ali's family comprised four members. Ali, 47, worked as an engineer, and was happily married to a 40-year-old Palestinian, Afra. They had two children: Ibrahim, 11 years old and Aminah, 22 years old. The family enjoyed a standard lifestyle. I experienced the hospitality of this family quite often. On 3 November 2001, Ali had organized a dinner at his home to which he invited me along with his friend Ahmad, a 29-year-old Algerian. The dinner would be special not only because of the fantastic Arabic food Afra cooked, but also because al-Jazeera would broadcast one of the recurrent Osama bin Laden videotapes inciting Muslims to act against the Afghan war.

That evening, at about seven, Ahmad and I reached Ali's home. Ali, despite his modern lifestyle, had maintained some of his family traditions, the most radical of which culminated in gender-segregated dinners. So, after serving our meal, his wife and daughter relegated themselves to the kitchen, which also proved to be a taboo area for a curious anthropologist interested in Algerian food. The first time I had dinner with Ali, Afra and her daughter emphasized that they preferred the gender-segregated dinners, which took place only when guests were invited (something that happened quite often). Indeed, it seemed that the two women could not bear Ali and his guests' preferred topics of discussion: sport, politics and, in particular, business. In the large kitchen Afra could enjoy the company of guests' wives and have their gossip while her daughter was entertaining the other children. I started to worry about what Afra said about 'enjoying gossip' when my own wife expressed grateful appreciation for these gender-segregated dinners!

The first time I became aware of this ritual, I expected that the 'segregation' would have extended to other gatherings, activities and spaces, yet I proved to be very wrong. Despite the fact that the house had a living room and a lounge, both equipped with televisions, Ali's wife and his daughter used to join us in the living room to watch the TV. Before my last visit, Ali had bought an outstanding super-slim TV screen, and he proudly illustrated the futuristic qualities it had. The select channel of the night was al-Jazeera, which remained as background noise to our conversation. This was until al-Jazeera broadcast the last of bin Laden's messages promptly subtitled in Arabic. Afra asked me whether I could understand it. Before I was allowed to answer, she translated the message while the others focused on Osama bin Laden's gentle words.[9] At the end of the message, Ali and Ahmad commented on bin Laden's words. Partially cut off from their discussion, I could observe it in detail. Ali's son, Ibrahim, had just moved to the right side of my armchair. Excited by being part of my research, Ibrahim helped me to understand the conversation when it started shifted to shift to a fast Arabic dialect. Osama bin Laden's message triggered off an animated discussion between Ali, Ahmad, Afra and her daughter.

Afra stated that Muslims could disagree with bin Laden's actions or ideas, but should recognize that Osama bin Laden was a 'faithful Muslim'. Her husband seemed less convinced yet she defended her viewpoint, 'Brother Osama has abandoned his rich life and wealth for defending Islam.' Ali observed that he could not know how much *din* (faith) bin Laden might have, because only Allah could know, then he said, 'Yet his actions could jeopardize the peaceful lives of many Muslims and families like us.' Afra was convinced that since bin Laden had escaped American punishment, this might have been a sign that Allah had accepted his jihad. In any case, Afra refused to believe that bin Laden had planned 9/11 and argued, 'Allah would have punished him, but since He has not, this means that Bush and the Zionist members of his government planned the plot.' Ali disagreed, 'Bin Laden has acted as a "prima donna" without thinking of the consequences for Muslims and Islam.' Ahmad agreed with Ali that bin Laden's actions could jeopardize the image of Islam among non-Muslims, but Ahmad added, 'Osama is shaking Muslims out of their torpor. Something good for us who are so passive.' Although the people who were sitting around me offered different opinions, I had the impression that everybody was ready to agree on the most popular conspiracy theories available. They were reading 9/11 not just as an attack on 'the West' but on Islam. So, Ali's daughter, Aminah, supported her mother's viewpoint that Allah had allowed 9/11 to happen. She emphasized, 'Americans believe in God's punishment, so why do they want to blame others for something that only God could allow? Why do they not understand that this was a punishment for all their mistakes and dirty wars.'

While some crude images passed over Ali's slim screen, Ahmad started to notice that al-Jazeera had not cut bin Laden's message and, laughing, he observed, 'the Americans should be mad about it. They [Americans] speak of freedom of speech, but they don't like our freedom of speech. Americans like American style of freedom that is like American food, junk.' At this point, an emotional al-Jazeera anchorman announced to his audience that during the holy month of Ramadan the invading forces had not stopped the bombing of 'Afghan Muslim families'. While speaking, graphic pictures of attacks on Kabul's eastern area were screened. The news outraged my hosts. With a quick exchange of remarks they agreed that, yes, Islam was under attack. The fact that Bush had ordered the continuation of bombing during Ramadan was producing an uproar within the family. Afra exclaimed, 'try now to convince me [speaking to her husband and daughter] that this was not a Crusade against Muslims and Islam'. Ali points his finger to his expensive technological screen and told me, as if he needed to convince me of the terrible acts the USA were perpetrating,

They [Afghans] are poor people; they don't have anything, and watch here, watch these powerful explosions against a country that has virtually nothing. What do these poor Muslims have? They have only Islam and their din. Poor children, Ramadan is so important for them; Ramadan for Afghan children is more than Christmas here, because they do not have all the things we can have all the days of the year. They [Americans] do not respect Muslim blood; for them our blood is the cheapest in the world. In Afghanistan, think about that, they are killing people that don't even know why they are killed. But I am pretty sure that they could erase Afghanistan itself and the rest of the world, but if Allah wants bin Laden to survive, well, he will survive. Wait and see.

Aminah observed that during one of the talk shows she watched on al-Jazeera it had been suggested that the USA had decided to attack Islam because Bush needed a counter-ideology to fight in the same way that Reagan had with communism, so she argued, 'They [Americans] are a very divided society who oppress the poorest and therefore they could have a revolution.' Ali generally agreed and with an empathetic voice told me, 'They fear Islam because Islam imposes social justice. So Islam appeals to the black community and Muslims know very well that Islam is a revolutionary force.' Ahmad challenged his friend, 'if you are right, are there sufficient reasons to conduct a defensive jihad?' The question, however, remained unanswered.

Afra wished to show me that the Western mass media tries to mislead their non-Muslim audience by hiding Muslim suffering, so she switched to the BBC News 24. After a while I could recognise some familiar images, indeed the BBC was broadcasting some of al-Jazeera's images, but the shocking and crude ones, showing some mutilated women and children, had disappeared in the BBC version. Afra was repeating, 'Cut! Cut! All cut. The horrible war now is just a new videogame. They [the Western mass media] want to show a clean war. No blood, and no amputations caused by cluster bombs, just fake happy Muslims who are grateful for democracy.' While speaking and waving the TV controller, she turned to her husband, 'Do you remember what the CNN journalist, who stood on the hotel roof said the first time the Americans bombed Baghdad [1991]?' Ali immediately answered 'Fireworks! The journalist on the top of the hotel roof said fireworks … could you think that … people were dying, but for him the powerful explosions were just fireworks! A party, you see?' Unexpectedly, Amhad turned towards me and said sarcastically, 'I guess that they [the Americans] did not compare 9/11 to a pyrotechnic show, did they?'

Although I am an anthropologist and tend not to judge my respondents, at the beginning I could not help feeling disappointed at the lack of sympathy the family and the guest had shown for the victims of 9/11. However, when I started to analyse their discourses, I noticed that even in the case of Muslim casualties they emphasized that Islam had lost Muslims rather than saying that people have been killed. They observed the tragedy of this terrible new war from a different perspective. This family seemed to interpret bin Laden's actions and the consequences they had brought to the Muslim world, through the concept of *qadar* (predestination). In other words, each of these events happened because they were part of Allah's plans. Yet qadar does not imply passivity or fatalism but Allah's will does take place and Muslims should act. The crude pictures available on al-Jazeera and al-Manar had subjected the family members to two emotional processes, the raising of feelings such as fear, frustrations and anger, and at the same time exporting them to a systematic desensitization to suffering which leads to a particular interpretation of qadar. This rapidly sucked Ali's family into the 'circle of panic'. The second ethnographic example that I shall discuss below confirms this dynamic.

Majd is a 58-year-old Iraqi Shi'a married to Asma, a 50-year-old Iraqi Sunni woman. They have four children, three daughters, Amal (27 years old), Ilham (22 years old), Jamilah (17 years old) and one son, Azhar (10 years old). The family had bought its detached house in a mainly white British neighbourhood. All of them hold British passports of which they used to be very proud before Blair ordered the war in Iraq. The members of these families saw themselves as British Muslims. In the aftermath of 9/11, Majd's business had suffered some economic hardship, since the non-Muslim customers declined in number, but the worst Islamophobic event took place when some local youngsters started to hurl abuse at his children. Yet Majd and Asma had continued to trust British society and repeatedly told me, 'The truth is that we are more respected as Muslims here in Britain than we were in Saddam's Iraq. We can be good Muslims here.' Notwithstanding the assimilation process, their faith in the justice and democracy of Western countries collapsed when the British soldiers had to attack Iraq despite the British people's massive opposition to the war. Since the beginning of the new Iraqi war, Asma had started wearing the *hijab* (headscarf), despite her husband's concerns, who feared his wife could become a victim of Islamophobic attack. Islam was a constant presence during the everyday life of Majd's family.

That night, after a superb Iraqi-style dinner and while Majd was settling down for his satellite TV news, Asma revealed, 'Since the beginning of the [Iraqi] war, Majd has spent every night looking for new information about Iraq. You know, we have relatives there.' Since Majd is a Shi'a Muslim. I would have expected him to support the war to topple Saddam's regime. On the contrary, from the beginning of the war I came to know that Majd openly supported the Sunni dictator; the very same tyrant whom had killed thousands of Majd's co-religionists and forced him into self-imposed exile. Majd justified his controversial position by arguing that Bush had declared a war not just against Saddam but the whole Islamic world. None of Majd's family members could understand why their host country (the UK), which was their children's country, had opted for a dangerous conflict which finally would result in thousands of dead civilians.

Werbner (1994) has correctly observed that in 1991 the British Pakistanis made a counter-productive choice in supporting Saddam Hussein. She has suggested they had access to two narratives which she called 'fabulations'. Indeed, Werbner has distinguished between 'myth', which achieves significance by detaching from the time flow, and 'fable', which achieves significance by detaching from space. Therefore, she has suggested that, on the one hand, the non-Muslim fable had 'cast Saddam as a vicious, tyrannical, insane villain', on the other, the Muslim fable had transformed the Iraqi 'insane villain' into an Islamic super-hero (1994: 213). Werbner has concluded, 'significant current affairs have the potentiality to become fables shared in space by a Islamic global community as "simultaneous consumers" in calendrical time' (1994: 21). But analysing the following account of what happened in Majd's home that night, we can go further than the culturalist interpretation Werbner has suggested.

Majd and his wife told me during an interview that the images they watched on Arab satellite channels had left them deeply shocked. Yet they *needed* to see them, and no effort was made to protect the youngest son from the grim pictures. After our dinner, Asma, who as usual held the TV remote control, was zapping between BBC News 24, al-Jazeera, CNN and al-Manar, while Majd complained of the hypocrisy of our Western governments and their ways of presenting and justifying the war. Majd made the same argument I heard so many times during my research, 'they show Muslim prisoners, dead Iraqi soldiers, but if one of the Muslim channels dares to show even two British soldiers bloody dead, they [politicians?] immediately make an outcry'. Of course, Majd was referring to what had happened the day before (26 March 2003), when Al-Jazeera made the controversial decision to broadcast a video showing two dead British soldiers. The al-Jazeera decision had provoked great indignation among the British and American public, politicians and Western journalists. Nevertheless, the indignation that the British politicians showed upset many Muslims such as Majd, since the same disgusted expression was missing from the Prime Minister's face when the mutilated bodies were Muslims. So Majd noticed,

I might be sorry for them [the soldiers] as human beings, but I am not sorry for them as soldiers. OK, I know I will become unpopular, I know that you will write these words, but should I lie? British soldiers and in particular Americans have to kill Muslims that never attacked Britain or America, and of course these Muslims defend themselves and their families. This it the right of any Muslim, I mean, to defend Islam. Come on! You did not need a war to topple Saddam, we needed the British and American intelligence services to reinforce the existing Shi'a militia. The reality is different. American and British politicians do not like Islam, they do not want a real Islamic state anywhere, so they did not

help the Shi'a people but bombed them. Freedom? Bollocks! They want to
prevent people living according to Islamic principles. It is important to show
these pictures so that British people can understand what Tony Blair is ready to
do to our and their children. You know, his children are safe at home in their
beds, aren't they? Saddam is surely an evil man and Muslims should have fought
him, but I am sorry to say that this time he is bloody right.

The British government and its war certainly have no support in this
British-Iraqi house, and, let me say, why should there be? For Majd's family,
and also for millions of other British people, the war is unjustified. However,
Majd is expressing his resentment against the British government not in
nationalistic terms, as an Iraqi, but in religious terms, as a Muslim. He told
me that an attack against Islam requires a defensive jihad, which any
Muslim, despite their origin, nationality, ethnicity, financial means, is
required to perform everywhere. 'I foresee a fiercely Islamic resistance in
Iraq and for the craziness of politicians lots of people will die on both the
Muslim and non-Muslim sides.' If Ali had only alluded to the concept of
qadar, Majd and his wife mentioned it overtly, 'people, said Majd, will die
because of their qadar, but Muslims are fighting for justice and will see the
Garden (Paradise).'

Asma was watching al-Manar and interrupted Madj to tell me that she
liked the channel because of its *dua'a* for the mujahidin, its jihadi songs, of
which their ten-year-old Azhar seemed to know some words. We watched
some of the video clips. As any other child, Azhar liked to play soldiers, yet
I could observe that within Azhar's childhood fantasies, the soldier was not
wearing any camouflage jacket and helmet, but rather a green bandana and
a dark cloak typical of the Hezbollah's mujahidin. Azhar was not playing war
but jihad. The propaganda song was playing, I could watch fully armed
young people walking in an anonymous countryside with their faces
covered, apparently they were reaching their next battlefield. A deep masculine baritone voice accompanied the images with words from the Qur'an
and Shi'a songs on a military soundtrack. Asma praised the Muslim
mujahidin in Arabic and asked Allah to protect them and their families,
Azhar parroted the martial steps of the soldiers, while his father and sisters
smiled at him. Nobody but the telly had explained to Azhar what jihad is.
Jihad is cool on al-Manar!

Conclusion

Different theories have tried to explain the processes through which some
people are radicalised and start to follow a fundamentalist version of their

faith (see Bruce 2000; Esposito 1999; Hafez 2004; Sayyid 1997). Some scholars, such as Halliday (1997), have de-emphasized the role that religion might play in fundamentalism; others, such as Bruce (2000), have argued the opposite, and suggested that certain religions may encourage fundamentalism and radicalism. Indeed, in these theories, Islam has been portrayed as the religion which may easily push worshippers toward radicalization. Bruce has compared several religions (but in particular Christianity and Islam) and reached the emphatic conclusion, 'I cannot accept that, as matter of principle, we should suppose religion to be without consequences' (Bruce 2000: 103). According to Bruce a tendency to fanaticism characterizes religion, but each doctrine differs in the degree to which it could become fundamentalist. This, the scholar has suggested, depends on the theological characteristics of the particular faith. Consequently, Bruce has ended in arguing that the most fertile ground for the development of fundamentalism may be found in Islam, because 'for Islam, religion is matter of obeying the Holy Law. As what God requires is obedience to the Law, then its imposition is not just acceptable but necessary' (Bruce 2000: 107).

I consider Bruce's statement, 'Fundamentalism is perfectly consistent with the logic of the religious tradition from which it grows' (Bruce 2000: 116) to be flawed. Bruce, by focusing on what he calls 'the fundamentalist mind', has axiomatically linked people's personal faith to people's theological knowledge. For these reasons, he has stated, 'Fundamentalism is a rational response of traditionally religious people to social, political, and economic changes that downgrade and constrain the role of religion in the public world' (Bruce 2000: 117). In short, Bruce has brushed up the old-fashioned theory which says that fundamentalism is derived from a counter-reaction to modernization and economic changes. Nevertheless, he has failed to observe that in the majority of worshippers of any religion the axiomatic link between personal faith and theological knowledge does not exist. Many Muslims do not have a clue about what Islam is beyond the practical aspects of their prayers and festivities, and what imams may say to them.

Certainly, some Muslims may start to develop a fundamentalist interpretation of their religion, yet this does not mean that they have to know particular theological aspects of their religion, and this does not mean that they reject modernity only because they are Muslims. The members of the two families, which I have presented, have combined strict cultural-religious traditions with a radical modern lifestyle, particularly in the case of their children. Their personal interpretations of Islam influence both the modern and traditional spheres of their lives. According to the theory of identity I have explained in Chapter 3, we know that Islam, and in these cases, jihad, could go beyond the sphere of religion and faith and become part of a complex mechanism shaping personal selves thanks to the role that emotions have in their lives.

Since the 1991 Gulf war, Arab satellite channels have played a fundamental role in shaping Muslims' social, political and religious views on the Middle East and the international crisis (Taylor 1992 and Werbner 1994). Nevertheless, in the aftermath of 9/11, these channels have exercised an unusually persuasive power over their Muslim audience, sometimes erasing the independent analytical capacity of some of their audience. The main Arab satellite channels (which also have a consistent non-Arab audience) portray themselves as not only Arabic but also Muslim. Nisbet et al (2004) have argued that satellite television news has amplified Muslim resentment towards the United States of America and the West. Some of these satellite channels have facilitated the development of the common misrepresentation that the West is monolithic and is so represented by the USA. By contrast, Osama bin Laden has received via Muslim channels the status of rebel rather than that of mass-murderer. But it is the overuse of shocking images that, as I have argued, facilitated the pushing of some Muslim families into the circle of panic, through two processes. On the one hand, these images overexpose Muslims, particularly if young, to emotions that are translated into feelings such as frustration, oppression and anger, on the other, they are exposed to processes of systematic desensitization to suffering and compassion. Furthermore, many Muslims living in the West are sitting on their sofas, eating crisps and drinking Sprite and Coca-Cola in front of their televisions while they watch their Muslim brothers and sisters suffering and being killed in that *dar al-islam* from which they have sought refuge. The guilt they might feel is another element that facilitates the circle of panic, which leads to acts of identity expressed through the rhetoric of jihad. Nonetheless, Western politicians seem to be unaware, or ignore, the circle of panic affecting part of the Muslim population, and are dangerously increasing the schismogenetic elements. Indeed, some of them have emphasized that there exists a clash of civilizations between the 'Occident', the expression of the most 'civilized' people because marked by Christian values, and a 'bad' version of Islam.

Was Stephan right in suggesting that Muslim families watched and enjoyed jihads? After analysing the facts, I strongly do not believe it to be so. Bruce (2000) has interpreted fundamentalism as the direct result of an Islamic theology. The families I spent time with clearly had no specific knowledge of jihad from a theological perspective. Some members of these families were discussing jihad not because it was part of their religion, but because it was part of their emotional reactions; their idea of jihad was beyond Islam but 'within' their identity.

Notes

1. In Britain Saddam received the moral support as an antagonist of the USA, not only from Muslim Arabs but many South Asians as well (see Werbner 2002).

2. Yet Kurdish migrants supported the war since the Iraqi dictator had killed and oppressed Kurds and their hope of an independent Kurdistan. By contrast Iraqi Shi 'a migrants showed a less homogenous opinion.

3. From http://news.bbc.co.uk/1/hi/uk_politics/1579043.stm

4. The *burqu'* is a traditional Pashtun Islamic veil that the Taliban imposed on all the women of the country despite their ethnic origin (El Guindi 1999).

5. It is interesting to observe here how Karim saw the terms 'Arab' and 'Muslim' as interchangeable.

6. Tamerlane (or Timur the Lame, 1336–1405), sacked Baghdad in 1401 killing thousands of people and devastating hundreds of towns.

7. See http://www.manartv.com/.

8. www.observer.guardian.co.uk, 7 September 2003.

9. A translation of this bin Laden message can be found at http://news.bbc.co.uk/1/hi/world/monitoring/media_reports/1636782.stm

CHAPTER 6

Baraka, Coca-Cola and Salah al-Din

In this chapter, I shall discuss some of my youngest Muslim respondents' understanding of jihad. I refer to the children of Muslim migrants as 'Western-born Muslims' instead of the more common 'second generation'. In doing so, I wish to respect my respondents' opinion that the appellative 'generation' misrepresents the relationship that they have with their societies, which are indeed their parents', or even grandparents', host societies. As Assad put it, 'You can like it or can dislike it, but the West is part of us and we are part of the West, we are not just Muslim and Paki, we are Western Pakistani Muslim.' Nonetheless, the most recurrent question these young people have been asked, 'Are you ... or Muslim?', aims to deny such a reality. Please, feel free to fill the gap with whatever adjective of Western nations may come to your mind (i.e. British, French, Italian, American and so on).

The question may not surprise a philosopher, our (Western?) common sense suggests that A could not be B, and although it admits 'in-betweens', these are often perceived as 'deviant'. So, the identities of those whom academia has labelled 'second generation', who seem to fit neither A nor B, we just defined as 'in-between'. Yet I very soon became aware that my respondents, like probably other Western-born Muslims, did not feel 'in-between' but just themselves. Individuality has a central role in the way these young people perceive themselves, though the Islamic concept of *ummah*, as we shall see, is relevant to their feeling Muslim. I shall suggest that their idea of the ummah is shaped in a 'community of emotions' rather than, as often suggested, in a sort of imagined community (Anderson 1991). Both their conceptualization of ummah as well as their strong individualism has produced an 'a-cultural' understanding of Islam, an Islam without 'contamination'. Before we discuss their idea of Islam, we must observe the effect of this loyalty questioning, which eventually became a nagging issue.

Are You ... or Muslim?

'Are you British or are you Muslim?', 'Are you French or are you Muslim?',
'Are you American or Muslim?', in other words, 'Are you one of us?' Here
is the Shakespearean dilemma which Western-born Muslims are asked to
answer. It is a rhetorical question of denial, a rhetorical question of
ostracism, it dichotomizes 'otherness' by transforming difference into 'cul-
pability'. This is the very process that could easily transubstantiate into persecution, with the Holocaust being the most horrible example. Today,
rather than being worn on coats, 'yellow stars' take the form of re-imagined,
stereotyped, crisped, imposed, social identities. This imposition forces the
person into a cage of objectification in which restraints have been imposed
on their identity affirmation. This process has contributed to a new
Orientalized, post-modern, neo-colonial freak show, but the 'abnormal', the
'monster' *which* repulses, but intrigues, is the Muslim, the more so if
Western born.

Because of the 1991 Gulf war, this reality powerfully epiphanied in
Nusarat. Still a teenage Muslim boy of Pakistani origin, his teacher asked
him to explain why the *Muslim* tyrant, Saddam Hussein, had invoked a jihad
against the West. Nusarat had just wanted to be a student among the others.
Yet the teacher turned him into the school's 'Grand Mufti' of what for
Nusarat was still a foggy family tradition, Islam. The now 25-year-old
Nusarat recalled,

> I felt uncomfortable to stand in front of the other pupils. I mean, maybe the
> teacher thought that it might have been a good idea to ask me, the Muslim, to
> explain something to the class. But, at that time, I was Muslim because my
> family was and I did not want to be seen as 'different'. By the way, I did not
> know what to say. The teacher's focus on my religion was enough to frame me
> as the 'evil' Muslim who wanted British soldiers dead. I started to dislike school
> because the other pupils started to bully me.

By highlighting Nusarat's otherness, the teacher (I presume unintentionally)
had metamorphosed him, the *black Paki* Nusarat, into *the evil Muslim*,
whose new nickname became 'Saddam' (of course, with evident geographic
and ethnic licence).

Twelve years later, another Gulf war, another classroom, another Muslim
child, another teacher; yet the same question: 'Umar, are you British or
Muslim?' The eleven-year old-boy answered, 'I have a British passport'.
The teacher seemed to be fazed by the politically correct answer. Then, the
teacher loudly read a newspaper article about the Iraqi war. The article was
about to end and with it Umar's happy school life. The teacher raised his

head and then the 'question' struck again. But this time the question 'are you … or Muslim' was shaped into a much more sinister, grimmer and inquisitorial sentence. 'Umar', asks the teacher, 'if you were a British soldier would you have killed Muslims?' Checkmate. 'I am Muslim', replies Umar, 'I would rather conduct jihad.' So, the tolerated 'other' Umar has metamorphosed into Umar the 'enemy within', Umar the symbol of the eternal traitor. The micro-social process, which years earlier had affected Nusarat's life had started again. Paradoxically, Umar's iron mask did not reproduce Saddam Hussein's face, but rather Osama's, the archetype of the terrorist. Umar's childish heroic imagination of the modern Islamic chevalier, the *mujahid*, had affected his answer disrupting his previous British standard student life. Umar's family have been living in the UK for more than twenty-five years and had easily integrated into its host country. Of course, Umar was as Western as his schoolmates but this fact had not shielded him from discrimination and ostracism. After the teacher's provocation, Umar was no longer the joyful child I had met previously; all his 'friends' were calling Umar 'terrorist' and 'bin Laden'.

Other Western-born Muslims have experienced the same discrimination that Nusarat and Umar suffered. For instance, in the aftermath of 1995 GIA's (The Armed Islamic Group) terrorist attack against the Parisian metro station 'Place de l'Etoile', Western-born Muslims, in particular those of North African origin, suffered similar discrimination. People often nicknamed them 'terrorists'. In 1999, one of my Parisian respondents recalled, 'They [French people] saw us as enemies. It did not matter whether you were French or Algerian, you had an Algerian face and surname and this was enough to dislike you. Sometimes I felt that I had no control over whom I was, because they decided who I had to be.' Immediately, his last words recalled to my mind a paragraph of Luigi Pirandello's novel *One, None and a Hundred Thousand*. Written in 1927 by one of the most famous Italian writers, the story narrates the identity crisis of Vitangelo Moscarda, a simple man living in an anonymous south Italian province. Vitangelo suddenly realizes that the nature of man is not essence but appearance. He does not have one personality but rather a hundred thousand that people are able to discern in him. Below, I quote the very moment in which he grasped this insight,

[Vitangelo stands in front a mirror during a storm while outside there is lightning] Was it my image, which I saw in a flash of lightning? Am I the thing that I saw, and people see from the outside, which while living I cannot feel? Thus, for the others I am that alien whom I have caught in the mirror: I am that person, and not that 'me' that I know myself to be. I am that alien whom I am, myself, unable to recognize while I see him. I am that alien, whom I can see living only through unthinkable time. I am the alien whom only the others can know and I cannot. (Pirandello 1927: 42, translation mine)

'Are you British or Muslim?', 'Are you French or Muslim?', 'Are you ... or Muslim?' These questions, many of my respondents have observed, are just a form of rhetoric. Since 9/11 and in particular after the Afghan war, politicians, journalists, scholars as well as ordinary people have challenged and questioned the loyalty of young Muslims to their countries. Hundreds of newspapers and magazines articles have periodically alleged that Western-born Muslims are turning against the UK and the rest of the West, by fighting British and American troops in Afghanistan and Iraq. This has reinforced the spreading view that Western-born Muslims might be a threat to Western 'civilization' and 'democracy'. This loyalty-paranoia has created its victims among Western-born Muslims, some have been arrested under the different national anti-terrorist legislation, some have been accused of 'jihading' shoulder to shoulder with the West's number one enemy Osama bin Laden but often no evidence is provided. The witch-hunt has begun and in a short time will affect the life of millions of our fellow citizens. For instance, the *Guardian* has reported (20 November 2001),

> Detectives ... are expecting to gather more evidence about the involvement of Britons from prisoners captured by the Northern Alliance. 'Any individual who arrives back in the UK having fought for the Taliban in Afghanistan could be arrested under the Terrorism Act 2000 for a number of different offences,' a security source said. 'We are waiting for these people to arrive back in the UK.'

The innocent British Muslims who were held in Guantanamo (and recently released without charges) or the repeated anti-terrorist action against UK mosques (without the police having reliable evidence of terrorist activities) have increased the fear that the barbaric 'others', the 'collaborationists' hiding among us are ready to strike with their jihad. Yet, these controversial headlines[1] and such an overemphasis on young British Muslims being involved in suicide operations[2] have achieved a dangerous effect: the spreading of panic among non-Muslims and Muslims alike. On the one hand, non-Muslims, but also Muslims,[3] fear becoming victims of jihad, on the other only Muslims fear becoming victims of Islamophobic attacks.

Bhabha (1994) has suggested that stereotyping is not only a fixed representation of the subject in the construction of the colonial 'other', but also a process similar to fetishism. 'The fetish or stereotype gives access to an "identity" which is predicated as much on mastery and pleasure as it is on anxiety and defence, for it is a form of multiple and contradictory beliefs in its recognition of difference and the disavowal of it' (1994: 75). In this complex process, contradictions between the known and imagined become the reality of representation. In other words, the object is understood not in its integrity but as metonymy. Bhabha has emphasized how the identity of the 'other' becomes fetishized not for the sake of false representation which may become 'the scapegoat of discrimination', but for 'the fantasy that dramatizes the impossible desire for a pure, undifferentiated origin' of the colonizer (1994: 81). The rhetorical question 'Are you ... or Muslims?', this metonymical re-imagination of Muslim identity through stereotypes, emotionally destabilizes young Muslims' identities and induces a sort of Pirandellian 'I am one, none and a hundred thousand'.

Ali a 29-year-old of Algerian origin, described his experience in these terms,

> You start your school life with other children; you are very young and don't feel any real difference between you and them. Actually, you don't even think about it. Then you go on, you grow up, and you understand that there are differences; the other students will tell you, often just bullying you. This stage is very hard because the bullying is aimed at your religion. When you become a teenager, you start to rationalise your position within the society and so you start to see the differences between you and your parents. You feel confused and ask yourself 'who am I?' The answer is not so simple: or at least it was in my case. I felt like a patchwork that needed just one colour and one pattern. This colour and pattern became Islam.

Identity confusion and identity ubiquity are common experiences among many young Western-born Muslims. So, the majority of my respondents have mentioned these difficult processes in order to define their 'I'. Adolescence is also the time in which conflicts with both family and society may arise (see Lepoutre 1997).

The young Muslims find themselves projected into parallel dimensions in which ethical and moral, as well as political, values may become cacophonic, almost schizophrenic. For some Western societies, such as the British and French, these Western-born Muslims represent the materialization of an unwanted and unplanned post-colonial present, as their parents represented the objectification – this time, desired and wished – of a glorious colonial empire (see Doty 2003: 44–57). The colonizer's resistance to the self-determination of the colonized used to repeat 'you belong to us'. Now, in an inverted performance of power, the former colonizer feels colonized and asks 'are you one of us?' Bhabha has discussed this process under the label of 'mimicry', 'Mimicry is the desire for a reformed, recognizable Other, *as subject of a difference that is almost the same, but not quite*, which is to say, that the discourse of mimicry is constructed around an *ambivalence*; in order to be effective mimicry it must continually produce its slippage, its excess, its difference' (1994: 86, italics in the original). The colonized, through mimicry, become part of the process that defines the colonizer. In other words, the colonized claim power by being the 'Other' of him/herself. Mimicry is a form of political and identity mockery that may leave the subject personal self because, as Bhabha has observed, he/she is *almost the same but not white*: the visibility of mimicry is always produced at the site of interdiction. It is a form of colonial discourse at the crossroads of what is known and permissible and that which though known must be kept concealed' (1994: 89 emphasis in the original). Almost the same *but not* British (French, Italian, German, etc.), the denial of authenticity became, for some of my respondents, the trap of their 'I' set in a difficult ubiquity, a form of eternal questioning that if they wanted to become 'real' they had to answer. A 27-year-old man of Bangladeshi origin living in Scotland emphasized,

> I really could not recall how many times somebody has asked if I was British or Muslim or if I was from here or where my home was. Home, well this word became my problem: where is my home? Am I from here or Bangladesh? I feel myself to be part of this [British] society but people seem to question my idea of myself. Do we need that others recognize us as part of something before we can claim to be part of it? I do not think so, I am what I am, despite what people think I should be. However, I grew up with many questions and all the answers seemed to be wrong until I understood that I am Muslim. In Islam it does not matter what you are and what others say you are; if you are Muslim, you have a Muslim identity.

'I'm Muslim' was the usual answer I received from the majority of my young respondents. But what does it mean to them to be Muslim in their contemporary societies?

Looking for Baraka while Drinking Coca-Cola

Studies of youth subculture have particularly focused on the analysis of style as counter-hegemony in the class conflict (cf. Cohen 1980; Hebdige 1979). This led to the interpretation of youth subculture identities as marked by dichotomies. Later sociologists criticized these 1970s works for their lack of attention to other relevant factors such as gender and ethnicity (see , Cohen 1980; McRobbie 1991; Thornton 1995). If we observe studies on young Muslims, we may invert this criticism, since ethnicity and gender have been over-scrutinized. The real issue is how scholars have discussed the identity of these young people. Indeed, in Chapter 3 we have seen that identity has been often interpreted as 'fluid', 'hybrid' and 'multiple'.[4] This has facilitated the false impression that Western-born Muslims may lack self-determination. Reacting to such overgeneralizations, other more recent studies, some of which I shall briefly discuss below, have tried to 're-empower' Western-born Muslims.[5] These studies, however, have based their understanding of identity on implicit or explicit social identities and culturalist theories, missing the vital relationship existing between the autobiographical self, identity and Islam. The undesired side effect of these theories is that they end in emphasizing the problems that Western-born Muslims have, instead of observing the solutions that they have developed. So, in her analysis of young Asians' identities, Archer even used a pathologizing language when she observed, 'second and third generation young Asians *suffer* from "mixed up" and "confused" identities because of the *"cultural clash"* that results from occupying a *contradictory* location between *conflicting* 'majority' and 'minority' *cultures* and *identities.*' (2001: 82, emphasis added).

Other scholars have instead undervalued the emotional role that Islam plays in young Muslims' formation of identity; for instance Jacobson (1998: 101) sees Islam as merely,

> a source of guidance in the young people's lives; guidance which allows them to undertake a 'quest for certainty', and thereby to resolve some of the ambivalence over identity engendered by their social circumstances. Second, I argue that the persistence of religious identities can be understood in terms of the boundaries which practising Muslims, by virtue of the demands of their religion, construct and maintain between themselves and others.

The statement 'I am Muslim', as I have explained in Chapter 3, expresses something deeper than just affiliation, culture and acknowledgement of moral guidance for young Muslims' lives. So, the 'in-between two cultures' theory raises more questions than it may answer (Baumann 1996). Nielsen has suggested, 'Culture is a rather more complex phenomenon to speak of in-betweenness' (2000: 27), and Werbner has observed that Muslims do not perceive Islam simply as 'culture' but as something more rooted in their identity. In making her point, Werbner has told us about an experience she had during her fieldwork. She saw some English louts insulting a Pakistani mother and her child and the mother and child did not react at all, nor did they report the matter to anyone because 'unknown to the English louts, there is an invisible shield protecting the little boy and his mother. That shield is Islam. Despite the insults, they feel protected, morally *superior*' (2002: 133).

I had occasion to observe something very similar, but this time the louts verbally abused some young British Pakistanis. From that experience, I have concluded that my respondents did not dichotomize their social space and environment through Islam as religion, but Islam as identity. The 'invisible shield' that Werbner has described does not represent a Muslim versus non-Muslim contraposition, by which Muslims feel 'superior' to other human beings. As some of the young British Pakistani Muslims abused by the louts in the middle of the street explained, as Muslims, they have *baraka* protecting them. Baraka (from the Arabic root *brk*, 'blessing') is a divine supernatural power and energy. In Sufism, people believe that holy men achieve this divine essence through their spiritual journey toward Allah. But baraka, as any other form of energy, could pass from one point to another; so holy men could impart baraka to other people or even objects. The Islamic tradition of visiting shrines resides in the pilgrims' belief that holy men's dead bodies emanate baraka that the visitor is able to absorb (Werbner and Basu 1998). Yet my respondents, as we shall see in the next paragraphs, have reinterpreted such an ancient Islamic concept, since the majority of them disagree with the practices often followed by their relatives living in Muslim countries of visiting shrines and give offerings to holy men. They see these traditions as derived from human superstition and the 'unorthodox' within *real* Islam.

So, 22-year-old Yasir, of Pakistani origin, strongly criticized his relatives in Pakistan and labelled them as 'shrine addicted'. He argued, 'They dissipate fortunes in offerings to *pirs* [holy men].' He went on to explain that his relatives had hoped the *pir* could bless them and their business with powerful baraka. Yasir was very quick to tell me that his criticism was not showing disrespect to part of his family but to emphasize that 'only the One (Allah) may bless you and give you baraka'. He added, 'we do not need human agents to receive baraka'. Because of the opinions of baraka I had started to collect, I thought that Western-born Muslims might have rejected this idea. Yet I observed that they do not deny the existence of baraka, rather they reinterpret it a mono-directional flow of divine power descending from Allah, through the Qur'an and the Prophet's example, to reach the believer; baraka for them means the *embodiment* of Islam itself. An Algerian whom I met in a local mosque in Saint Denis, Paris, said,

> Baraka has nothing to do with *marabouts* (holy men). Baraka is the power of Islam, the power that you feel by reciting the Qur'an, the power, I mean, that you feel while fasting during Ramadan. Of course, you need to detach yourself from the cultural contamination of Islam. You have to go to the root of Islam if you want to have baraka.

If, as we have seen in Chapter 4, some Muslim migrants saw a certain paradox in being Muslim and living in the West, the paradox dissolved in the comments of their children. Islam, the 'real' one, has no geographical space, no culture, no interpretation. Islam could only be lived and embodied in the soul of the believer.

Therefore, 19-year-old Ajaz, of Pakistani origin, could not find any contradiction between his Western lifestyle and his Muslim (he preferred the term Islamic) identity,

> I can tell you that I do not see any contradiction between seeking baraka and drinking Coca-Cola. Both of them are part of my world. Maybe the others can see contradictions or find it strange. I want to obtain baraka from the Qur'an and from the Prophet's example. If you want, I am both a Coca-Colaholic and a proud baraka-seeking Muslim.

The re-imagination of the concept of baraka has another relevant implication. Although the relationship with Islam is individualistic and the achievement of baraka can change from one person to another, Muslims share their faith, emotion and experience through the ummah. The individualistic experience of Islam does not mean the self-isolation of the single believer. On the contrary, believers are part of a spiritual community in which they can share their experience of Allah.

The Ummah: From Discourse to Emotions

Nowadays, it is not unusual to read the word *ummah* in newspapers and popular books on Islam. Conventionally, the *ummah* has been translated as the 'community of believers'. So, what is a community? Anthropologists, as well as other social scientists have answered the question in different ways. Some, such as Hillery (1995), have even listed several definitions of 'community' on which he thought scholars might agree. Of course, an agreement was never reached and attempts such as Hillery's have been dismissed as pointless. Others have taken the extremist path and asked whether we still need the word 'community'.[6] Nevertheless, community, as a culturally constructed concept, still remains central to anthropological studies. Olwig (2002) has suggested two main notions of community as culturally constructed. In the first, communities have been portrayed as 'belonging entities', in the second, as imagined units based on 'sentiments' (cf. Appadurai 1996). If we understand communities as 'belonging entities', face-to-face relationships play a fundamental role (Rapport 1993; Strathern 1982). By contrast, if we understand communities as being based on 'sentiments', it is the symbolic relationship that matters. Following the latter, Anderson has argued:

The members of even the smallest nation will never know most of their fellow-members, meet them, or even hear of them, yet in the minds of each lives the image of their communion. ... it is imagined as a *community*, because, regardless of the actual inequality and exploitation that may prevail in each, the nation is always conceived as a deep, horizontal comradeship. Ultimately it is this fraternity that makes it possible, over the past two centuries, for so many millions of people, not so much to kill, as willingly to die for such limited imaginings. (1991: 5–7)

This interpretation has become fashionable in the analysis of 'diasporic and transnational communities' (Clifford 1994; Vertovec 2001).

The Internet, satellite TV and mobile technology facilitate contacts as well as community formation. So, in his studies of migration and mass media, Appadurai has further developed Anderson's theory, suggesting that the complex media network connecting the world enables people to rethink their lives through the circulation of cultural domains (Appadurai 1995, 1996).

The Muslim migrants I have interviewed present the ummah as an Andersonian 'imagined community' in which local and global dimensions are entangled, but within which individuals might maintain, if not national, at least religious differences. I have argued in previous researches (Marranci 2003a and 2003b) that Muslim migrants live the ummah more as an instrumental answer to their environments than as religious dogma. In other words, they develop what we call an *ideology of ummah*. Emotions play a role in their experience of ummah, since emotions facilitate unity beyond locality, which 'seems to have lost its ontological moorings' (Appadurai 1995: 204). For this reason, Appadurai has suggested the term 'neighbourhood' to represent this new dimension (Appadurai 1995) So, in the case of immigrants, we may argue that the ummah becomes an ideology through which they can share (in order to make sense of) analogical experiences of displacement or colonial (as well as neo-colonial) memories.

By contrast, I have observed that the idea of ummah among Western-born Muslims may carry a different meaning. Grown-up and educated in the West, Western-born Muslims develop an Islamic knowledge that is more influenced by, for instance, Islamic websites (Brückner 2001; Bunt 2003) than their cultural heritages. Furthermore, lacking the experience of displacement their parents knew, Western-born Muslims tend to categorize the concept of local and global as their non-Muslim peers do. Therefore, I noticed that within the same Muslim family living in a Western country we could find different understandings of ummah. This became particularly evident during a visit to an Iraqi family I knew in Dublin. While discussing the last Iraqi war, the parents told me that we should not compare Iraq and

Arab Muslims to the 'still uncivilized Afghan Muslims'. Arabic religious nationalism and prejudice affected their concept of ummah. By contrast, their children (a 19-year-old daughter and a 23-year-old son) rejected their parents' opinions and rather emphasized the humiliation that the war had brought on Islam; cultures and nations had disappeared from their argument. This was not an isolated case, many Western-born respondents described the ummah as *a-national,*

> The concept of ummah is central to Islam but I think that because we were born here [Paris] we developed the authentic Islamic concept of ummah. Remember that Islam is one and we should behave as one nation only. (France; Djamel, 19-year-old of Algerian origin)

> The ummah is like your hand, single fingers form it but when you close them together, they become a powerful fist. About Islam, Muslims share sentiments, this make us unique. Our parents have cultural traditions to defend, but I don't, ummah and Islam are just one. (Northern Ireland; Azan, 26-year-old of Bangladeshi origin)

> When you see what Palestinians and other Muslims around the world are suffering, you feel as if your family has been attacked and your brother or sister killed … the ummah is like … when you go to a concert of pop-music, you don't know anybody but you feel part of the group. (Italy, Nadia, 23-year-old of Egyptian origin)

Hetherington (1998) has criticized sociologists and anthropologists for overlooking emotions in their study of communities. Instead, Hetherington, starting from Maffesoli (1996), Bauman (1992) and Scheler (1954), has suggested that people form communities in order to share emotions and empathetic identifications. These, Hetherington has observed, are 'intentional "communities", that can be seen as either moral communities or emotional communities' (1998: 50). Although this process requires identification, Maffesoli has argued that personal identities find their expression in the community through a mutual transformation: 'this bond is without the rigidity of the forms of organisation with which we are familiar; it refers more to a certain ambience, a state of mind … It is a case of a kind of *collective unconscious (non-conscious)* which acts as a matrix for varied group experience, situations, actions or wanderings' (Maffesoli 1996: 98 emphasis in the original) I think that Western-born Muslims experience the ummah exactly as a 'community of emotion'.

Many Western-born Muslims argue that the ummah needs a spiritual (also political) leader who can catalyse the emotional powers of the ummah towards coherent action capable of changing injustices into 'justice', the only one which according to my respondents matters, Allah's justice.

Looking for a New Salah al-Din

My friends Labib, a 26-year-old Algerian student at the local university, and Nusarat, a 22-year-old Western-born Muslim of Pakistani origin, and a 30-year-old Italian anthropologist (me) met for one of their recurrent meetings at the 'same place', a local café. Labib and Nusarat's disagreements traditionally marked these conversations. The diatribes became particularly lively when they used to discuss *halal* (acceptable) and *haram* (unacceptable) in Islam. Since the different schools of Islamic thought have different approaches as to what might be harmful or halal, it is easy to grasp that Muslims from different backgrounds hold contrasting opinions. Basic questions such as 'May Muslims wash their mouth with an alcoholic mouthwash?, 'May Muslim men have long hair?', 'May Muslim women show their bare feet?' trigger endless discussions; at least they did between my two friends.

Thus they raised the hot topic of whether terrorism might be considered halal or haram in Islam. Labib argued that Islam rejects terrorism under any circumstances; so according to him actions such as 9/11 betrayed Islam and possibly (indeed 'only Allah knows') condemned the perpetrators to hell. Knowing that Nusarat was a nice guy, I confidently expected his agreement. My expectation remained frustrated. Nusarat rejected Labib's argument, and he was not joking. Although Nusarat emphasized that any loss of human life was regrettable to him, he argued, 'People call Islamic terrorism what in reality is an absolute justified jihad.' He explained that the word terrorism had been used to discredit the *mujahidin* that today have to fight unconventionally because 'they could not overwhelm Western forces or Western supported dictators'. So, according to Nusarat, Islam allows mujahidin to use stratagems, 'What both of you call terrorism, I call legitimate stratagems.' We, of course, noticed that Western bombs kill civilians no less than suicide operations. Nusarat described in vivid detail the horrible images he had seen in Birmingham when fellow Muslims showed him some MP3 videos recorded on mobile phones in Jenin during the Israeli retaliation (19 June 2002). This had strongly convinced him that jihad was required.

Our coffees cooled on the table. It was so strange to hear our friend Nusarat speaking in such terms. Nusarat realized how much we had been left surprised by his argument and tried to convince us:

I am not surprised that the mujahidin targeted the Twin Towers in New York. It was a strike against the American economic oppression of Muslims; so let me say that it was a legitimate target. Americans do the same during their wars, they target economic, military and political infrastructures to change, for instance, the regimes that they dislike. When they bombed a factory in Sudan because they [Americans] thought it was a WMD factory, they did not think about the civilians working there. During 9/11, the mujahidin had targeted economic, military and political symbols. Muslims have the right to retaliate. We'll win, no doubts. Muslims are ready to use their lives and become *shahid*. Try to find one non-Muslim ready to do the same. We have faith, we have a spiritual strength, we have baraka, and most important we have our Muslim identity.

Being an Algerian, Labib knew the consequences that 'terrorism' may have on ordinary people. Terrorism had devastated Algeria for years. Labib tried to persuade Nusarat that Islam forbids terrorism, that even Muslims might die in these random attacks, that the Prophet, 'was a great diplomat; he signed more treaties than declarations of war'. But I became aware that the two were just speaking two different languages: what for Labib was terrorism, for Nusarat was heroic jihad; who for Labib were terrorists, for Nusarat were mujahidin.

Nusarat had his philosophy. He emphasized that Muslims must believe in predestination (qadar), 'nobody could become shahid without Allah's allowing it, also nobody would die if it was not his last day,' he said. Nusarat was extending qadar to the issue of civilian victims; people die in terrorist actions only because it is their qadar and not because of the mujahidin decided to kill them. Thus, he declared, 'People die during war; it is not something new. Bush and Blair speak of "the war on terror", I say that the West started its war on Islam long before 9/11, but I agree with Mr Bush and Mr Blair at least on this, there is a war.' Nusarat believed, however, that the mujahidin would stop their global jihad when justice was restored and Muslims and Islam respected.

At this point, I became curious to know whether Nusarat saw Osama bin Laden as a leader of the ummah. In other words, if he would have accepted bin Laden as the rightful *khalifa*. First, Nusarat reminded me that this jihad was defensive, so it did not require any authorization but, he said, 'Each Muslim has to act according to his means and degree of faith.' Nonetheless, Nusarat did not consider bin Laden to be a good candidate for the post. He explained, 'He lacks respect from the majority of Muslims. I think that bin Laden is just an instrument of Allah to start jihad.' This was the first time I had seen Labib and Nusarat agree on something, beyond good Indian food. Labib, who had rejected any form of violence, reinforced Nusarat's viewpoint, 'the Muslim ummah needs a leader who is capable of creating a real

Islamic state'. This idea that Islam today needs a new khalifa (caliph) has been shared by the majority of my Western-born Muslim respondents. The main reason used to explain this is that today Muslims are disoriented, lack guidance and remain very weak.

At this point we may wonder which qualities a modern caliph should have. Although, as expected, my Shi'a respondents answered that 'Ali would have been the perfect example of an Islamic leader, the Sunnis showed a similar homogeneity in their answers. The archetype of the perfect Islamic leader was not to be found among either the well-known Ottoman caliphs or the contemporary Muslim leaders or scholars. The name that catalysed the imaginations of my respondents, came from an Islamic history that was entangled with the European medieval Crusades. The archetype had the name of Salah al-Din, the respected and feared Muslim commander. Salah al-Din al-Ayyubi (better known to non-Muslims as Saladin) was a name that for centuries the Muslim East had forgotten but the West feared and loathed. His name reminds us of the 1187 capture of Jerusalem. Despite the campaign of defamation that some Crusaders launched against the 'ferocious Saladin', the character achieved such fame that even the most 'Islamophobic' Italian poet, Dante Alighieri (1265–1321), who in his *Divine Comedy* sentenced Muhammad to eternal hellfire as a false prophet, granted Salah al-Din a place in Limbo (the acknowledged residence of pre-Christian souls).

During his studies Salah al-Din preferred religion over military strategies. Despite his inclination to philosophic and religious studies (Lyons 1982), he had to accept a military career and serve the state administration. In 1174, the caliph named Salah al-Din as the first *ayyubid* (Sultan of Cairo). When Salah al-Din retook the holy city of Jerusalem from the Christians he ordered that the captured Christians could leave the city after paying a ransom which Salah al-Din himself paid for the poorest. Since he decided not to take revenge on the 1099 Crusaders' carnage among Muslim civilians living in Jerusalem, his reputation of being a just warrior, who respected the *shari'a*, fascinated Muslims as well as non-Muslims. Furthermore, Salah al-Din followed the Qur'anic precept of respecting religious buildings and, against the suggestion of his advisors, preserved the Church of the Holy Sepulchre (Lyons 1982). Often romanticized, his character has appealed to young Muslims not only because of his Islamic devotion and his successful jihad, but also because of his efforts to unite the increasingly scattered Muslim ummah.

According to my respondents, Salah al-Din possessed baraka so that Islam guided all his actions. Kamil, a 25-year-old Muslim of Libyan descent, observed,

He [Salah al-Din] was an important historical character. Jerusalem and Palestine are now reoccupied, all Muslims hope that sometime in the near future a Salah al-Din will liberate Jerusalem. He was a just, respected and admired leader, even by his enemies. His jihad started from inside and for these reasons was successful outside. Allah blessed him. Today, we just have Muslims who want to protect their own interests, they do not really care about Islam and do not have spiritual power at all.

It is clear that Western-born Muslims, as we have seen in the case of Muslim immigrants, do not have a monolithic, standardized opinion on jihad. Yet for the sake of clarity, I shall categorize my respondents' opinions into three main viewpoints.

First, young Muslims such as Kamil, who reject violence, but do not renounce the idea of non-violent jihad to achieve Allah's justice. These young Muslims agree that the Islamic world is suffering but recognize that the ummah is too weak to oppose Western or Western-supported military forces. They argue that not only has Islam forbidden terrorism but also terrorist action further divides the ummah and damages the image of Islam. Said, a 22-year-old Muslim of Syrian origin observed, 'Stupid actions achieve stupid results. The more people fear Islam, the less Muslims can influence the West.' He argued for a jihad (a struggle) that could enable Muslims to achieve hegemonic positions within their Western societies.

The second category may be defined as the 'messianic'. Although these young Muslims have also rejected current international terrorism, the reasons are deeply different from those within the first category. They do believe in violent jihad but they think that some Muslims are jihading at the wrong time since Muslims need a leader first. The Muslims in this category consider resistance against 'Western' occupation justified, but they do not consider it as jihad, rather as an anti-colonialist struggle for independence. These young Muslims strongly believe in the Islamic concept of qadar by which they explain the sufferings of Muslims eschatologically. Hafiz, a 28-year-old Muslim of Pakistani origin, explained with regard to this idea of qadar,

The Prophet clearly reminded his ummah that Muslims must suffer before reaching the Day of Atonement. There are two kinds of signs, minor and major. Of course, we are not at the stage of the major signs, which are, for example, *Masih ad-dajjal* [the Antichrist] and the destruction of the Ka'bah. We are living in the final stage of the minor signs such as the disruption of nature in that we have acid rain, an increase in the number of poor people, the people of Iraq not receiving food and money because they are oppressed by Romans, that today means the Americans, corrupt Muslim leaders conducting an unjust war, fanatics who by their actions damage the reputation of Islam. We don't need to fight, we need just to wait and pray. Islam will reign at the Day of Judgement.

The final category is formed by a minority of radicalized Muslims for whom jihad means to kill the infidels, in other words, everybody but Muslims; so what for us is terrorism, for them is a defensive jihad. Here as well, the concept of qadar is used, but this time to explain why, for instance, suicide bombers are not required to ask whether Muslims are around before blowing up their victims (Muslim and non-Muslim alike). Those Muslims who believe that acts of international terrorism are defensive jihads, do not interpret death as something either good or bad. According to them, death is part of our human experience and you will die only when Allah decides. What matters is not death but after death. As Nusarat explained to me in a follow-up conversation, 'All the victims of a terrorist attack become martyrs and all their sins, whether they are Muslims or not, will be forgiven by Allah.' You can see that from this perspective, the victims and their relatives should even thank the terrorist who decided to bless them! It is clear that for the would-be suicide bombers, taking one's own life (and those of their victims) becomes a test of their Muslim Islamic identity, i.e. the supreme act of identity.

The few people I had occasion to interview from this last group had experienced two phases in their lives: what one of them defined as a 'denial of Islam' and a 'rediscovering of Islam', while his Pakistani friend preferred the joke expression, 'He saw the light.' The process brings some of these Muslims to sink deeply into the circle of panic. They suffer such a schismogenetic process that needs to test and retest their identities, ending with a possible desperate act of identity. Martyrdom becomes simultaneously the ultimate test and the final freedom from temptation.

Tensions and Divisions among Western-born Muslims

Having met both Western-born Muslims who sympathize with violent jihads and those who reject them, I wondered what they might think of each other. Do they consider each other as 'Muslims'? One fact was clear from the beginning, both groups represented the other through stereotypes. So, the respondents who rejected violent jihad represented the 'fake mujahidin' as Muslims who did not pray from their hearts, did not respect Ramadan, had girlfriends, and patronized pubs and bars. The reason for this behaviour was blamed on a lack of Islamic knowledge, difficult childhoods and depression. The latter suggestion was made to explain the suicide attacks. The majority of Muslims who rejected terrorism had a straightforward theory about

Muslim suicide bombers. They covered the sin[7] of taking their own depressed lives by the concept of holy martyrdom. Following this theory, Amir tried to analyse 9/11 and why the Muslim hijackers committed such an atrocity,

> We know that Atta [leader of the group who perpetrated the 9/11 attacks] was addicted to pornography, went to pubs, bars, and many people saw him in the 'red light district' of Hamburg. Atta had a conflict between his behaviour which was non-Islamic and his being a Muslim. He wanted to prove that he was a real Muslim. The Muslims who take their lives are often living in *fitna* [confusion, lack of order]. I mean, was the Shoe Bomber a Muslim with a nice and normal life? Of course not! These Muslims want to die but suicide is a terrible sin in Islam, they want to think that they will go to Paradise. So, here you are, they take their lives and kill innocent people and say 'we are *shuhada!*' when they have just committed one of the most horrible acts against Allah's Will.

Notwithstanding all this criticism, the majority within this category tend to consider the violent 'jihadi' as still being true Muslims. Amir, a 21-year-old of Pakistani origin, tried to explain why this is so. He observed that Muslims who are 'fake' mujahidin are still Muslims because they recite the *shahada* (the Muslim profession of faith). Despite their horrible actions, they have not disowned the shahada. Indeed, they would be judged by God for their actions, but they would still be judged as Muslims despite their unlawful killings. In other words, only Allah can judge whether people might be Muslims or not, since Muslims, unlike Catholics, do not have any form of excommunication.

While, for instance, Muslims such as Amir and Hafiz , who reject violence, argued that only Allah knows the degree of 'Muslimness' of each person, those supporting violent jihad saw Muslims like Amir and Hafiz as *munafiq* (plural *munafiqun*, hypocrites). In Islam, munafiqun indicates Muslim believers who in their hearts and actions deny Islam. The Qur'an (Sura 4:145) reminds Muslims that munafiqun will hold the lowest position among the damned souls. Shahid, a radical 22-year-old Muslim of Pakistani origin, observed,

> Muslims who deny that Islam is under attack and that we have the duty of conducting jihad are munafiqun. I hope, inshallah, that they would change their mind, maybe by speaking to me and understanding the situation. Nobody likes death but life is not in people's hands, is it? It is in Allah's hands. Allah asks you to sacrifice your life and wealth for Islam, it is your duty to perform jihad. When you do jihad you kill or die, or both. Muslims rejecting the call would die together with their kafirun friends. These Muslims are worse than kafirun, they

are munafiqun; they say and say that they are Muslims but they just play at it. I certainly do not want to be one of the munafiqun, I prefer to die in this world and be saved from hell in the afterlife.

As I have explained, the circle of panic traps the radical Western-born Muslims. They cannot accept Muslims with different ideas because for them Islam is one, Islam cannot be interpreted and must only be obeyed. Radical Western-born Muslims feel their identities jeopardized by non-Muslim environments and they react following their emotions. Many of them fear 'Allah's judgement' because they are aware of previous immoral conduct. For many of them Islam is merely providing a standardized terminology.

Conclusion

Western-born Muslims belong to the West like any other person educated and born in this part of the world. Yet Western people and governments have challenged this obvious fact by the mass questioning of Western-born Muslims' loyalty. The great majority of Western-born Muslims have reacted by strongly denying the existence of a contradiction in being British, German, American, French (just to mention only a few possibilities) and still Muslims. Yet others have reacted more emotionally and ended in the circle of panic. Immigrant Muslims (see Chapter 4) have lived their childhood at a distance from such a Western rhetoric of loyalty. The 'terrorist stereotype' marks both migrants and Western-born Muslims, yet the emotional significance for them is different; some members of Muslim migrant host societies may perceive Muslim immigrants as 'enemies within', but Western-born Muslims are perceived as 'traitors'.

Western-born Muslims actively reinterpret Islamic concepts such as the ummah and baraka in accordance with their experiences. Many of them reject the nationalistic and ethnic sectarianisms that still affect the relationships between Muslim immigrants. The Western-born Muslims' understanding of the ummah as a metaphysical place in which people can share emotions and empathetic identifications preserves the sense of a-cultural purity that they think Islam should have.

In the case of radical Western-born Muslims, the rhetoric of jihad goes beyond the theological aspects of Islam to become part of fundamental processes in the mechanism of human identity (see Chapter 3). In this, as well as in the previous chapters, we have focused on Muslim men. Yet, as we shall see in the next chapter, some Muslim women not only can become the victims of the circle of panic but actively develop an inspired rhetoric of jihad.

Notes

1. See for example, 'British Muslims take path to jihad', *Guardian*, 29 December 2000.

2. See for example 'British Muslim suicide bomber', *Guardian*, 1 May 2003, or 'British suicide bombers boast about killings' *The Times*, 9 March 2004.

3. Indeed Islamic terrorists and suicide bombers do not ask whether Muslims may be among their future victims. They just kill human beings irrespective of gender or age, skin, faith or nationality.

4. See for instance Bhachu 1993; Brah 1979; Knott and Khokher 1993; Mirza 1989.

5. For instance Archer 2001, 2002; Jacobson 1998; Roald 2001; Shaw 1998.

6. See for instance Baumann 1996; Cohen 1985; Guijt and Shah 1998; Lustiger-Thaler 1994; Macfarlane 1977.

7. Islam forbids suicide.

CHAPTER 7

Modern Nasibahs?

Al-Jazeera had just released another video of a new Hamas Palestinian suicide bomber. With explosive belt and Kalashnikov, he explained his jihad which a few hours later would culminate in his body being torn apart and his blood being mixed with his victims'. The day after, I met a group of Muslim women, both immigrants and Western-born, outside the local mosque. They were speaking while waiting for their children from the *madrassa*. I could hear their repeated '*shahid*' while discussing in English (the only language common to all them). The shahid was the man whose video al-Jazeera had shown. Yet there was another word that attracted my attention: honour. I asked one of the Western-born women I knew why she was mentioning such a word. She explained that this 'brave' Muslim had 'brought honour to his family', but particularly to his mother, by immolating himself successfully in jihad. The woman recalled the *hadiths* testifying to the divine blessing that the shahid's families would receive through their shahid. The shahid would be able to intercede for his mother and other members of his family, and would see Paradise. I knew which hadiths these women were referring to, yet the women had overlooked an important fact about these hadiths: none of the protagonists took their own lives for Islam, they had fought as heroic soldiers to save their lives and their religion. These historical shahida were ready to die but did not seek death.

Notwithstanding this historical fact, the conversation I witnessed challenged the stereotype that support for jihad is only given by men. As we shall see in this chapter, Muslim women have their opinions of jihad, though they see it from a different perspective than their fathers, brothers and husbands. Yet we have observed in the previous chapters that to understand the rhetoric of jihad we need to observe the environment in which these ideas formed.

Muslim Migrant Women and their Daughters

Reading some sociologists' and anthropologists' analyses concerning Muslim women, we may receive the impression that Muslim women are passive objects, without a will, unable to act either socially or politically. In other words, they are commodities that violent and sexually jealous Muslim men exchange like gifts. A minority of scholars, who have a very essentialist vision of Islam, suggest that Islam transforms Muslim women into such objects. For instance, Shankland, in his ethnography, observes:

> A girl is also controlled first of all by parents. When she marries she becomes the responsibility of her husband. She remains under his control until she becomes a widow, when she may enjoy a greater degree of freedom. At any time, though, she remains constrained by male relatives and the other men of the settlement, all of whom feel the right to control her behaviour. (2003: 54)

Although Shankland has been right to denounce the oppression that some women suffer in certain Turkish families, he has presented a black-and-white picture that does not take into consideration the strategy that many women (Muslim and non-Muslim) develop. Yet this is not so surprising, if we consider that he has never mentioned a female respondent in his book, leaving him only with the option of caricaturing Muslim women through the boasting maleness of his Muslim men informants. Unfortunately, like many other authors who have depicted Muslim women as passive beings, Shankland does not tell us whether he was prevented from interviewing them, or in an andro-centric fashion, he did not even try. If the latter were the case, it would mean that Shankland had failed as an anthropologist. Feminist studies have demon-strated that the representation of Muslim woman as passive has often been the result of the male authors' exotic, if not erotic, ethnocentric fantasies (cf. El-Solh and Mabro 1994; Mernissi 1975). The scholarly debate about women in Islam became topical after the 1970s; by contrast, the studies concerning Muslim immigrant women tend to be very recent.

We had to wait until the 1990s for anthropologists, together with other social scientists, to realize that in the field of migration studies they had to focus on the overlooked aspects of gender and in particular give back women their missing voices. For too long, scholars have considered immi-grant women as incidental factors in a more relevant male migration. In some studies (particularly French), sociologists reduced Muslim immigrant women to nothing more than another piece of luggage carried by Muslim immigrant men. In other words, immigration had been studied as a male phenomenon. Lutz (1991) has criticized this 1980s academic disinterest and has argued that the colonial representation of Muslim women as merely sexually passive was so deep-rooted that it was increasingly difficult to avoid reproducing the stereotype (see, for example, Sabbah 1984). She has argued that Western scholars may consider Muslim immigrant women to be passive because 'the Western woman serves as counterpoint: as the standard for measuring women elsewhere' (Lutz 1991: 2). The over-discussed *hijab*, clearly confirms Lutz's argument. We do not need much observation to grasp that the Muslim headscarf and its possible symbolic value has been read through the eyes of Western Christian women as a symbol of male sexual oppression. This is opposite to the symbolic value that Muslim women say it has.

Yet Lutz has made another relevant observation. She has argued that there is an overemphasis on the difficulties and 'foreignness' of Muslim immigrants. These academic attitudes of focusing on the problems instead of the solutions can undermine the efforts sociologists and anthropologists are making to understand the identity of Muslim immigrant women. So, Lutz has suggested that scholars need to 'look at them [immigrant women] as newcomers, needing time to adjust to both differences and similarities in the host societies life-styles' (1991: 23).

The number of Muslim women migrating towards the West as refugees, economic migrants and for family regrouping has been continually increasing. The 1990s saw an increase of Muslim women seeking jobs mainly in European countries. The case of migrant Muslim women shifted from being an academic 'curiosity' to being a cause for social scientific research. A milestone in the study of immigrant women is the book *Migrant Women: Crossing Boundaries and Changing Identities* (Buijs 1993). The collection of articles has demonstrated that men and women experience displacement and migration differently. The book explores controversial topics, such as domestic violence, discrimination against women within and outside their families, and immigrant women's adaptation to host societies. In one of the chapters, Abdulrahim has observed that migration may induce fundamental changes in the 'traditional cultural codes' of Muslim women:

Instead of the traditional method of taking refuge with relatives or neighbours, young women had the opportunity to turn to a German women's centre'. These women, in the majority of cases, return to the family household, but a small and increasing number of exceptions is significant. Taking refuge outside the community, even if temporarily, indicates that an alternative to family organisation now exists for women. By using it as a threat, young women have increased their power in a conflict situation. (1993: 70)

Abdulrahim, like the other contributors to Buijs's book, has emphasized the social advantages that migrating towards Western countries would bring to

Muslim women. Nonetheless, emphasizing the positive aspects, often linked to processes of modernization, has hidden the other side of the coin: the distress and suffering that migration could provoke. The disintegration of family and friendship networks upon which Muslim immigrant women used to rely is one of the commonest sources of distress I have documented. Yet this has been one of the aspects most overlooked by academics. So, Abdulrahim has stressed the positive aspects of the fact that many Muslim immigrant women suffering domestic violence or facing forced marriages decide to seek asylum in 'refuges for women'. But Abdulrahim has not observed that these desperate Muslim migrant women, cut off from the protective extended family network they enjoyed in their homelands, had no other choice. They had to accept the help of associations and end up in 'women's hostels'. During one of my interviews, a Muslim woman, who had suffered domestic abuse, described how humiliating, degrading and upsetting the experience of going to a 'women refuge' was. She commented that, 'Only prostitutes, in my country end in these institutions. I mean, I have a good family and good friends back home who would have supported and helped me during those difficult times. But here I had no choice other than ending in the women's refuge.' Some Muslim immigrant women could perceive what Abdulrahim has said is a modern positive choice rejecting patriarchal and traditional schemes as yet another distress to add to the many they have to face.

Although academic studies have overemphasized the economic and social problems experienced by Muslim immigrant women, there are other aspects which are fundamental to the experience of immigration for these women. Therefore, Mozzo-Counil, a French social worker, has written an interesting (but unfortunately little known) book (1994) with a powerful ethnography and analyses concerning the immigration experiences of North African women. Being a social worker, Mozzo-Counil was able to observe the other side of the coin which some social scientists have missed. Not only has she recognized the relevance that women's networks played in the pre-migration lives of these women, but she has also recognized that Muslim immigrant women are unable to recreate those models of solidarity among women they used to enjoy in their homeland. Some of Mozzo-Counil's respondents have suffered depression and isolation because of immigration. The surprise in Mozzo-Counil's book is how she focused on the human aspect, disclosing the emotions and thought processes these women went through. So, the sentiments of these women as well as their complex psychological relationship with their own bodies become part of Mozzo-Counil's narration and argument. She has reminded the anthropologist, 'the Maghribi women of the first generation communicate through their bodies, the cry of their suffering bodies, the joy of their dancing bodies' and through them the experience of their immigration (1994: 9, translation from French is mine).

The year 1994 was also when Clifford, needing to reaffirm the centrality of gender in immigration studies argued, 'Diasporic experiences are always gendered. But there is a tendency for theoretical accounts of diasporas and diaspora cultures to hide this fact, to talk of travel and displacement in unmarked ways, thus normalizing male experiences' (1994: 313). Women, according to him, retain a particular position within the immigrant family; they propagate the cultural traditions of their families. Because of immigration, however, some of them may achieve an economic and social freedom outside their families. French scholars[1] have radicalized the idea that migration axiomatically means the emancipation of Muslim women. The main argument is that the difficulties experienced by men during immigration give the opportunity for Muslim women in the family to emancipate themselves from patriarchal structures. According to this viewpoint, the children, and in particular daughters, would be the family members who would benefit most from the disruption of the father figure within the immigrant family. For instance, in a family in which the father suffered unemployment and the mother had to find low-paid jobs in order to maintain the family, the French educational system might become the only point of reference for the children.

These facts help us to understand why an influential scholar such as Lacoste-Dujardin interprets as positive, for example, the experience of divorce for Muslim migrant women. In contrast with Mozzo-Counil, Lacoste-Dujardin has failed to observe that Muslim immigrant women and their daughters may have different opinions about female emancipation from those of Western women. But Lacoste-Dujardin is not interested in what these people think, but only what is conducive to their assimilation: 'emancipation is more relevant to daughters and especially the older daughters in a family, although even the younger children, both boys and girls, may benefit by being brought up by an emancipated mother, more able to stimulate them in their studies and to incite them to social success' (2000: 66). Before arguing against the supposed dynamics that these theories present, let me say that I see a degree of collusion between these French social scientific researches and the controversial French assimilation policy. Reading some of these French scholars, I had the impression that the discussion was not about understanding the system and structure of Muslim immigrant families, but how to transform the children of Muslim parents into 'acceptable' French citizens. There is nothing wrong with this (although I do not believe in the French way of *l'assimilation*), but this has more to do with political policy-making than social scientific research.

These kinds of studies have clearly failed to observe the consequences of the disruption of traditional Muslim family structure.

Recent anthropological studies have finally focused on the 'dark sides' of family immigration. Although Pels in his studies on Moroccan families in the Netherlands (2000) has confirmed the social disempowerment that Muslim men suffer within and outside their families, he has rejected the idea that the disempowerment of Muslim men could improve the lives of Muslim women. Pels has suggested that Muslim immigrant men suffer disempowerment within their family because of unemployment or low-paid jobs, which effectively reduce the possibility of their being the family breadwinner. Some may think that this might be just an economic issue, but the fact is that Islamic law requires Muslim men to be *the* family breadwinner. Unemployment or, more often, their husbands' low-paid jobs 'force' Muslim women to experience role reversal economically speaking. In other words, there is a dramatic inversion of the Islamic precepts structuring the traditional Muslim family. It was exactly this inversion that Lacoste-Dujardin (2000) and other French scholars (i.e. Lepoutre 1997; Souilamas 2000; Tribalat 1995) have interpreted as extremely positive for Muslim immigrant women, but the anthropological study provided by Pels has revealed a considerably less idyllic picture. He has noticed that a majority of Muslim women he interviewed rejected Western-style gender relations and parenthood because, according to him, they 'are not willing to give up their central position within the family and their power over internal family affairs.' (Pels 2000: 88)

Indeed, Muslim immigrant women tend to retain and protect the cultural tradition of their families and resist assimilation. So, Salih, who has conducted an anthropological study concerning Moroccan immigrant women living in Italy (2000) has argued, 'Immigrant women contextually negotiate the boundaries of inclusion and exclusion of Self and Other, according to the diverse and sometimes intersecting hegemonic discourses that they may face in different places and phases of their lives' (2000: 323). Salih has emphasized the abilities of Muslim immigrant women to renegotiate new boundaries instead of passively assimilating the host 'Western' models. She has reminded us that Muslim immigrant women actively take part not only in their families, but also in their host societies. While the majority of French scholars we have discussed seem to interpret Islam as an obstacle to assimilation, Salih has argued that Muslim immigrant women integrate Islam in their complex negotiation processes, which involve not only their host societies but also their former homelands. Indeed, Basch, Glick Schiller and Szanton (1994) have argued that immigrants are part of 'deterritorialized nation-states' (i.e. a state that 'stretches beyond its geographical boundaries') so that 'the nation's people may live anywhere in the world and still not live outside the state so that 'wherever its people go, their state goes too' (1994: 269). However, Smith (1999) has criticized Basch's idea of 'deterritorialized nation-states', arguing that it might affect the concept of diaspora. Smith has reminded us that, despite the available communication technology, in their host countries Muslim immigrant women may still experience displacement.

Avoiding the radicalism of Basch et al. (1994), Salih, in another article (2001), has suggested that Moroccan immigrant women are plurinational subjects. This highlights the fact that Muslim women experience 'embeddedness with multiple hegemonic structures operating at more than one national level which conditions their potential to move, their identities and their transnational activities in a gendered way' (2001: 669). It is precisely because Muslim immigrant women are 'plurinational' that they cannot be politically passive subjects as some have suggested. Indeed, far from being passive 'repeaters' of men's discourses, Muslim immigrant women develop their own political and religious views. Fifteen years after the 'head scarf affair' (Dayan-Herzbrun 2000), the French government has enforced a controversial law which bans all visible religious symbols; in reality, this legislation aims to stop Muslim female students wearing hijabs, since the French government reads the Muslim headscarf as anti-secular, hence anti-French. A considerable number of Muslim women in France have fiercely opposed the new government's legislation in different ways, from writing passionate e-mails to the unknown cyber sisters within the 'virtual *ummah*', to political protests and marches. Their protest has had an international audience and spread the protest not only to other European Countries but also to many Islamic countries.

The resistance to this legislation, however, has moved beyond political and religious arguments to become an emotional experience of an anti-colonialist denial of identity (see Chapter 5). Indeed, many Muslim women linked the anti-hijab legislation to France's colonialist past. Concerning the role that memory may have in post-colonial discourse, Ganguly has observed,

> Re-making the past, then, serves at least a dual purpose. It is a way of coming to terms with the present without being seen to criticize the status quo; it also helps to recuperate a sense of the self not dependent on criteria handed down by others – the past is what women can claim as their own. The past is seen as autonomous and as possessing an authority not related to the privileges acquired through marriage and emigration. Since self representation is so tied up with the representation of the past, it is no wonder that some of the memories have more to do with how things ought to be rather than how they were. (1992: 40 emphases in the original)

Personal memories are also essential in the redefinition of 'home' as a place of belonging, as Ahmed has observed, 'Nostalgia and memory also take what Gopinath calls "a generative or enabling" form when it is used for the reinterpretation of homes and homelands' (Ahmed, Castañeda, Fortier and Sheller 2003: 9). Yet for some daughters of Muslim immigrant mothers, the hijab and Islamic dress emphasize their re-imagined, 'mythologized' connection with a pure, a-cultural, essential Islam.

As in the case of their brothers, even recent studies[2] have represented the identities of Western-born Muslim women as in-between the West and Islam. Yet as in the case of their mothers, they have been represented as passive human beings, shaped by the culture Islam has provided. Other studies have rejected this representation and suggested a more dynamic relationship between Islam and Western-born Muslim women. Basit has studied the aspirations of British Muslim girls and observed:

> While British Muslims are not a homogeneous group, a collective Muslim identity transcends the regional and sectarian differences when living in a non-Muslim country which is their adopted homeland. Shaw (1994) argues that the assumption that these young people are 'torn between two cultures' is both inappropriate and misleading. And the implied dichotomy between 'modern' and 'traditional' is in effect quite unsustainable as Muslim identity now provides them with a powerful and ideologically effective justification ... (1997: 430)

The authors who, like Shaw, suggest that Western-born Muslim women are 'torn between two cultures' discuss identity exclusively from a culturalist viewpoint. Yet we have seen that another understanding of identity could be brought to the fore, in which emotions and feelings play the major role.

Gender and Jihad

Khadijah was fifty-seven when I met her in 1998. She had been living for twenty-seven years in Seine-St-Denis, a Parisian suburb in which one-third of the population was at the time Muslim. A mother of four, she succeeded in joining her husband when the French government allowed the *regroupement familial* (family regroupment). I always had my meetings with Khadijah in her small kitchen, in which scents of different spices were pleasantly hanging around. As usual, that day Khadijah was 'force-feeding' me with another and another (and another) handmade piece of terrific *baqlaw*,[3] while we were speaking of her favourite Algerian Raï singer (Marranci 2000b). The audiocassette was playing the melancholic singer's voice singing a song in Algerian dialect, which Khadijah translated word by word for me in her peculiar French accent while cooking her meal. Unexpectedly one word, *gorba*, stopped both Khadijah's translation and her rhythmical stirring. *Gorba* means 'foreigner land' or 'exile', but had a particular emotional flavour for all Algerian immigrants. Speaking more to herself than me, she said,

> To emigrate is suffering. You miss your homeland, your parents and your friends with whom you have shared your life. But the most difficult thing was to educate my children in another country that was so different from mine. If I had not been Muslim, I would have not survived all the problems I had to face. I can tell you, and I am not joking, that Islam prevented me from taking my life. I was depressed but I am a Muslim and suicide is a really really bad thing. I had to fight against my depression and against this racist society. France wants our children to change and they corrupt them. I had to struggle as a mother to keep my children on the right path and this was my jihad. When I go back to my country and I meet young Muslim women who want to come here, I repeat to them that Muslim women who want to emigrate should be ready for nothing less than a jihad.

For the first time, I heard the word jihad from the mouth of a Muslim woman. By 'jihad' Khadijah meant a fight against nostalgia depression, as well as her effort to educate her children as Muslim. Although she was the first, she was not the last Muslim woman who mentioned jihad to emphasize the hardship she had to endure during the adaptation to the host country lifestyle.

The jihad was often marked through the symbolic Muslim headscarf. So, 'A'ishah who was twenty-three when she migrated alone from an Egyptian village to cosmopolitan Paris, told me how she used to perceive the new Western environment as threatening and dangerous. By contrast with the majority of teenagers leaving their homes for a new student life, 'A'ishah worried about her new uncontrolled freedom. She explained that the women of her village rarely travel without at least one *mahram* (a male member of the family) but her father had trusted her to go to Paris to complete her studies. 'A'ishah explained, 'I feared that I could not resist the many temptations around me,' and provided some examples: 'Drinking alcohol, going to parties, eating during Ramadan, and finding a non-Muslim boyfriend or having premarital sex'. She, however, decided to conduct what she defined as a 'jihad against temptations'. To mark the beginning of her jihad she decided to wear the hijab everywhere and not just at the mosque, 'I felt strongly Muslim and I wanted to show that I was Muslim, that this is my main identity.'

Before the second Intifada, I noticed that many of the Palestinian women I had met charged jihad with a similar meaning to Khadijah and 'A'ishah's.

Although they openly spoke and supported the Palestinian cause and the war against the Israeli occupation forces, they avoided the word jihad and preferred to use the generic *muqawamah* (resistance).[4] In 1999, Fadwa, a Palestinian wife of an influential member of the mosque in Pisa, told me why she did not use jihad in that context, 'Jihad is a very, very important word, and too many journalists use it. Italians do not know what jihad really means, they say holy war and this creates lots of confusion.' This was before 28 September 2000, the date on which the second Intifada started. Afterwards, desperation, fear and anger replaced the hope that Palestinians had for a peaceful end to the conflict. But the tension and the violence had to increase not only in Palestine and Israel, but also internationally. September 11 saw an increase of Islamophobia and the abuse of Muslim women: some of them had their hijab ripped off, others unfortunately, were physically attacked.[5] My women respondents believed that Islam was the target of this Islamophobia and the circle of panic became particularly noticeable.[6] They shifted from describing jihad as mainly an inner struggle to violent action.

Fatimah is a 52-year-old Palestinian woman. She migrated to the UK fifteen years ago and has a 22-year-old daughter and a 12-year-old son. Fatimah today did not show the same wariness 'A'ishah had in calling Hamas's operations jihad so she argued,

> In Palestine men, women and even children are conducting a jihad against the Zionists. Jihad means that they cannot stop us; that we'll kill them for what they have done to us, Jews kill our children every day, nobody cares about them anymore. So don't tell me that our shuhada [martyrs, but here she meant suicide bombers] are wrong when they go to Israel to do their jihads.

The only concern she seemed to have about the word jihad was that I should be convinced of the terrifying 'power' of it. Fatimah's daughter, Lya, shared her mother's opinions. Lya had, like many Western-born Muslims, a more international understanding of the conflict. She argued that after 9/11 non-Muslims had to take into consideration that Muslim blood would no longer be cheap since jihad could reach everybody and strike everywhere. She then observed, 'the suffering of Palestinian people and all the other oppressed Muslims have been brought to the nations that hate us [Palestinians] and Islam'. Lya believed in international jihad, 'Every time a non-Muslim has been killed, people make a lot of fuss, but when a Muslim child dies because of the terrorist actions of the West, nobody cares. If every time a *kafirun* kills a Muslim the world had to show respect [followed by a minute of silence], we would enjoy endless holidays here.' During all our conversations, Lya never mentioned the Qur'an, the hadiths or other

Islamic texts. Her idea of jihad had originated from a different source, her identity.

After the interviews and discussions I had with Fatimah and her daughter, I had to recognize that I felt more uncomfortable listening to these arguments from Muslim women than Muslim men. Maybe the reason is that, despite years of feminism, we still see women as mothers. This is partially confirmed by the fact that the most effective pacifist rhetoric resorts to the figure of 'the mother' as a dissuasive symbol against war.[7] In Christianity, the paramount symbol of maternal pain for the loss of her child is Mary. Finally, we tend to think that a mother might be more sympathetic to the pain of other mothers. In other words, in the choice between death and life we expect mothers to choose the latter. Yet not all cultures have the same myths, as Sparta teaches.

We have just seen in Chapter 5, that women may support jihad no less than male members of their family. Let me share an anecdote that happened quite recently at Azhar's home. Ten years ago Azhar emigrated to the UK with his wife Jamilah. They came from a middle-class Lebanese family and quickly adapted to the new British lifestyle. During my research, I asked if I could interview them together on their experience of immigration. The day arrived and Azhar invited me to his home. They seemed very pleased to share their experiences with me and the atmosphere was very relaxed. One of my usual questions focuses on the aftermath of 9/11 and whether the tragic event had modified their neighbourhood relationships. Before answering the question, Azhar gave an introduction in which he defined 9/11 as a criminal act against Islam and humanity. He then acknowledged that people could have problems in trusting Muslims since, 'people do not have something like terrorist detectors; but they know that there is more chance that Azhar could blow up their flight than my friend John'. Then laughing Azhar added, 'What they do seem to forget is that Azhar himself is as worried as they are that the Pakistani men sitting on his left on the plane could blow him up.' I noticed that Jamilah was becoming increasingly disappointed. She was not laughing at all and she was looking at the other side of the room.

Azhar did not seem to pay any attention to his wife's expression and stated, 'Muslims have a duty to rebuild the relationships with non-Muslims and not the other way around. The terrorist acted in the name of Islam, we have to show that they were wrong.' Jamilah could not help but interrupt her husband in quite a rude manner. This would not be so surprising or wrong, if I had not been there. In even the most modern and liberal Muslim family, Jamilah's rebuke would have sparked tension, since I was not part of the family and I was conducting research. Jamilah started to speak while her husband tried to make strange (quite funny) facial expressions as if asking her to avoid something. But she did not pay any attention and said, 'Palestinians have suffered because of Israel and Lebanese Muslims like us know what the Israeli oppression is like.' Of course, I could understand that this was just the beginning. Jamilah holds a very different opinion from her husband. From his expressions I thought that he probably knew that. She went on accusing the Americans of supporting Israel and selling powerful weapons to Israel. With an expression of disgust she added, 'the same weapons have not only killed Palestinian *mujahidin* but also innocent children and women'. Jamilah seemed to like her husband's incredulous expression when she said, 'Americans used to feel secure in their homeland, and they thought that our Muslim suffering could not reach them. 9/11 just taught them that America is vulnerable to jihad as we are vulnerable to their bombs and violence.' Azhar was visibly annoyed but unable to stop his wife, perhaps fearing that I might be embarrassed. For this traditional family to have such a dispute was beyond the pale. Jamilah's final comments during that day left Azhar evidently embarrassed and ashamed, 'too many Muslims', she said, 'are Westernized and doing nothing for Islam or their families. They only think about money and business. I wonder whether they are still men.' Was Jamilah challenging Azhar's masculinity? Perhaps this was the impression that Azhar had, since I was never invited again and was unable to meet him again.

Jamilah was very critical of the Islamic behaviour of Muslim men and she, as other women I met, seemed to guard the faith of the members of the family.[8] For instance, on many occasions I observed how Muslim women checked and made sure that their children (in particular boys) respected Ramadan and the prayers. Yet it was not only the mother but also older (sometimes even younger) sisters who encouraged their brothers to read the Qur'an and go to the mosque on Fridays. Inayah, a 21-year-old British-Pakistani girl, explains in these terms the role of 'guardian of the faith' she has within her family.

We have to remind our brothers and sometimes our fathers that Islam is important. They [male members of the family] have many distractions so my brothers do not want to go to the mosque. I have to tell them that they have to visit the mosque. Our family wants to be a respected Muslim family within this community. We want to be good Muslims otherwise others would speak about us behind our backs or refer to our family as a bad example. Islam asks women to be shy and lower their eyes so that their family honour can be protected but our father and brothers have to show good Islamic behaviour if they want to make us an honourable family that people can refer to as a good example. So we should help our brothers to respect their din [faith]. I mean, within the Muslim family there is a relationship between the Muslim women's chastity and the men's honour but also between the men's respect for Islam and the respect that others show to the women of a certain family. If you have a very good Muslim father, people will respect you as a Muslim daughter.

We might be tempted to link honour to masculinity and the patriarchal sexual control of the family's women. Yet the concept of honour is not, as we shall discuss in the next section, mono-directional from women to men. Muslim women care about their family honour no less than their Muslim male relatives do. As Inayah seemed to be aware, respected fathers, husbands, sons, and brothers enhance Muslim women's status among their peers. In other words, if the degree of sexual control imposed on their family's women may define Muslim men's honour, the degree of din of their family's men may define Muslim women's respectability.

Re-gendering the Honour Shame Complex

The honour and shame theory suggests that in certain societies men's honour depends on their ability to control women's sexuality.[9] Extreme attempts to control and regulate the sexuality of the family's women can lead to some men performing honour killings in the hope of re-establishing their forfeited honour. Peristiany (1965) suggested that the 'honour and shame complex' has only characterized Mediterranean societies. However, Brandes (1980) has criticized Peristiany's monolithic view and has argued that the relationship between honour and shame is not restricted to particular ethnic, cultural or religious groups. A short review of the British news confirms Brandes' opinion. For instance, the BBC reported that during 2003, Scotland Yard had registered twelve 'honour killings' in the whole of the UK. Not all of them, however, saw a Muslim charged. Among the perpetrators figured Sikhs and several British Christians.[10]

Stewart (1994) has suggested that 'honour' has a bipartite system: the concept of 'honour' should be relevant to both the honour acknowledged and the honour acknowledger. Therefore, the members of a group must share similar moral codes because they are then able to recognize an action as honourable or dishonourable. In the case of honour and shame syndromes, neither the single man nor the social group sharing the 'honour code' has sole control over the dynamics of how honour is achieved and kept. Women have the power to jeopardize or enhance the honour of their male relatives through sexual behaviour. In other words, wives and daughters retain the, presumably, undesired power to dishonour their men by breaking the shared group's sexual norms and 'bringing shame' on their families. In the worst cases in which social sexual norms have been broken, the husbands, fathers and brothers of the woman have to act quickly to re-establish their honour within their social group.

This is achieved through public violent acts (Akpinar 2003), which unfortunately are rarely merely symbolic and can culminate in the murder of the 'culprit' woman. On 12 October 2003 Abdullah Yones stabbed to death Heshu Yones, his 16-year-old daughter. She had planned to run away from home and live with her Lebanese boyfriend. Because of his daughter's behaviour, Abdullah felt that his honour was jeopardized and his position within the local Kurdish Muslim community ruined. His daughter's pre-marital relationship represented the tangible evidence of his failure as a Muslim and Kurdish father. The fact that he was an immigrant, distant from his family network and suffering from long-term unemployment surely had a dramatic impact on his tragic action which ended his daughter's life. Abdullah saw himself as humiliated both as a member of the Kurdish community and as a Muslim model father.

When I discussed the case of Abdullah Yones with a Kurdish man I had met in an Edinburgh mosque, the worshipper observed, 'Only weak Muslims, who have problems being respected even by their families commit honour killings.' He then explained that these Muslims use violence against their daughters and wives because they want to stop their communities speaking about their failure as Muslim men. 'I tell you the truth, if you are a failure as a father and husband the community do not take you seriously as Muslim. Muslim men know how to deal with their children and wives.' He acknowledged that in 'Kurdistan', as in other Muslim places, if one's daughter behaved like Abdullah Yones' daughter 'people there would certainly expect the father to act'. Yet my Kurdish interlocutor made an interesting observation, 'Abdullah Yones allowed his daughter to be educated among non-Muslims here in the West; so, since Allah gave him a daughter, he had to think carefully about the problems he had to face if Abdullah wished to stay in Scotland.' This was not the only critical opinion I collected, others pointed out that if Abdullah Yones were a 'real Muslim man' having a strong faith, his daughter would have respected his honour and the tragedy would have been avoided.

At this point, we can wonder whether honour is only a masculine feeling. In other words, could a Muslim man make the women of his family feel ashamed because of his actions or lack of them? By studying the concept of honour among Egyptian Bedouins, Abu-Lughod (1986) has observed that in that society women hold codified 'honour' rules to which men (at least if they wanted to achieve a successful marriage) have to conform:

Women claim, for instance, that 'real men' control all their dependents and beat their wives when the wives do stupid things. One woman, whose daughter was about to marry one of the most respected men in the camp, said, 'my daughter wants a man whose eyes are open – not someone nice ... No, she wants someone who will order her around' ... One old woman told me, 'when a man is really something [manly] he pays no heed to women.' 'A man who listens to his wife when she tells him what to do is a fool' said a young woman ... many agreed adding 'if a man is fool, a woman rides him like a donkey.' (1986: 89, 95)

Is this just a peculiar characteristic of Egyptian Bedouin women? Apparently it is not. Some of my Muslim women respondents have expressed a clear preference for men who conform to the 'real Muslim man' model. The list below is based on the opinions that I have collected, and of course is over-generalized,

1. an observant Muslim who has Islam in his heart;
2. acts justly towards his family, in particular his wife;
3. is ready to defend his family and religion in any circumstances;
4. avoids too explicitly Westernized behaviour;
5. takes straightforward decisions;
6. is the bread winner;
7. controls his children and educates them in Islam, but without being unjust or oppressive.

In particular two aspects were linked to the concept of 'honour'. First, the man should show devotion to Islam; secondly, as the Qur'an requires, he should be the breadwinner.[11] Indeed, when I interviewed some Muslim women employed outside their families, they seemed felt compelled to stress that they kept their salaries for themselves since their husbands' salaries provided for the family.[12] By contrast, I have collected complaints from some Muslim women who found themselves forced to find a job because their husbands were unemployed. These women would have preferred to take care of their children instead of spending time outside their homes. In some cases, complaints turned into strong criticism of their husbands. In this case, immigration was blamed for the 'dishonourable' state of their men, some of whom, I came to know, had started drinking.

As we have seen, Muslim immigrant men face challenges within their host societies but also within their families because of their unusually weak position in both. Many of them went through the experience of family regrouping with mixed feelings of joy and fear since they could not provide the 'standard-Western life' which some of their wives expected. Shadi, a

Algerian 42-year-old living in Paris, expressed a kind of nostalgia for his first
years of immigration, when his wife and son were not with him,

> I had so many troubles in finding a job and when I found one, the salary was not
> good. How could I provide something for my family? My wife wanted to come
> here with our son. I couldn't refuse, could I? When she arrived, she was
> unhappy as I had expected in my worst nightmare. The house I rented was too
> small and in a very poor area but I could not afford any better. Women expect
> that their husbands are strong and pray and are good Muslims. At that time, I
> was weak, with lots of problems. Before my wife arrived, I had started drinking
> because I was desperate. I was such a bad Muslim that my wife asked for a
> divorce, she did not want to share her bed with a man left without any honour.
> I lost everything but then she agreed to take me back because I started to prac-
> tice Islam and stopped drinking.

Some feminist scholars have highlighted the problems and difficulties that
Muslim women face within their families and host societies and have rightly
criticized the androcentric perspectives that have affected sociology and
anthropology for a long time. Yet the effort to rebalance the lack of attention to women has had the unwanted result that 'gender', as category, has
become synonymous with femininity, when, of course, masculinity was also
part of it. So the honour and shame complex has been mainly observed from
an axiomatic assumption that men oppress women and women passively
suffer this oppression (see Akpinar 2003).

But we have just observed that Muslim women may form their own 'code
of honour' to which Muslim men have to conform. A distressed Muslim
woman in Ireland told me 'How can I feel proud of my husband when he is
even unable to achieve respect from his own children?' It is clear that Muslim
men may 'bring shame' upon their Muslim women so that Muslim women's
status can be disrupted. We now know that some Muslim men may resort to
violence to re-establish their lost honour, yet Muslim women seem to prefer
physiological and emotional pressure rather than physical violence.
Nevertheless, I have noticed that, contrary to all my expectations, during my
researches, I have come across a few cases of the violence of women against
their sons and husbands.[13] As we shall see below, the fact that in many
Muslim families in the West men are increasingly unable to match the 'real
Muslim man' model has some effect on some women's rhetoric of jihad.

Past, Memory and Islamic Heroines

Some Muslim women's circles emphasize that it is a Muslim's duty to
defend Islam and it is the duty of good mothers and sisters to remember that

this was particularly important for a Muslim man's honour. For instance, a Western-born Pakistani boy recalled how his mother 'constantly told me that if somebody abused the name of the Prophet, I had to act and punish the person; if I did not, I was not only a bad Muslim but also without honour'. Other women I met overtly stated that there was no more reward from Allah than being a shahid's mother or wife. Of course, they were not referring to Islamic history. Where did these ideas come from? What impact do they have on Muslim women's rhetoric of jihad?

The Islamic accounts of the most famous battles in the time of the Prophet emphasize honour and self-sacrifice as the main characteristics of the 'right-guided' Muslim hero. Muslim women have some archetypes which they may use to test the Muslim honour of their men. These tests may induce in some men forms of 'bravado' attitudes towards jihad, some of which we have observed in previous chapters. The weaker the Muslim man is within his family, the more effective and dangerous this rhetoric of jihad could become. Although, a bravado jihadi attitude is often the commonest reaction to male honour testing, there is the possibility that it could end in tragic terrorist action. The mass media have supplied us with many examples of these tragedies from Palestine and Chechnya, yet Asif Hanif became the first British citizen to act as a suicide bomber.

Asif Hanif (twenty-one years old) took his own life, killed thirteen people and injured many others. He was the first British Muslim to make a suicide bomb attack in Israel. Asif's father was a wealthy businessman and was able to provide his son with private and state education as well as a comfortable life. According to his friends, Asif had planned to become a teacher, in other words, he had a brilliant future in front of him. The imam of the local mosque that Asif used to attend said '[Asif was] honourable and very polite and I never heard about any kind of politics from him' (BBC 1 May 2003). The word 'honourable' appears repeatedly in the imam's words and as we have seen, Muslims use this word carefully. Asif had never expressed radical ideas, he came from a middle-class family, he was what some may call a perfect, happy, 'integrated' Western-born Muslim. So, what went wrong?

I discussed this tragedy with some Muslim friends. They used the case of Asif to challenge the stereotype that 'an integrated Muslim always means a safe Muslim'. Habib (a 23-year-old Syrian) has observed that some Muslims 'Westernized' because it may help their lives, yet, according to Habib the 'Westernization' means also that these Muslims had to compromise their Islamic life and identity. Habib, however, thought that notwithstanding the efforts that 'these weak Muslims make they quickly discover that they are becoming neither good Muslims nor good non-Muslims'. Habib then explained that these 'Westernized' Muslims rediscover their faith as part of their identity but they feel the need to prove it to themselves and to others. Indeed, it is not difficult to spot the schismogenetic process in which these Muslims become involved. However, Muhammad, a Western-born Muslim of Pakistani origin, pointed out other aspects that matches what I had discovered during my research,

> Our sisters [Muslim women] are becoming more religious and better Muslims than we [the men] are. They [Muslim women] have many occasions to remind us that we do not have much honour left. Some of these women are more radical than men in their arguments, believe me. It is only because Muslim women are considered weak and oppressed that people do not pay attention to what they say and police do not stop them so often as they stop us in the streets. Some Muslim brothers may feel uncomfortable with the fact that they are less good Muslims than their sisters and mothers; so they [Muslim men] have to show that Islam is everything for them if they do not want to be less than a woman.

The police have traced e-mails between Asif and his sister which would suggest that the girl had incited her brother to conduct the jihad (see *The Independent*, 27 April 2004). Probably, Asif had to show that he was an 'honourable Muslim man' by defending Islam. He became convinced that Islam was under attack, and his Muslim identity became trapped in the circle of panic, perhaps he was trapped. His jihad, which went beyond rhetoric to materialize in carnage, had more to do with emotions of feeling 'shame' for being too Westernized, than with Islam as a religion and jihad as a theological concept. As I have discussed above, the syndrome of honour and shame is never mono-directional; an increasing number of Muslim men are becoming 'victims' of their lost honour. Muslim immigrant women as well as their daughters may develop forms of rhetoric of jihad. Yet such female jihadi rhetoric is not new but part of a long established tradition.

Indeed, the first shahid was not a man, as some might think, but a woman: Sumayya bint Khubbat, who was killed by Abu Jhal (one of the fiercest enemies of the Prophet). Actually, her family became the first shahid family since her husband and then her son also offered their lives for Islam. Sumayya's story became popular (and still is) among Muslim women and they often narrate the story to their children. Indeed, Sumayya represents the perfect Muslim woman who educated her son in Islam and encouraged her husband to act honourably. Her story, like others involving Muslim heroines, is even available on audiocassettes, the majority of which are produced in Pakistan (Shalinsky 1993). These stories let me realize that during jihad the traditional Islamic distinctions between gender roles vanish; jihad has no gender. Shalinsky has observed,

women may have to redirect their loyalties and transcend their immediate
concern with family and kin. ... In ordinary times women express their *'aql*
[reason] by veiling and by appropriate concern for family and kin. In extraordi-
nary times like jihad too much concern with family and kin may actually be *nafs*
(self-indulgence). *'Aql* is expressed by a woman willing to sacrifice herself and
her kin during a time of jihad. Hence, the exalted figure of the Muslim mother
is turned into a more powerful figure: Islam's mother. (1993: 65)

Many other Islamic stories emphasize the role of Islam's mothers; and the
topical point is the sacrifice of maternal love for the sake of Islam.

Another of these 'brave women of Islam', as a Muslim female friend liked
to describe her, was Nasibah bint Kahf Yazidi. During the battle of Uhud
she stopped distributing water to the Muslim fighters and armed herself
with a sword to shield the Prophet from fierce attacks. While fighting, she
saw her son wounded and went to help him. After she dressed his wounds,
Nasibah urged him to fight and to die as shahid. During the battle, the
Prophet pointed her towards the person who had fatally injured her son and
she killed him saying 'Allahu akbar' (Allah is Great). Nasibah was wounded
in her shoulder and had to leave the battlefield. At the end of the battle, the
Prophet of Islam praised Nasibah's love for Islam and her heroism. 'A'isha,
the youngest and most loved wife of the Prophet, also participated in several
battles and led the Muslim army against her enemies after the death of her
husband. These Muslim heroines inspire the 'rhetoric of jihad' that some
Muslim immigrant women have developed. These examples of heroic, independent, brave, successful Muslim women, who facing terrible tasks only
succeeded because of their faith in Islam, inspire some Muslim immigrants
and their myth of the 'perfect Muslim woman'.

Today, new Muslim heroines have flanked Sumayya and Nasiba. These
new heroines are the female Palestinian suicide bombers such as Wafa Idris
who, on 27 January 2002, aged twenty-eight, killed herself and an elderly
Jew, injuring another 150; and Dareen Abu Aisheh (twenty-one), who just
one month after Wafa's jihadi action, injured three policemen while blowing
herself up. Yet the youngest were also the most quoted by my female
respondents: Ayat Akhras (aged eighteen) who detonated a bomb inside a
supermarket in Jerusalem on 29 March 2002 and killed, among others, a
17-year-old Jewish girl and a mother of two children; and Hanadi Tayseer
Jaradat (aged twenty-nine), who on 4 October 2003 killed herself and
another other nineteen people and injured fifty. Some of these women witnessed Israeli soldiers brutalizing or even killing their relatives and we can
imagine how their determination formed.

Discussing the topic of female Palestinian suicide bombers with both
Muslim men and women, I noticed two different opinions. The majority of

non-Palestinian Muslim immigrant men and some Palestinian men, argued that the first duty for a Muslim woman is her family and children and then to support their Muslim men during jihad. In conclusion, these men believed that these women's actions went against Islamic teachings. Muslim immigrant women, showed a less homogeneous point of view. Palestinian women tended to exalt the courage and faith that these women had shown in giving up their own lives. Yet non-Palestinian women saw these female suicide bombers as controversial. By contrast a larger number of Western-born Muslim women I interviewed showed respect and appreciated the courage of these suicide bombers. They called them *shahida* and emphasized that 'they loved Islam more than many Muslim lads living in our [Western] cities'. Jamila (a 23-year-old Muslim girl of Pakistani origin) compared these female suicide bombers to the great Islamic heroines,

> I think that their actions have shamed Muslim men who are doing nothing for Islam. If these women had such a strong *iman* [faith], why should Muslim men have less than they had? I think that today Muslim women should be as strong as they were in Muhammad's time because the modern kafirun have attacked Islam as fiercely as the Meccans did.

Probably I do not need to mention that Jamila overtly supported violent jihadi actions and she thought that the majority of her 'brothers in Islam' lacked honour because they even criticized her radical position. Like the Bedouin women studied by Abu-Lughod (1986), some of the Muslim women I met had their model of the 'perfect Muslim man'. Yet the archetype often clashed with the reality of everyday life. To mention just one thing, Jamila's father was an unemployed man for whom Islam meant only Jamila's hijab.

Conclusion

In some historic battles, in which the enemies of Islam tried to wipe out the newborn religion, some Muslim men ran for their lives leaving the Prophet in danger. By contrast, women such as Nasibah and Summaya offered their lives and encouraged even their wounded sons to accept martyrdom for Islam. Today, some Muslim women refer to these stories to challenge the honour and the Islamic identity of their male relatives. Indeed, when the first American missile hit Afghanistan during the last war, a Muslim girl of Indonesian origin sent me this little poem,

> If you want to believe that you're doing all that you can
> then remember Sumayya who lay in the burning sun with blood flowing

freely from a fatal wound, yet her heart and lips overflowing with La Illahe Illalah [the Muslim proclamation of faith].

If you want to believe that your struggle is the most difficult

then remember the wives, sisters and daughters of the Ashab who fought along-side the Prophet.

Remember Nasiba bint Ka'b who took her *saber* [sword] and went to fight with the Prophet when the archers disobeyed his orders at the battle of Uhud;

Remember Nasiba bint Ka'b at the battle of Uhud when her son was injured;

Remember how she took care of his wounds and told him to keep on fighting,

Remember how the Prophet pointed out her son's injurer and she boldly hit the *mushrik* [infidel] across his knees causing him to kneel before her making the Prophet smile so that his molars showed.

Remember Nasiba bint Ka'b and the fire of *iman* [faith] inside her heart and the hand she lost during the battle of Yamam;

Remember 'A'isha, the mother of believers and the pregnant Umm Sulaym who went with her husband into jihad and remained firmly with the Prophet while the Muslims fled from the battle of Hunayn,

Remember her fury for the sake of Allah when she asked the Prophet to kill all of those who had upon the conquest of Makkah accepted Islam but had turned away when their lives were at stake.

Remember Umm Ayman who gave water to the thirsty and cared for the wounded at the battles of Uhud, Haybar, Mu'ti and Hunayn.

Remember all these *Mujahidas* [female fighters] and so many more true Muslimas [Muslim women] who struggled for the cause of Allah,

Remember them and compare your *iman* and struggle to attain theirs not to the shells of women living today and see whether you're truly an exception or a poor excuse for a Muslim Woman.

Searching the Internet, I became aware that e-mail by e-mail this little poem had achieved certain success among Muslim girls. This text confirms the relevance that the Muslim heroines have for many Muslim women. But at the same time the total absence of any male figure tells us how Muslim women feel that Islam needs them because, as in the traditional Islamic stories, men had fled; Muslim women could save Islam; as Sumayya, Nasibah, 'A'isha, Umm Sulaym. However, they have to renounce their role as mothers and their femininity, jihad has no gender.

Notes

1. See for instance, Tribalat 1995; Lepoutre 1997; Manço 1999; Souilimas 2000.

2. See for instance, Anwar 1981; Archer 2002; Qureshi and Moores 1999.

3. Algerian sweets made of many layers of paper-thin dough with a filling of crushed nuts and sugar between layers.

4. It is interesting to note that Hamas is the Arabic acronym for *Harakat al-Muqawamah al-Islamiyya* meaning 'The Islamic Resistance Movement'.

5. Muslim immigrant women or their daughters are even less likely to report aggression and abuse to the Police than their husbands and brothers.

6. The number of Muslim female respondents who believed that Islam was under attack exceeded the number of my Muslim male respondents holding the same opinion.

7. The most virulent campaigns against the last Iraqi war centred around the figure of the mother. In Scotland soldiers' mothers have organized protests against the war.

8. Other researches (see for instance Buijs 1993; Lutz 1991; Pels. 2000; Salih 2001 and Timmerman 2000) have highlighted this role of 'guardian of the faith' that some Muslim women have developed after emigrating.

9. For a discussion of the honour and shame complex in different societies, see Abu-Lughod 1996; Gilmore 1987; Murphy 1983; Wikan 1984.

10. BBC News website, on 30 September 2003: http://news.bbc.co.uk/1/hi/england/london/3149030.stm

11. This does not mean that women are not able to work, rather that the most important economic element of the family should be the man. For this reason Islam allows working women to keep their salary and contribute to the expenses of their families only if they want to do so.

12. More than once, I discovered that some families depended upon the wives' wages.

13. Unfortunately, studies concerning domestic violence among immigrant families (but also non-immigrant) have failed to acknowledge male victims. Men tend to hide their status as victims within their families but also tend to receive less support from their peers.

CHAPTER 8

Anti-Semitism, Westernophobia and Jihad

People enter the gates of Auschwitz: pilgrims forgiving but not forgetting. Today, Jews, Christians, Muslims, Buddhists, Agnostics, Spiritualists, Humanists and people with any genre of philosophy, visit the monument to Nazi hatred. The ashes, which still shame humanity, had spoken different languages, believed different faiths, hoped for different vanished dreams. Together (one body over another) were cremated Jews, Muslims, Christians, Communists, Gypsies, political antagonists and disabled people. Stop a second and there, in the little wired square, you may hear the silence of their voice repeating, 'never again.'

Unfortunately, anti-Semitism is still among us, in our jokes, stereotypes, political language, ideas and behaviours. We can surf the Net and find many examples of how the experience of the Holocaust can be often denied or even invoked. The Palestinian–Israeli conflict has ignited waves of anti-Semitism. Muslims, particularly if they are Arabs, have been singled out as the new archetypes of 'anti-Semitism'. Sometimes, the language of *some* of my respondents and their conspiracy theories let me wonder whether this might be the case. They called the Jews names, they blamed them for any Muslim tragedy and they saw them as the worst creatures on earth. It would be easy at first glance to admit that the still existing Nazi anti-Semitism has been supplanted by a new Muslim and Arab anti-Semitism. Yet I am an anthropologist and I tend not to think that the first glance should also be the last. As in the case of the word 'identity', 'anti-Semitism' has often been used without any critical understanding. It is one of those words that suffer from a long history of clichés. Although, the long, cruel history of anti-Semitism within and outside Europe is beyond the scope of this chapter,[1] we need to study what anti-Semitism might be before venturing upon the task of understanding what has been called 'Muslim anti-Semitism'.

The majority of people are united in condemning anti-Semitism as unacceptable, but laymen as well as experts have been unable to agree on a single definition. Some time ago, I tested the divergences when I asked some of my students, friends and colleagues to suggest their definition of anti-Semitism; below I categorize their answers,

1. when people hate Jews;
2. a form of discrimination against Semitic people, such as Jews and Arabs;
3. hostility towards Jews;
4. a form of racism and xenophobia;
5. intolerance towards Judaism;
6. the attempt to destroy the Jews as a people and Israel as a nation;
7. anti-Zionism and hatred against Israel.

I observed that nobody noticed the most important characteristic of anti-Semitism, the fact that it is informed by fable. Hate or hostility cannot distinguish anti-Semitism from other existing forms of discrimination and xenophobia, as Klug (2003), with a good sense of humour, has demonstrated.

Klug has used the fictional character of Mary, a London bus conductor, to make his point. In all these hypothetical scenarios, Mary will repeat the same action, angrily throwing Rabbi Cohen off her bus. In the first story, Rabbi Cohen was smoking. Although the Rabbi was wearing his *kipah* (which marked his Jewish identity), anti-Semitism has not guided Mary's decision to angrily throw Rabbi Cohen off her bus, but the bus company's anti-smoking policy. Indeed, whoever wants to smoke on Mary's bus would share Rabbi Cohen's fate (and probably a heavy fine). In the second story, Rabbi Cohen was singing *zemiros* (Jewish hymns) at the top of his voice when Mary promptly angrily threw him off her bus. Again, Klug has argued that Mary evicted the Rabbi not as a Jew but 'as a lout' (Klug 2003: 122). The third scenario makes Mary a much grimmer character. Mary has been depicted as a bigot, but she has no clue what a Jew might look like. Mary spotted Rabbi Cohen on her bus and thought that he was one of the many foreigners invading her country and challenging her British culture. Consequently she angrily threw Rabbi Cohen off her bus. Klug has explained that we might accuse Mary of being xenophobic,[2] but certainly could not define her as anti-Semitic. In the fourth scenario, Mary mistakes Rabbi Cohen, who has a flowing beard, for a Muslim imam, angrily throwing Rabbi Cohen off her bus. Of course, in this case, Mary would have behaved as an Islamophobe but not as an anti-Semite. Finally, Mary *knew* that Rabbi Cohen was a Jew and *only for this reason* did she evict him from her bus. Klug has suggested that *only in this case* could we label Mary as anti-Semitic. But Mary did not hate Rabbi Cohen as a person, rather as the *personification* of the 'Jew' she had in her mind.

Defining anti-Semitism

Among definitions of anti-Semitism, Fein's one is the best known and the most used:

> Anti-Semitism is a persisting latent structure of hostile beliefs towards Jews as a collective manifested in individuals as attitudes, and in culture as myth, ideology, folklore and imagery, and in actions – social or legal discrimination, political mobilisation against the Jews, and collective or state violence – which results in and/or is designed to distance, displace, or destroy *Jews as Jews*. (1987: 7)

In its report *Manifestations of anti-Semitism in the European Union*, the European Monitoring Centre on Racism and Xenophobia (EUMC) has adopted it and invited others to adopt it (Bergman and Wetzel 2004). Klug has argued, however, that Fein's definition needs a tiny but essential edit. Anti-Semitism means hostility towards Jews as 'Jews'. In other words, the inverted commas tell us that the anti-Semitics' Jews exist only in the anti-Semites' minds and not on our streets. Langmuir (1990b) has coined the neologism *chimeria*[3] to define this characteristic of anti-Semitism.

However, we might ask why we just do not interpret anti-Semitism like any other form of xenophobia. Langmuir has answered, 'Chimerical assertions have no "kernel of truth" while xenophobic have' (1990b: 334). In other words, xenophobic stereotypes manipulate real-life elements. To say that all Italians are 'Mafiosi' is certainly xenophobic but it is not a chimeria, since there is 'a kernel of truth' in the fact that some Italians are 'Mafiosi'. For the same reason Langmuir has described the hostility against Jews in ancient Alexandria[4] as xenophobic rather than anti-Semitic. By contrast, chimerical stereotypes formed ideological Nazi anti-Semitism of the 1930s. Certainly, some medieval myths were utilized to trap European Jews into enduring chimerias. The historian Langmuir (1990b) has provided us with some examples of historical chimerias, such as the 'blood libel' and 'ritual crucifixion'. The 'blood libel' accused Jews of killing and drinking Christian children's blood each year for the celebration of Passover (Jewish Easter). Alternatively, the accusation of ritual crucifixion alleged that Jews ritually crucified a Christian child to mock Jesus' death. Surprisingly, some of these chimerical beliefs, such as the blood libel, are still part of anti-Semitic fantasies today.

Langmuir has suggested that these chimerias started and spread because of political interests. An example he has provided is that of St William of Norwich's beatification. In 1144, villagers in Norwich discovered a young child's corpse with alleged signs of crucifixion. Five years later, the local authorities called the monk Thomas of Monmouth to investigate the murder.

Thomas of Monmouth concluded that a local Jewish family had ritually crucified the young William of Norwich. Probably, Thomas of Monmouth
turned the incident into one of the most disgraceful lies in history. Langmuir
has suggested Thomas of Monmouth's interests lay behind his false claim, to
be a part and master of the canonization of St William of Norwich.

These medieval fables won the battle against time and dramatically they
have repeatedly surfaced in modern and contemporary times. The most
notorious example of modern chimeria against the Jewish people is the
Protocols of the Elders of Zion (also known as *the Protocols*). This was a proven
hoax that the Czarist police fabricated at the end of the 1800s and widely
publicized in 1905. The plan aimed to blame the Russian Jewish population
for the country's ills. The Protocols purport to be the minutes of the Jewish
ruling clique's secret meetings describing a complex plot to take control of
the world. Unsurprisingly the *Protocols* found a privileged place in Hitler's
Mein Kampf (1933). Langmuir has acknowledged that the term anti-
Semitism might be useful to designate 'the peculiarly horrifying example
that marked European culture for seven centuries and killed millions of
victims during the "Final Solution"'. But he has also observed: 'If we con-
tinue to use that literal term, we as social scientists, should free "anti-
semitism" from its racist, ethnocentric, or religious implications' (1990b:
352). Langmuir's arguments have appealed to and influenced many students of anti-Semitism such as Bergmann (1998), Chevalier (1998), Fein
(1987) and Poliakov (1993). Yet Langmuir's position has attracted not only
praise but also strong, often ideological, criticism.

Smith has branded Langmuir's analysis as 'significantly flawed' (1996:
212). Smith has alleged that Langmuir's chimeria have overgeneralized the
concept of anti-Semitism. She has polemically suggested that 'chimeria' is
so general that scholars might even apply it to witchcraft accusations (1996:
212). But this observation of Smith indicates the degree of her misunderstanding of Langmuir's 'chimeria'. Smith has failed to notice that, following
Langmuir's distinctions between chimeria and other forms of stereotype,
witchcraft accusations have a 'kernel of truth', something that anti-Semitism
does not. Witchcraft accusations often stem from exaggerations of 'real
facts' among people living in a superstitious society (see, for instance,
Evans-Pritchard 1956).

Smith's article reveals, however, less academic and more political reasons
for rejecting Langmuir's viewpoint. Her concept of chimeria may deprive
anti-Semitism of its *uniqueness*. Indeed, Smith has warned her readers:

> Not every exaggeration is equal. Not every lie is a Big Lie … Muslims and
> Asians or Turkish migrants may be reviled, but currently *only Jews* have the mis-
> fortune to be the object of a globally diffused conspiracy theory. … Not until fear

of 'fanatical Islam' is as delusional as Manichaean antisemitism will it qualify as a form of chimeria; and even then it would remain a minor chimera until it captures the imaginations of tens of millions of people. (1996: 225, emphasis added)

Although Smith wrote before 9/11, it is certainly difficult to argue that chimeria have not affected Islam and Muslims. Even a superficial knowledge of medieval representations concerning Muslims and Islam or reading Dante's *Divine Comedy* or a casual visit to Bologna's main church, San Petronio, would disclose the chimerias that Muslims suffered.[5] But for Smith could anti-Semitism be regarded as a unique phenomenon? Because according to Smith the 'mythical Jew' is *the* symbol of 'democracy demonized'. In other words, anti-Semites hate Jews because they hate democracy:

The antisemite's enemy is the authoritarian nightmare, the democrat perceived as anarchist (personified as Antichrist). This is why the mythopoesis of anti-Jewish chimeria has special appeal for antidemocrats. Democratic opponents are eternally present *in potentia*. 'The Jew' as master metaphor for this eternal enemy, can never be destroyed, no matter what happens to actual Jews. Every new antiauthoritarian current can be subsumed under the rubric 'Jewish'. (1996: 233)

Smith's point of view may sound very Judaeo-centric, but the reason we may cast doubts on this theory is that some historical facts ask us to reject the alleged axiomatic relationship between anti-democracy and anti-Semitism. For example, not all Jewish people have been pro-democratic and not all anti-democracies have been anti-Semitic. For instance, Fascism and anti-democratic regimes fascinated Jabotinsky, a Zionist leader (Brenner 1983) and in Chile, under the anti-democratic and oppressive Pinochet's rule, Jews did not suffer from anti-Semitic[6] attitudes.

Langmuir's distinction between stereotypes and chimerias remains a valid and good guide in our attempt to understand whether today Muslims are becoming anti-Semitic or, as some commentators in Israel have suggested, the international jihad is nothing other than a jihad against Jews and Israel.

The Qur'an as the Muslim *Mein Kampf?* Discussing Misleading Interpretations

In the early 1980s, after the shocking Iranian revolution, Daniel Pipes (a historian by training and a controversial journalist and politician by vocation) together with Bernard Lewis (1986) called for a greater awareness within and outside academia of the danger that Muslim anti-Semitism may present for Jewish people. Like Smith, Pipes, in his article 'the politics of Muslims anti-Semitism' (1981) reminded us that anti-Semitism should refer *only* to anti-Jewish sentiments and not, as some have suggested, to Semites in general. He invited his readers to observe that Arabs[7] 'are as capable of this [anti-Semitism] as anyone speaking an Indo-European language'. Nevertheless, Pipes had to recognize that Jews, despite Muslims considering them as *dhimmi*,[8] had lived better and safer under Islamic rulers than under Christian kings. Pipes's historical interpretation of such an 'unexpected' phenomenon suggested that Islam, far from being tolerant, had relegated the Jewish population to being second-class citizens. In the article, he has argued that such a degrading status for the Jewish population prevented Muslims from developing anti-Semitism, at least until the creation of the state of Israel.

Let me say that, as with many other of Pipes's articles, his argument misleads more than it clarifies. The state of dhimmi did not imply a 'second-class citizen status'. Indeed, I doubt that Muslims even had the concept of 'second-class citizens' we possess today. In medieval kingdoms money, power and knowledge, more than religion, ethnicity and nationality, made status. Medieval Spanish documents prove that Islamic courts employed Jewish teachers, military commanders and accountants. Reguer (2000) has explained that in Muslim societies, although dhimmi, Jews could reach influential positions. He has provided us with the example of Samuel ibn Nagrela:

> Samuel ibn Nagrela [a Jew], who rose to become vizier [adviser of the khalifa] of Granada, was a statesman, poet, scholar and military commander. His political career marks the highest achievement of a Jew in medieval Muslim Spain. In 1027, the Jews conferred on him the title of *nagid*, designating him head of the community. (2000: 134)

Pipes's argument may suffer from faulty reasoning. Had the second-class position of Jews within Muslim societies saved them from anti-Semitism, in Christian Europe, where Jewish populations suffered ostracism and persecution rather than second-class status, the pernicious and long-standing anti-Semitism we can observe until today would have been non-existent. The reason why this is not the case is that Pipes's argument does not work.

Surely Pipes has appeared more convincing while arguing that the eighteenth-century colonial experiences had an influence on the formation of Muslim anti-Semitism. He has argued that the colonial forces employed Jewish people within their administration since Western colonizers trusted the hated Jews more than the 'barbaric' Arabs. According to Pipes, Muslims saw their former Jewish dhimmi achieve power and control over the Muslim population. Consequently, they borrowed anti-Semitic Western discourse to attack the former dhimmi. Yet this 'jealousy' hypothesis appears very weak and simplistic. Unfortunately, Pipes's academic arguments stop here since his 'anti' anti-Semitism is increasingly coloured by political anti-Arab and anti-Muslim thinking. Pipes has aimed to show that Muslims and Nazis share and shared their hate for Jewish people. Therefore, he has reminded us of the collusion between Muslim (in particular Palestinian and Arab) leaders and the 1930s' German Nazi government. By contradicting his previous arguments, Pipes has suggested that such a controversial relationship had its historical root in Islam itself because the Prophet, according to Pipes had some 'uneven relations' with Jews.[9]

Pipes has reminded his readers of the contacts that some Palestinian leaders had with Nazi and Fascist leaders. However, he has omitted another grim side of the dirty political battle for Jerusalem. Both some Arabs *and* some Zionist leaders (the so-called Zionist-Revisionists) had contacts with the German Nazi and Italian Fascist regimes in the attempt to achieve the same goal: a nation for their people in the contended Holy Land. While Arabs attempted to contact the Nazi authorities, in November 1934 the Zionist-Revisionists convinced 'Mussolini [to] set up a Betar squadron at his *scuola marittima* at Civitavecchia, where 134 [Jewish] cadets were trained by the notorious Blackshirts; in 1936, Il Duce himself reviewed his Zionist wards' (Brenner 1983, but see also the *Encyclopaedia Judaica* 1972: 175). Why should we be so surprised that both Arab and Zionists leaders tried to bargain with what they considered European superpowers? Both sides were only interested in the land rather than ethics. To read these historical events as the ultimate evidence of Arab anti-Semitism derived from the Qur'an or as the ultimate proof that Zionism is the Jewish version of Fascism would be seriously misleading and unethical.

In 1997, Pipes issued another of his 'fatwas' against Muslim anti-Semitism. This time his title featured the word 'new' in front of the old 'Muslim anti-Semitism'. In this more controversial article, he has labelled as anti-Semitic not just Arabs but Muslims: 'Antisemitism, historically a Christian phenomenon, is now primarily a *Muslim phenomenon* ... Muslims today are *the most vibrant and explicit* antisemites ... Jewish organisations should devote less of their resources to the Christian right and more to fundamentalist Islam' (1997: 2 emphases added). In this article Pipes has appeared more interested in rehabilitating the extreme American Christian right from its anti-Semitic 'sins' than in presenting a realistic analysis of anti-Semitic attitudes among Muslims. Despite Pipes arguing that Islam may facilitate anti-Semitism, he has at least avoided the common mistake of presenting the Qur'an as the Muslim *Mein Kampf.* By contrast, Kramer (1998) has observed 'It is a sign of the times that the study of Islam today, far from being an escape from anti-Semitism, is more likely to be an immersion in it.' Kramer has 'discovered' 'the origin of [Muslim] anti-Semitism' inside the Qur'an and in Muhammad's frustration with the Arabian Jewish tribes that had rejected the Prophet's message. Nevertheless, Kramer himself has accepted that the Qur'an lacks the 'eternal Jew' that Christian societies had developed.

Thus, Kramer has hypothesized that contacts with the Christian West enhanced the anti-Semitic features of both the Qur'an and Sunna. Yet Kramer, a scholar convinced of the beneficial effects of colonialism on Arabs and Muslims, could not, as at least Pipes suggested, blame Western civilizing campaigns for this 'enhancement'. Kramer blamed the Muslim immigrants invading Western countries, who, in this way, became exposed to anti-Semitic ideas and, like an infection that found good terrain, brought them back to their Islamic world. Kramer strongly believes that a solution to the Middle East conflicts would not defuse Muslim anti-Semitism, 'neither a break with tradition, nor a diminishing of the injustice, will stop it. It exists above all because it is needed to complete an irrational logic' (Kramer 1998), which, according to him, wishes the extermination of Jews. But do not be mistaken, this has nothing to do with Hitler's ideology, rather Kramer has revealed that Muslims wish to exterminate the Jews to revenge their arrogant denial of Muhammad's prophecy. Here it is easy to spot Kramer's political reasoning composed as an academic argument. Muslims are anti-Semitic just because they are Muslims, so do not blame Israel's occupation of Palestine and American policies in the Middle East. Kramer's argument may even suggest that Israel has the right to occupy and civilize Palestinians; otherwise Muslims, with their endogenous anti-Semitism, would wipe out the only democracy in the region (Kramer 1998).

Kramer has an essentialist approach to Islam, and, as we have seen in the introduction, his interpretation is based on the idea that the Qur'an exists above and beyond Muslims' interpretations. Although Kramer and extremist Muslims would agree that Islam is only one, we know that Muslims do have different opinions on Islam and anti-Semitism. Emotions, feelings and environment influence the ways in which they read the Qur'an, the *hadith* and live Islam. We may certainly find Muslims who think exactly what Kramer would like them to think but these Muslims do not develop their extremist views starting from Islam or, as Kramer and others seem to suggest, because the Qur'an is an older version of *Mein Kampf.*

The 'Anti' Anti-Semitism and New Chimerias

Earlier we saw that Smith has suggested that Muslims never suffered from chimeria. Smith has probably never read Bat Ye'or (a pseudonym meaning 'daughter of the Nile'). Bat Ye'or is certainly a less romantic scholar than her name might suggest. She mixes concepts such as jihad, dhimmitude and anti-Semitism to form what we can read as *anti-Muslim Protocols* (see Bat Ye'or 2004). To understand her 'scholarly' production it is necessary to know that she is an independent Jewish scholar living in Switzerland who suffered the emotional experience of exile when in 1948 Egypt expelled, among others, her family. Reading her last production, incessantly less academic but increasingly influential in the discussion of Muslim anti-Semitism, we may get the impression that Bat Ye'or is crusading against Islam and Muslims.

Her argument is popularly straightforward; Islam means submission, all contemporary Muslims dream of submiting non-Muslims and transforming them into dhimmi. So, Muslims conduct two jihads, one violent and criminal, the other manipulative in trying to Islamicize the European political left. This is the gist of Bat Ye'or's main argument. Recently she has concluded,

> Europe's hidden war against Israel is wrapped in the Palestinian flag, and is part of a global movement that is transforming Europe into a new continent of dhimmitude within a world strategy of *jihad* and *da'wa*, the latter being the pacific method of Islamization. The implementation program [*sic*] of this policy of dhimmitude for the Euro-Arabian continent [*sic*] is set forth in the *Rapport du Comite de Sages* submitted to the European Commission President Romano Prodi in October 2003. This program, entitled 'Dialogue between Peoples and Cultures in the Euro-Mediterranean region' was accepted by the European Union in December 2003. Unfortunately, the policy of 'Dialogue' with Arab League nations, wilfully pursued by Europe for the past three decades, has promoted European *dhimmitude* and rabid Judeophobia. (Bat Ye'or 2004)

Not only does Bat Ye'or have to decontextualize the Islamic concept of dhimmi but she has also suggested that Muslims could use it in the same way they have done since the time of the first *khalifa*. She has tried to create new chimeria in which Muslims are the conspirators against the Judaeo-Christian civilized world. A new 'Protocols', a new chimeria: a new Holocaust? This, of course, is a provocative question, but the process through which Europeans discriminated against Jews as the enemy within and then persecuted them does not appear to be so different from the ways in which some scholars and politicians have demonized Muslims as the 'anti-civilizing' forces attacking our democracies. Someone who thinks that these anti-Muslim chimerias would not have any impact on academia and political circles might discover that such anti-Muslim arguments have already found willing ears (see for instance Bodansky 1999; Wistrich 2002).

Although we must reject such ideologized and misleading anti-Muslim arguments, we have to acknowledge that something is going wrong among young European Muslims. The European Monitoring Centre on Racism and Xenophobia (EUMC) has recently observed (Bergmann and Wetzel 2004) that young Muslims have verbally and physically attacked Jewish people and institutions. However, again politics has overwhelmed scientific accuracy, the report that the EUMC commissioned from Bergmann and Wetzel (2004) was supposed to be an analysis of all forms of European anti-Semitism. On the contrary, Bergmann and Wetzel have written a *j'accuse* against *all* European Muslims. Even worse, it has been discovered that the Bergmann and Wetzel report is far from being an original piece of analysis; it is a patchwork[10] of other more politically and ideologically motivated studies, among which the most dilapidated was Wistrich (2002).

Wistrich (2002), in his approach to Muslim anti-Semitism, has quoted and adopted the works of Pipes and Bat Ye'or. Wistrich has tried to convince his audience that Islam is as violent and anti-Semitic as Nazism had been. Like others who before him decided to support such a false argument, Wistrich (who is Neuberger Professor of Modern European and Jewish History at the Hebrew University in Jerusalem) has fragmented and decontextualized the Qur'anic *suras* and selected controversial hadiths to suit his argument. Then, like Pipes, Wistrich has emphasized the historical links that existed between Palestinian leaders, Arabs, Muslims and the Nazis in 1930s.[11] Wistrich's work (on which the reputation of the EUMC's report is based) has even suggested that the perpetrators of 9/11 knew about Hitler's dream of burning New York and, as good Nazis, implemented it (Wistrich 2002: 15).

Wistrich's political discourse highlights another interesting argument within some contemporary ideologically right-wing 'anti' anti-Semitism. Wistrich has (probably rightly) argued that the majority of Muslims share anti-Zionist and anti-Israel sentiments. Yet to support his viewpoint, he has ventured into a very controversial syllogism to affirm that, since Zionism, Israel and Judaism are the same reality, Muslims who criticize Zionism are in reality spreading anti-Semitic propaganda. In other words, Wistrich has supported the idea that Israel has substituted for the 'Jew', Israel embodies Jewishness and Judaism. Consequently, Wistrich has told us that today anti-Semitism 'is nothing else that *Israelphobia.*'

Wistrich's argument is flawed in many respects but what makes it unacceptable is that he imposes a social 'Israeli identity' upon all the Jewish people, some of whom might have developed other identities and would reject such a generalization.[12] However controversial his idea might be, Bergmann and Wetzel's EUMC report has officially institutionalized it: today 'Israel is the "Jew"':

> In the form of anti-Semitism it could be said that the tradition of demonising Jews in the past *is now being transferred to the state of Israel.* In this way, traditional anti-Semitism is translated into a new form, less deprived of legitimacy, whose employment today in Europe could become part of the political mainstream. (2004: 10, emphasis added)

They end ten pages later by presenting anti-Zionism as anti-Semitism:

> a form of anti-Semitism, because Zionism is described by the extreme right, the extreme left and also by parts of Arab-Muslim circles as the evil of the world and therefore can be used easily as a wanted scapegoat. This implies the fight against the existence of Israel. (2004: 22)

Nevertheless, this new definition of anti-Semitism has not convinced the majority of experts on anti-Semitism. Klug has gone even further and suggested that such a parallel between anti-Zionism and anti-Semitism may be a political attempt to put Zionism and possibly controversial Israeli military backlashes, beyond discussion and criticism:

> In short, the empirical evidence overwhelmingly supports the view that hostility towards Israel, at bottom, is not a new form of antisemitism; it is a function of a deep and bitter political conflict ... They [Arabs and Muslims] see the state [Israel] through the lens of their own history and their own interests, and why shouldn't they? ... But, if Palestinians and people who take their side are partisan, this does not mean they are being anti-Semitic, they are just not being Jewish. The mere fact that they are biased does not make them anti-Semitic, any more than those whose sympathies lie with Israel are *ipso facto* Islamophobic. (2003: 133)

I provide here an example that may support Klug's view. In May 2004, the Israeli army conducted some internationally condemned retaliation raids in southern Gaza which killed and injured mainly Palestinian civilians. On 20 May, BBC News Online collected interviews from Israeli citizens;[13] some of their comments showed an appalling lack of sympathy towards the suffering innocent Palestinian families. For example, Ranaan Bavli, forty-four, said 'I don't think that collective punishment is the intention of this raid. But even if it is, I think that this is justified because I think the whole Palestinian population supports the terror and you never hear voices against it.' Could we label Ranna Bavil as Islamophobic or anti-Palestinian? To do so would be misleading and cheap propaganda rhetoric. Mr Bavil, like others who have expressed similar viewpoints, see themselves as involved in an endless conflict and, like many Palestinians and Muslims, as emotionally trapped in a similar circle of panic.

Today there is a need to understand what has been called (or miscalled) Muslim anti-Semitism. Kressel (2004) has rightly observed that there are few studies on 'Islamic anti-Semitism', particularly in the field of social sciences. Nevertheless, I deeply disagree with Kressel's general idea of 'Islamic anti-Semitism' and particularly with his opinion that only Jewish and Israeli scholars could successfully and without bias study the subject. Indeed, if we do not distance ourselves from the political implications of anti-Semitism and its entanglement with the Israeli–Palestinian conflict, we could never answer the question, why increasing numbers of immigrants and Western-born Muslims use and develop 'anti-Semitic' attitudes.

Anti-Semitism or Westernophobia?

It is Friday, the day of the sermon: the imam of the mosque stands up in front of the congregation. Bethlehem besieged, the Middle East in turmoil, the congregation angrier than ever. The imam gives an impromptu speech, something unusual for him. His voice emotionally sends a message of hope: the Palestinians' sufferings will be rewarded; and the oppressor's arrogance punished. This is Allah's promise: justice. Pause, then he adds 'In the same sura Allah says that those following Jewish as well as Christian scripture with a sincere heart, will be saved on the Day of Judgement'. Another emphatic pause, then, the imam stresses slowly, 'Allah will not punish a Jew only because he is a Jew but because of his or her personal evil actions. Sharon will not go to hell because he is a Jewish person but because he is a bad Jew who is doing evil actions against his religion.' As the imam ends his sermon, I can hear some worshippers whispering, one of them clearly complaining to another, 'Is he really saying that Jews will be in *al-janna* [paradise]?' The other, smirking, 'maybe he [the imam] likes to have pigs in paradise'.

As Muslims differ in their nationalities, ethnicities and languages, so they differ in their opinions and interpretations of their Holy Book. In that congregation, many appreciated the imam's khutba, some opposed it and others denigrated it. I came to know that the imam had decided to say what he said because he knew that the deteriorating conflict in the Middle East and the besieged Church of the Nativity (in which some Palestinian gunmen had found refuge) were exacerbating the congregation's anger against Jews. Although I believe that the end of the Middle East conflict might decrease

Islamophobic and anti-Arabic attitudes among Jewish people, I am very sceptical that it might stop 'anti-Semitic' feelings among immigrant and Western-born Muslims.

The end of October 2003, Ramadan: the shadows over a destabilized Iraq, the constant deaths of Palestinian civilians, and the torments and sufferings of Chechen Muslims irremediably mark this joyful event. I do not know many people in this local Muslim community but the Holy Month is the ideal time for starting new friendships and trying to find an inner peace. After a while I visit the same mosque, I meet a group of North Africans. Hakim, Samir and Rabah are Algerians, Mohammed and Sayf Moroccans and Hazim Tunisian. We speak of this and that, when Hakim asks if I watch al-Manar. They seem quite disappointed when I told them that I have still not bought a satellite TV,

> *Sayf*: So you do not know *Al-shatat*?
> *Me*: No, what is it? (*They seem to enjoy my lack of knowledge.*)
> *Hazim*: Well … it is a TV series written for this Ramadan. Al-Manar is broadcasting the series and it's such a success! You must …
> *Rabbah*: (*interrupting*) I do not like it. You know, it says such incredible things that I can't believe the stories. I think that at the end these stories damage us, I mean, us, the Muslims.
> *Hazim*: (*pointing his finger toward Rabbah*) You don't know any Jews, do you? We have lots of them in Tunisia and we know that they do lots of strange things. Believe me I have heard lots of strange stories about Jews and their secret rituals.
> *Mohammed*: Hey, I think that Jibril [my name in Arabic] needs some info about the series. I don't think he could understand anything of what we are saying, (*looking toward me*) eh, Jibril you could not understand but it is simple … the …
> *Hazim*: (*interrupting*) … look, Jibril, it's [*Al-shatat*] the real history of Zionism, that Allah will destroy all of them inshallah (*the others say inshallah*). The authors knew that people would accuse them so they used only Jewish texts, sources; to document the dirty things Zionists have done and do even today everywhere they live.
> *Sayf*: They [Zionists] are so evil … you must watch it, we know that you are a nice guy but if you see what these people do you cannot worry. They killed a Christian child to drink his blood and even killed a Jew in such a horrible way only because he refused to do what Zionists said …
> *Me*: Ermm, I see …
> *Rabbah*: I don't like it, but I will tell you the truth, there are some professors working in prestigious universities that helped [to produce the fiction] … I don't know what to say … but maybe *opening his arms* …some of what they say could be correct … well … I still think that today these things sound too incredible … but what to say … today we read incredible things that then are true like you and me …

Mohammed: (*to Rabbah*) Be careful! You start to trust the West too much. You are becoming like them [people in the West] and this is not good for you ...

Hakim: Rabbah look, Jews have infected the West with their wrong ideas and practice but they became like that because they Westernized after the Romans destroyed their temple. You see, they want everything, they cry and cry and want to show that they are weak and victims, but in reality they are responsible for lots of things. They [Western countries] lost their colonies so they sent their Jews to take back our lands and control the region. Who has created Israel? Americans. And they have done so because they hoped that these pigs would spread the Western corruption to the Islamic world by force, but they failed, or buying corrupt Arab and Muslim regimes, and they in this case succeed. You know, Arab politicians are easily corrupted ... is it not the same in Italy, Jibril?

Me: Well ... we had our problems ... uhmm ... corruption is everywhere ...

Hazim: You are right Hakim, the Jews are the worst part of the West, they represent the worst, they are the worst colonizers and they like power but they depend on Americans and Europeans ... [the conversation goes on]

Although from the conversation, I expected that *Al-shatat* would be astonishingly anti-Jewish, I could not appreciate the level of anti-Semitism the series broadcast until I had occasion to watch some of it. *Al-shatat* employs conspiracy theories similar to those presented in the *Protocols* as well as a certain number of medieval chimerical aberrations such as the 'blood libel'.

The spread of xenophobic and chimerical stories are not limited to Muslim men. Some Muslim women told me that Jewish soldiers systematically rape Muslim women because Jewish women are frustrated. Palestinian houses are demolished without reason because Jewish people believe that the destruction of a Muslim house brings fertility to their families and Jews even kill Muslim children in order to have transplant organs to save their own children. Other stereotypes focus on the violence within the Jewish families and the lust of Jewish men. I have also recorded disapproving expressions such as 'I'm not a Jewish woman', 'These are things that only Jewish women do' and so forth. Many reasons might be brought to the fore to explain why some Muslims may have resentments toward Israel and Jews, such as the conflict in the Middle East, which has acquired a global and symbolic meaning that goes far beyond the territorial issues. Yet these arguments do not answer the questions that many Western people and Jews seem to ask: 'are Muslims (or some of them) as anti-Semitic as the Nazis were? Is Muslim anger directed against Israel as the "Jew"?'

My answer to both questions is negative. Analysing how Muslims speak of Jewish people and Israel, I have found a constant that I can express in an equation *Colonialism : Israel :: West : America*. Yet, this equation needs to be flanked by a second: *Islam : Justice :: West : a-Justice*. I prefer the term *a-justice* rather than injustice because many Muslim respondents have often emphasized that 'the West' lacks the very concept of justice which for Muslims can only be divine. For instance, Qays, a 29-year-old Western-born Muslim of Bangladeshi origin, told me that Americans and their allies could not understand their 'unjust actions' because they 'genuinely think that they were bringing *Justice* when they were spreading unacceptable injustice'. He explained that Americans could not have done it differently because their justice is based on human values and is not divinely guided. When I asked how Muslims could achieve the justice they needed, Qays mentioned jihad as the way to impose what was right and forbid what is wrong.

Many Muslims see Jewish people as colonizers, Israel as a colony, and *both of them as Western products*. Hakim's idea that the Western powers have replaced their direct colonialism with Jewish explicit and implicit colonialism is not an isolated opinion, but a spreading commonplace among young Muslims. For instance, Jamila, a 20-year-old girl of Pakistani origin observed,

> It was different before the *al-nakba* [the catastrophe]. Muslims and Jews had many things in common, they shared places and lifestyles. Although they had a lot of things in common with Muslims and they were part of the *ummah* for a while today they have changed because they have become part of the West, and the West today is against divine justice.

From a Muslim perspective, *a-Justice* is nothing less than *jahiliyya* (a state of ignorance, a term also applied to pre-Islamic societies). Some Muslims fear that jahiliyya could spread among themselves and affect their identities. By fighting Western jahiliyya these Muslims fight their fears, the most threatening of which is to lose their sense of Islamic 'I'. Some Muslims use Western prefabricated discourses of anti-Semitism. Others, like Rabbah, are aware that these anti-Semitic discourses are only propaganda. Yet they do not speak against it. They feel that discrediting these *chimerias* against the 'Jew' would accredit jahiliyya and the most power symbol of it: 'the West'.

Conclusion

Some of the scholars we have discussed in this chapter have argued that Muslims are anti-Semitic because of Islam. They have scrutinized Islamic history, the Qur'an and the Sunna looking for the roots of such Islamic anti-Semitism. Breaking up suras, isolating lines, employing weak hadiths, highlighting some historical events and de-emphasizing others, they have certainly succeeded in finding what they looked for. Recent events such as the kidnapping and brutal beheading of Jewish hostages such as Daniel Pearl and Nick Berg have reinforced the idea of Muslims as dangerous people because of their faith. These arguments originate from a sort of faulty logic, arguing that human beings become the expression of their religions. However, as with any other religion, people can find in the Islamic faith and sources whatever they want to find. My criticism of the previously discussed analysis of 'Muslim Anti-Semitism' is that the ideological and political efforts to label Islam as anti-Semitic as Nazism fail to provide a real answer to why some Muslim immigrants and their children increasingly employ chimerical representations of Jews.

Lewis (2000 and 2003) has argued that Muslims failed in their modernization because they rejected the separation of church and state, the path that brought Europe towards modern secularism. For this reason, according to Lewis, the Islamic countries, which used to be the advanced societies, witnessed the rise of Western culture and technology and the consequent decline of their Islamic states. Lewis argues that Muslims have still not found an answer to their decline but instead of blaming their religio-political system, they have victimized the West, which for this reason they have learnt to hate. Lewis's historical reconstruction highlights what may be called a 'jealousy theory'. In fact, Lewis has suggested that the decline of the Islamic state was just the effect of the structure of its religion, Islam, which did not allow the state, as well as Muslims, a modernization comparable to that enjoyed by the West. Lewis does not mention colonialism and the Western post-colonial countries preserving their economic and geopolitical interests as one of the most important factors contributing to the crisis of the Islamic world.

As an anthropologist, I prefer to suggest a different, if not opposite, scenario. It was not the lack of adaptation to Western models that undermined what Islamic societies had achieved, but rather the unsuccessful attempt to mimic them. The attempt to mimic Western models prevented the Muslim world from discovering its preferred route toward modernity. The mimicry of the West is evident in the case of Arab nationalism. The religio-political views of Islam do not promote the idea of nations, rather they exalt the concept of ummah.

Langmuir (1990b) has contributed to the understanding of anti-Semitism by distinguishing between xenophobia and *chimeria*. We have seen that 'Muslim anti-Semitism' does not derive from an ideological and planned anti-Semitism as in the case of Nazi ideology. Rather, these 'anti-Semitic' attitudes should be interpreted as a symptomatic expression of the 'circle of panic' spreading among many Muslims that Western jahiliyya could not only wipe Islam from the earth but also erase their Muslim identity. Today, Muslims wish to reject the passivity affecting the Islamic world. Some Muslims feel threatened by the continuous contact they have with 'Western jahiliyya'. They see Jewish people as the negative example of a successful assimilation within the imagined and so-called monolithic West. Jewish people, who used to be an integral part of the Muslim world are not any longer. These Muslims think that the same corruption thought to have affected Jews could disrupt their Islamic identity. The circle of panic starts, so the emotions and feelings connect. Indeed, behind the anti-Semitic attitudes of some Muslims *Westernophobia* may epiphany.

Notes

1. Readers interested in a historical viewpoint may read Katz 1982, Langmuir 1990a and 1990b.
2. Xenophobia is hatred of people that natives perceive as outsiders.
3. The root of 'chimeria' comes from ancient Greek, referring to a hideous monster.
4. In 68 BCE, and again in 38 BCE, the Egyptians organized themselves against the Jews of Alexandria. In particular, the 38 BCE revolt against Jewish people was apparently caused by the privileges that some Jews had.
5. In both, Muhammad is depicted as co-Lucifer in the Hell.
6. But of course, the Jews opposing the regime were persecuted not as Jews but as rebels.
7. It is important to note that, despite using 'Muslim' in the title, throughout the article, Pipes speaks of Arabs.
8. Dhimmi indicates what Muslims called 'the people of protection': free non-Muslims who were levied in Muslim countries. By paying a tax called *jizyah*, non-Muslims were granted the freedom to practise their religion and the protection of the Muslim army.
9. I wonder whether it might be the Jewish tribes that initially had 'uneven relations' with Muhammad and his new religion. Indeed, as the case of Christianity may show, from a Jewish perspective all these 'new sects' were only heretical versions of their true religion.
10. See, for example, pages 7–8 of the report.
11. Of course, Wistrich did not mention the similar contacts that some Zionist circles had.
12. For instance, on 18 July 2004, during a meeting of the American Jewish Association in Jerusalem, Sharon, the Israeli Prime Minister, invited all Jewish people in the world and in particular French Jews, to leave their actual countries and move to their 'real home'. Sharon was arguing that the five million Muslims were an unacceptable threat to the French Jews. The French Jewish community

has rejected Sharon's fundamentalist appeal, arguing that their home is in France, where Jewish people have contributed to establishing a democratic, multicultural nation.

    13. http://news.bbc.co.uk/1/hi/world/middle_east/3728137.stm

CHAPTER 9

Conclusion: The Sword of Damocles

Damocles lived in Greece under a despotic king, Dionysius, who was his best friend. Indeed, the tyrant's wealth only surpassed his cruelty. One day, during a party, Damocles addressed his cruel friend with these words, 'Lucky you! You can have everything that any man could wish.' The king asked Damocles if for one day he would like to be Dionysius. Damocles, fascinated by his friend's power and wealth, accepted the offer without thinking twice. Dionysius exchanged the throne with Damocles, who immediately started to enjoy the king's life. However, when Damocles had the chance to look up toward the ceiling of the room, he saw something that frightened him to death: a sharp sword attached to horsehair hanging over his head, 'Get me out of here! I am your friend!' screamed Damocles. Laughing, Dionysius replied, 'You wanted to be me, but I am not only the most rich but also the most hated; my life is endangered each second I am the king. So, I have a sword over my head all the time.' Damocles understood and was happy to give back the throne to his friend. Indeed, it is not nice to live with a sharp sword over one's head.

Today, different swords are over our heads but we do not have someone with whom we may exchange places. The throne that we wanted and achieved is modernity, of which globalization represents the richest pearl. During these last two centuries, our social life has changed as never before: faster, global, entangled with unknown others. Yet in many aspects we, human beings, are still the same. Despite the 'evolution' from *Homo sapiens* to 'Homo technologicus', we still depend, as most of our ancient ancestors did, on those bodily changes and reactions that our relationship with the environment provokes. In this book, following Damasio's observations, I have called such automatic reactions 'emotions' and explained how they are perceived in the form of feelings that may affect the human self (Chapter 3). I have argued that emotions and subsequent feelings are fundamental to an understanding of Muslim interpretations of jihad, because jihad can only exists within a mind and without consciousness the personal mental object we call 'jihad' would never have existed.

Today, a minority of individuals feel that to be Muslim allows one to fly
planes against buildings, kill children on their first day of school, blow themselves up among innocent people at a tube station and call it jihad. At the
same time a majority who feel they are Muslim reject and condemn these
actions and call them mass murder. In *Jihad beyond Islam*, I have argued that
it is only by focusing on that 'feeling to be' rather than the 'Muslim', that
we can go to the root of these tragic events. Traditionally, social scientists
have studied societies. Anthropologists, for instance, have relegated the
individual to the far-flung parts of their interpretations. For a long time, any
attempt to foreground an individual as part of a composite society would
expose the adventurous scholar to the denigrating label of being ethnocentric. In the study of jihad this lack of focus on individual identities has, to
use a Batesonian (2002) expression, facilitated the mistake of seeing the
map as the actual territory. Many religious, social, political and economic
factors have been suggested for the different understandings of jihad among
Muslims. Yet by starting from the viewpoint of individuals, in *Jihad beyond
Islam* I have demonstrated that some radical Muslims do not speak of and
act for 'jihad' because they are Muslims but rather they *feel* Muslim because
of jihad (see Chapters 4, 5 and 6).

I have suggested that many Muslims today may be subjected to a schismogenetic process that I have called 'the circle of panic'. Through contacts
with different emotional triggers, such as pangs of guilt about the status of
Muslims and Islam, rejection from host societies (Chapter 4); shocking
images and particularly TV reportage of Muslim tragedies around the world
(Chapter 5); challenges of identity and loyalty (Chapter 6); emotional
dynamics of gender relationships (Chapter 7); and fear of Westernization
(Chapter 8), the idea has arisen that Islam (seen as religion but also as an
element of identity) is under attack from 'the circle of panic'. The circle of
panic, being schismogenetic, changes the relationship between the autobio-
graphic self and identity, so that to stop the identity crisis an 'act of identity'
becomes required. The rumour producing this circle of panic not only suggests that Crusaders are attacking Islam but also that the West is spreading
jahiliyya among Muslims, weakening Muslims' Islamic identity. In Chapter
8, I have explained how the fear of jahiliyya plays a role in the anti-Semitic
attitudes of some Muslim immigrants and Western-born Muslims. Rejecting
essentialistic theories, which tend to scrutinize the Qur'an to collect evidence against Muslim anti-Semitism, I have suggested that some Muslims
interpret the creation of Israel and the support it receives as the final evidence of the endogenous Western incapacity for justice. So, accepting the
distinction between stereotypes and chimeria that Langmuir (1990b) has
advanced, in Chapter 8, I have concluded that anti-Semitism is not the

reason for Muslims' jihad. This does not mean that some Muslims in the West, while trapped within the circle of panic, have not used anti-Semitic language.

In conclusion, the rhetoric of jihad, in certain contexts, becomes the most suitable act of identity to break the schismogenetic circle of panic. I have shown in this book that Muslims do not need to know very much about Islam at the theological level to develop their rhetoric of jihad. Today our global world subjects us (Muslims and non-Muslims alike) to unprecedented schismogenetic processes. Every morning, millions of us wake up waiting for the next suicide bomber, war, extradition, kidnapping, Guantanamo bay, Abu Ghraib torture, shoot-to-kill (the wrong man) policies, unjustified arrests, Islamophobic attitudes and terrorist threats. The jihads that are inflaming our cities and countries are beyond Islam but part of one of the many 'circles of panic' into which people are sucked. The question is whether we will be able to avoid the fate of Damocles.

Glossary

Adhan: The call to prayer, which the *mu'adhdhin* (q.v.) chants five times per day.

Al-janna: The Garden, i.e. Paradise.

Al-nasikh-ua-al-mansukh: Literally 'the abrogating and the abrogated', it indicates the controversial practice that allows the abrogation of some early Qur'anic verses and their replacement with others revealed subsequently. *Nasikh* indicates the verse, which, abrogating, replaced the *mansukh*, the abrogated.

Amir: Commander. Originally it was a military title, then it was also attributed to caliphs and some sultans as *amir al-muminin*, the commander of the faithful', i.e. the commander of all Muslims.

Baraka: Divine blessing. It is a characteristic of *pirs* and it can be transferred to places and objects.

Da'wa: Propaganda or mission

Dar al-harb: The abode of war. In Islamic jurisprudence it indicates the lands not under Muslim rule.

Dar al-Islam: The abode of Islam. In Islamic jurisprudence it indicates the lands under Muslim rule or in which Muslim institutions were established.

Dhimmi: Non-Muslim people living in Muslim countries which, under the *shari'a*, were granted protection and freedom of worship. Exempted from military services, they had to pay *jizyah*.

Din: Faith and religion.

Du'a: Supplication to Allah. It is also performed at the end of *salat*.

Fatwa: Legal advice of a religious scholar or mufti.

Fiqh: Interpretation of the *shari'a* on which the Islamic legal system is based.

Fitna: Chaos and temptation. It could also indicate historical times in which Muslims did not respect Islamic teaching. For instance *fitna* also indicated the Muslim civil wars that started 200 years after Muhammad's death.

Hadiths: Reports or narratives about the teaching, saying and actions of the Prophet of Islam.

Halal: What is permissible.

Halqat: Circles often organized in the mosque to study the Qur'an recitation and the teaching of Muhammad.

Haram: What is forbidden in Islam.

Hijab: Veil traditionally worn by Muslim women in public (its real Arabic meaning is 'screen').

Hur: Virginal female companions of the Islamic paradise.

Imam: The Arabic word means 'the person who stands in front' and indicates those responsible for the Muslim community, and also the person who is in charge to lead the prayers.

Iman: In Qur'anic language the word means belief in Islam.

Isnad: The chain of authorities transmitting the *hadiths*

Istidsha: Martyrdom

Jahiliyya: The pre-Islamic ignorance

Jihad: Striving physically and spiritually to achieve an Islamic result.

Jizyah: Poll tax which *dhimmi* had to pay for their exemption from military services.

Kafir (often pl. *Kafirun*): The people who deny God.

Khalifa: Deputy. During Islamic history it indicates the successor of Muhammad as leader of the ummah.

Khutba: The sermon that the imam delivers on *yawm al-jum'a*.

Madhhab: Movement or ideology. It indicates the five different schools of *fiqh*.

Madrassa: Religious schools.

mu'adhdhin: The person which intones the *adhan*.

Mufti: Trusted religious scholars expert in *shari'a* who is able to give *fatwas*.

Mujahidin: Muslims who are conducting *jihad*.

Munafiq (often pl. *munafiqun*): A person who declares that he is Muslim, but his behaviour or intentions are not truthful, i.e. a hypocrite.

Naf: Soul, mind, spirit but also a human being. This word needs to be contextualized in order to find its proper meaning.

Pirs: Sufi master considered to be an holy man

Qadar: Predestination

Razzia: A pre-Islamic term, *razzia* indicated a quick raid against non-Muslim territories conducted not for conquest but to provide essential resources for the Muslim tribes, which at that time were living in hospitable places.

Sahaba: The companions of the Prophets.

Salat: The Muslim worship which is performed five times per day. *Salat* is one of the most important pillars of Islam.

Shahada: The Muslim profession of faith, 'I testify that there is no God but God and Muhammad is the Prophet of God'.

Shahid: Martyr, the person who offers his or her life for Islam and will be rewarded with immediate access to Paradise.

shari'a: Divine law.

Shaykh: A respected Muslim, often an elderly person. Today even young devoted Muslims are addressed with this title to show respect for their Islamic knowledge.

Sura: A chapter of the Qur'an.

Tajweed: The correct recitation of the Qur'an.

Ummah: The community of believers.

Yawm al-jum'a: Friday. It also indicates the congregational prayer that Muslims perform at midday. It is the only congregational prayer in which the imam delivers a sermon.

References

Abdulrahim, D. (1993), 'Defining Gender in a Second Exile: Palestinian Women in West Berlin', in G. Buijs (ed.), *Migrant Women*, Oxford: Berg, pp. 55–82.

Abu-Lughod, L. (1986), *Veiled Sentiment: Honor and Poetry in a Bedouin Society*, Berkeley, CA: University of California Press.

Ahmed, S., Castañeda C. Fortier A. and Sheller, M. (eds) (2003), *Uprootings/ Regroundings*, Oxford and New York: Berg.

Akbar, M. J. (2002), *The Shade of Swords: Jihad and the Conflict between Islam and Christianity*, London: Routledge.

Akpinar, A. (2003), 'The Honour/Shame Complex Revisited: Violence against Women in the Migration Context', *Women's Studies International Forum* 26 (5): 425–42.

Al-Qari, A. (1986), *al-asar al-marfu 'a fi al-akhbar*, Beirut: dar al-kitab al-masri.

Alsayyad, N. and Castells, M. (eds) (2002), *Muslim Europe or Euro-Islam: Politics, Culture, and Citizenship in the Age of Globalization*, Lanham, MD: Lexington Books.

Al Theidi, A. (2003), *Al-Jazeera Satellite Channel: from Regional to Global: a Question of Objectivity and News Flow*, Brighton: University of Sussex.

Amersfoort, V. H. (1998), 'Ethnic Residential Patterns in Dutch Cities: Class, Race or Culture?', in T. Gerholm and Y. G. Lithman (eds), *The New Islamic Presence in Western Europe*, London: Mansell Publishing, pp. 91–115.

Anderson, B. (1991), *Imagined Communities: Reflections on the Origins and Spread of Nationalism*, London: Verso.

Anwar, M. (1981), *Between two Cultures: A Study of Relationships between Generations in the Asian Community in Britain*, London: Commission for Racial Equality.

Appadurai, A. (1995), 'The Production of Locality', in R. Fardon (ed.), *Counterworks: Managing the Diversity of Knowledge*, London: Routledge, pp. 204–25.

—— (1996), *Modernity at Large: Cultural Dimensions of Globalization*, Minneapolis: University of Minnesota Press.

Archer, L. (2001), '"Muslim Brothers, Black Lads, Traditional Asian": British Muslim Young Men's Constructions of Race, Religion and Masculinity', *Feminism & Psychology* 11 (1): 79–105.

—— (2002), 'Change, Culture and Tradition: British Muslim Pupils Talk about Muslim Girls' post-16 "Choice"', *Race, Ethnicity, and Education* 5 (4): 359–76.

Arjomand, S. A. (ed.) (1984), *From Nationalism to Revolutionary Islam*, Albany: State University of New York Press.

Armstrong, G. and Giulianotti, R. (eds) (1997), *Entering the Field. New Perspectives on World Football*, London: Berg.

Asad, Talal (1990), 'Ethnography, Literature, and Politics: Some Readings and Uses of Salman Rushdie's *The Satanic Verses*', *Cultural Anthropology* 5 (3): 239–69.

Ashmore, D. R. and Jussim, L. (eds) (1997), *Self and Identity*, New York and Oxford: Oxford University Press.

Barth, F. (ed.) (1969), *Ethnic Groups and Boundaries: the Social Organization of Culture Difference*, London: Allen and Unwin.

Basch, L., Glick Schiller, N. and Szanton C. B. (1994), *Nations Unbound: Transnational Projects, Postcolonial Predicaments and Deterritorialized Nation-States*, New York: Gordon & Breach.

Basit, T. N. (1997), '"I Want more Freedom, but not too Much": British Girls and the Dynamism of Family Values', *Gender and Education* 9 (4): 425–39.

Bateson, G. (1936), *Naven*, Cambridge: Cambridge University Press.

—— (2000), *Steps to an Ecology of Mind*, Chicago: Chicago University Press.

—— (2002), *Mind and Nature*, Creskill, NJ: Hampton Press.

Bauman, Z. (1992), *Intimations of Postmodernity*, London: Routledge.

Baumann, G. (1996), *Contesting Cultures*, Cambridge: Cambridge University Press.

Benedict, M. (2002), 'Fact Versus Fiction: An Ethnographic Paradox Set in the Seychelles' in W. A. Haviland and L. A. Vivanco (eds), *Talking about People Readings in Cultural Anthropology*, London: McGraw-Hill, pp. 6–9.

Bergmann, W. (1998), 'Approaches to anti-Semitism Based on Psychodynamics and Personality Theory', in W. Bergmann (ed.), *Error without Trial: Psychological Research on Antisemitism*, Berlin and New York: Walter de Gruyter, pp. 9–34.

—— and Wetzel, J. (2004), *Manifestations of anti-Semitism in the European Union*, Vienna: EUMC.

Bhabha, H. (1994), *The Location of Culture*, London and New York: Routledge.

Bhachu, P. (1993), 'Identities Constructed and Reconstructed: Representations of Asian Women in Britain', in G. Buijs (ed.), *Migrant Women: Crossing Boundaries and Changing Identity*, Oxford: Berg, pp. 99–118.

Binder, L. (1988), *Islamic Liberalism: a Critique of Development Ideologies*, Chicago: University of Chicago Press.

Blumer, H. (1969), *Symbolic Interactionism*, Englewood Cliffs, NJ: Prentice-Hall.

Bodansky, Y. (1999), *Islamic Anti-Semitism as a Political Instrument*, Houston, Texas: The Freeman Centre for Strategic Studies.

Bonnett, A. (2004), *The Idea of the West: Culture, Politics and History*, London and New York: Palgrave Macmillan.

Boyd, D. A. (1999), *Broadcasting in the Arab World: a Survey of the Electronic Media in the Middle East*, Ames: Iowa State University Press.

Brah, A. (1979), 'Inter-Generational and Inter-Ethnic Perceptions: A Comparative Study of South Asian and English Adolescents in Southall', unpublished Ph.D. Thesis, University of Bristol.

Brandes, S. (1980), *Metaphors of Masculinity: Sex and Status in Andalusian Folklore*, Philadelphia: University of Pennsylvania Press.

Brenner, L. (1983), 'Zionist-Revisionism: the Years of Fascism and Terror', *Journal of Palestinian Studies* 13 (1): 66–92.

Bruce, S. (2000), *Fundamentalism*, Cambridge: Polity Press.

Brückner, M. (2001), 'IslamCity, Creating an Islamic Cybercity' *ISIM Newsletter* 8: 12.

Buijs, G. (ed.) (1993), *Migrant Women: Crossing Boundaries and Changing Identities*, Oxford: Berg.

Bunt, G. R. (2003), *Islam in the Digital Age*, London, Sterling and Virginia: Pluto Press.

Burke, P. J. and Reitzes, D. C. (1981), 'The Link between Identity and Role Performance', *Social Psychology Quarterly* 44: 83–92.

Burton, J. (1994), *An Introduction to the Hadith*, Edinburgh: Edinburgh University Press.

Buruma, I. and Margalit, A. (2004), *Occidentalism: a Short History of Anti-Westernism*, London: Atlantic Book.

Chevalier, Y. (1998), *L'Antisémitisme*, Paris: Les Editions du Cerf.

Choueiri, Y. M. (1997), *Islamic Fundamentalism*, London: Printer Press.

Christiansen, C. C. (2004), 'News Media Consumption among Immigrants in Europe: The Relevance of Diaspora', *Ethnicities* 4 (2): 185–207.

Clifford, J. (1994), 'Diasporas', *Cultural Anthropology* 9 (3): 302–38.

Cohen, A. P. (1985), *The Symbolic Construction of Community*, London and New York: Tavistock Publications.

Cohen, S. (1980), *Folk Devils and Moral Panics*, London: Granada.

Cook, D. (2005), *Understanding Jihad*, Berkeley: University of California Press.

Cooley, C. H. (1992), *Human Nature and the Social Order*, New York: Scribner's.

Cooley, J. K. (2000), *Unholy Wars*, London: Pluto Press.

Dabbagh, N. T. (2005), *Suicide in Palestine: Narratives of Despair*, London: Hurst.

Damasio, A. R. (1995), *Descartes' Error: Emotion, Reason and the Human Brain*, Hayrer Collins: New York.

—— (2000), *The Feeling of what Happens: Body, Emotion and the Making of Consciousness*, London: Vintage.

—— (2002), *Looking for Spinoza*, London: William Heinemann.

Davies, B. and Harré, R. (1990), 'Positioning: the Discursive Production of Selves', *Journal for the Theory of Social Behaviour* 20: 43–63.

Dayan-Herzbrun, S. (2000), 'The Issue of the Islamic Headscarf', in J. Freedman and C. Tarr (eds), *Women, Immigration and Identities in France*, Oxford and New York: Berg, pp. 69–82.

Dewitte, P. (ed.) (1999), *Immigration et integration l'etat des savoirs*, Paris: Éditions la découverte.

Donnan, H. (ed.) (2002), *Interpreting Islam*, London: Sage.

Doty, R. L. (2003), *Anti-Immigrantism in Western Democracies*, London and New York: Routledge.

Duquin, M. (2000), 'Emotion in sport' in J. Coakley and E. Dunning (eds), *Handbook of Sport Studies*, London: Sage, pp. 477–89.

Eickelman, D. F. and Anderson, J. W. (eds) (1999), *New Media in the Muslim World*, Bloomington and Indianapolis: Indian University Press.

El Guindi, F. (1999), *Veil: Modesty, Privacy and Resistance*, London and New York: Berg.

El-Nawawy, M. and Iskander, A. (2002), *Al-Jazeera: How the Free Arab News Network Scooped the World and Changed the Middle East*, Oxford: Westview.

El-Solh, F. C. and Mambro, J. (1994), *Muslim Women's Choices*, Oxford: Berg.

El-Zein, A. H. (1977), 'Beyond Ideology and Theology: The Search for the Anthropology of Islam', *Annual Review of Anthropology* 6: 227–54.

Erikson, E. H. (1968), *Identity, Youth and Crisis*, London: Faber & Faber.

Esposito, J. L. (1999), *The Islamic Threat: Myth and Reality?* New York: Oxford University Press.

—— (2002), *Unholy War: Terror in the Name of Islam*, New York and Oxford: Oxford University Press.

Evans-Pritchard, E. E. (1956), *The Nuer*, Oxford: Clarendon Press.

Fein, H. (1987), 'Explanation of the Origins and Evolution of Antisemitism' in H. Fein (ed.), *The Persisting Question*, Berlin and New York: Walter de Gruyter, pp. 3–22.

Freedman, L. (1993), *The Gulf Conflict, 1990–1999: Diplomacy and War in the New World Order*, London: Faber & Faber.

Fuss, D. (1989), *Essentially Speaking: Feminism, Nature and Difference*, New York: Routledge.

Ganguly, K. (1992), 'Migrant identities: Personal Memory and the Construction of the Selfhood', *Cultural Studies* 6 (1): 27–50.

Geertz, C. (1964), 'The Transition to Humanity' in S. Tax (ed.), *Horizons of Anthropology*, Chicago: Aldine, pp. 37–48.

—— (1968), *Islam Observed*, New Haven and London: Yale University Press.

—— (1973), *The Interpretation of Culture*, New York: Basic Books.

Geest, S. (2003), 'Confidentiality and Pseudonymous', *Anthropology Today* 19 (1): 14–19.

Gellner, E. (1981), *Muslim Society*, Cambridge: Cambridge University Press.

—— (1992), *Postmodernism, Reason and Religion*, London: Routledge.

Gerholm, T. and Lithman, Y. G. (eds.) (1988), *The New Islamic Presence in Western Europe*, London: Mansell Publishing.

German, T. C. (2000), 'The Russian Federation in Transition and the Causes of the Chechen War (1994–1996)', PhD Thesis: University of Aberdeen.

Gilmore, D. D. (ed.) (1987), *Honor and Shame and the Unity of the Mediterranean*, Washington, DC: American Anthropological Association.

Gleason, P. (1982), 'Identify Identity: A Semantic History', *The Journal of American History* 69 (3): 909–31.

Goffman, E. (1959), *The Presentation of Self in Everyday Life*, Garden City, NY: Doubleday.

Goldziher, I. (1971), *Muslim Studies*, London: Allen & Unwin.

Greenberg, B. S. and Thompson, M. T. (eds) (2002), *Communication and Terrorism: Public and Media Responses to 9/11*, Mount Waverly: Hampton Press.

Guijt, I. and Shah, M. K. (1998), *The Myth of Community*, London: Intermediate Technology Publications.

Haddad, Y. Y. (2004), *Not Quite American? The Shaping of Arab Muslim Identity in the United States*, Texas: Baylor University Press.

—— (ed.) (2002), *Muslims in the West: from Sojourners to Citizens*, Oxford & New York: Oxford University Press.

—— and Esposito, J. L. (eds) (2000), *Muslims on the Americanization Path*, Oxford: Oxford University Press.

Hafez, K. (2001), *Mass Media, Politics, and Society in the Middle East*, Cresskill, NJ: Hampton Press.

Hafez, M. M. (2003), *Why Muslims Rebel*, Boulder, CO: Lynne Rienner.

Hall, J. (1985), *Powers and Liberty: the Causes and Consequences of the Rise of the West*, Harmondsworth: Penguin.

—— and Jarvie, I. (eds) (1996), *The Social Philosophy of Ernest Gellner*, Amsterdam: Rodolphi.

Halliday, F. (1984), 'Review of in the Path of Good; Islam and Political Power by Daniel Pipes, *Political Science Quarterly* 99 (3): 583–4.

—— (1997), 'Review Article: "The Politics of Islam" – A Second Look', *British Journal of Political Sciences* 25 (3): 399–417.

Hallowell, A. I. (1955), *Culture and Experience*, Philadelphia: University of Pennsylvania Press.

Harré, R. and Van Langenhove, L. (1991), 'Varieties of Positioning' *Journal for the Theory of Social Behaviour* 21: 391–407.

Hebdige, D. (1979), *Subculture, the Meaning of Style*, London: Routledge.

Heck, P. L. (2004), 'Jihad Revised', *Journal of Religious Ethics* 32(1): 95–128.

Henry, B. (2002), 'Identities of the West: Reasons, Myths, Limits of Tolerance' in H. Friese (ed.), *Identities: Time, Difference, and Boundaries*, Oxford and New York: Berghahn Books, pp. 77–106.

Hess, S. and Kalb, M. (eds) (2003), *The Media and the War on Terrorism*, Washington: Brookings Institution Press.

Hetherington, K. (1998), *Expressions of Identity: Space, Performance, Politics*, London: Sage.

Hillery, G. A. (1955), 'Definitions of Community: Areas of Agreement', *Rural Sociology*, 20: 86–118.

Hitler, A. (1933), *Mein Kampf*, Munchen: Nachfolger.

Hodgson, M. G. S. (1993), *Rethinking World History: Essays on Europe, Islam, and World History*, New York: Cambridge University Press.

Hoffman, V. (1995), 'Muslim Fundamentalists Psychosocial Profiles' in M. E. Marty and R S. Appleby (eds), *Fundamentalism Comprehended*, Chicago: University of Chicago Press, pp. 199–230.

Holland, D. (1997), 'Selves as Cultured, as Called by an Anthropologist who Lacks a Soul', in D. R. Ashmore and L. Jussim (eds), *Self and Identity*, New York and Oxford: Oxford University Press, pp. 160–190.

Hunter, S. T. (ed.) (1988), *The Politics of Islamic Revivalism: Diversity and Unity*, Bloomington: Indiana University Press.

Huntington, S. (1996), *The Clash of Civilizations*, New York: Simon and Schuster.

Ibn Hazm al-Andalusi, (1986), *An-Nasikh wal-Mansukh*, Beirut: Dar al-Kotob al-'Elmeyah.

Ingold, T. (1992), 'Culture and the Perception of the Environment, in E. Croll and D. Parkin (eds), *Bush Base: Forest Farm*, London: Routledge, pp. 14–32.

—— (1993), 'Globe and Spheres: The Typology of Environmentalism', in K. Milton (ed.), *Environmentalism: The View from Anthropology*, London and New York: Routledge pp. 31–42.

—— (1996), 'Against the Motion' in T. Ingold (ed.), *Key Debates in Anthropology*, London: Routledge, pp. 112–18.

Jacobson, J. (1998), *Islam in Transition: Religion and Identity among British Pakistani Youth*, London and New York: Routledge.

James, W. (1890), *Principles of Psychology*, New York: Holt.

Johnson, J. T. (1997), *The Holy War: Idea in Western and Islamic Traditions*, Pennsylvania: The Pennsylvania State University.

Kant, I. (1781/1990), *Critique of Pure Reason*, Buffalo: Prometheus.

Katz, J. (1982), *From Prejudice to Destruction: anti-Semitism, 1700–1933*, Cambridge: Harvard University Press.

Kelsay, J. and Johnson, J. T. (eds.) (1991), *Just War and Jihad*, New York: Greenwood Press.

Kepel, G. (1997), *Allah in the West. Islamic Movements in America and Europe*, Cambridge: Polity Press.

—— (2002), *Jihad: The Trial of Political Islam* London: I. B. Tauris.

—— (2004), *The War for the Muslims. Islam and the West*, Cambridge, MA: Belknap Harvard.

Khadduri, M. (2002), *The Islamic Law of Nations*, Baltimore: Johns Hopkins University Press.

Khan, M. M. (1995), *The Translation of the Meanings of Summarized Sahih Al-Bukhari: Arabic-English*, Riyadh, Saudi Arabia: Maktaba Dar us-Salam.

Khan, Z. (2000), 'Muslim Presence in Europe: The British Dimension–Identity, Integration and Community Activism', *Current Sociology* 48 (4): 29–43.

Khellil, M. (1991), *L'integration des maghrébins en France*, Paris: Presses Universitaires de France.

Kitayama, S. Markus, H. and Liberman, C. (1995), 'The Collective Construction of the Self Esteem; Implication for Culture, Self and Emotion', in J. A. Russell, J. M. Fernández-Dols, J. M. A. S. R. Manstead and J. C. Wellenkamp (eds), *Everyday Conceptions of Emotion: An Introduction to the Psychology, Anthropology, and Linguistics of Emotion*, Dordrecht, Holland: Kluwer Academic, pp. 1–15.

Klug, B. (2003), 'The Collective Jew: Israel and the New Antisemitism' *Patterns of Prejudice* 37 (2): 117–38.

Knott, K. and Khokher, S. (1993), 'Religion and Identity among Young Muslim Women in Bradford', *New Community* 19 (4): 593–610.

Kolocotronis, J. (1990), *Islamic Jihad: An Historical Perspective*, Indianapolis: American Trust Publications.

Kondo, D. K. (1990), *Crafting Selves: Power, Gender, and Discourses of Identity in a Japanese Workplace*, Chicago: University of Chicago Press.

Kraidy, M. M. (2002), 'Arab Satellite Television between Regionalization and Globalization', *Global Media Journal* 1 (1): 1–15.

Kramer, M. (1996), *Arab Awakening and Islamic Revival: The Politics of Ideas in the Middle East*, New Brunswick, NJ: Transaction Publishers.

—— (1998), 'The Salience of Islamic Antisemitism', www.ict.org.il/articles/

Kressel, N. (2004), 'The Urgent Need to Study Islamic anti-Semitism', *The Chronicle Review*, http//chronicle.com/free/v50/i27/27b01401.htm (accessed: 31 May 2004).

Lacoste-Dujardin, C. (2000), 'Maghribi families in France' in J. Freedman and C. Tarr (eds), *Women, Immigration and Identities in France*, Oxford: Berg, pp. 57–69.

Langmuir, G. I. (1990a), *History, Religion, and Anti-Semitism*, Berkeley: University of California Press.

—— (1990b), *Toward a Definition of Antisemitism*, Berkeley: University of California Press.

Lepoutre, D. (1997), *Coeur de banlieue*, Paris: Editions Odile Jacob.

Lewis, B. (1986), *Semites and anti-Semites: and Inquiry into Conflict and Prejudice*, London: Weidenfeld & Nicolson.

—— (1988), *The Political Language of Islam*, Chicago: University of Chicago Press.

—— (1993), *Islam and the West*, New York: Oxford University Press.

—— (2000), *What Went Wrong? The Clash between Islam and Modernity in the Middle East*, London: Weidenfeld & Nicolson.

—— (2003), *The Crisis of Islam: Holy War and Unholy Terror*, New York: The Modern Library.

—— and Schnapper, D. (eds) (1994), *Muslims in Europe*, London: Pinter.

Locke, J. (1694/1959), *An Essay Concerning Human Understanding*, New York: Dover.

Lustiger-Thaler, H. (1994), 'Community and Social Practices: The Contingency of Everyday Life', in V. Amit-talai and H. Lustiger-Thaler (eds), *Urban Lives: Fragmentation and Resistance*, New York: McClelland & Stewart Inc., pp. 20–44.

Lutz, H. (1991), *Migrant Women of 'Islamic Background': Images and Self-Images*, Amsterdam: MERA.

Lyons, M. C. (1982), *Saladin: The Politics and the Holy War*, Cambridge: Cambridge University Press.

Mabry, T. J. (1998), 'Modernization Nationalism and Islam: An Examination of Ernest Gellner's Writing on Muslim Society with Reference to Indonesia and Malaysia', *Ethnic and Racial Studies* 21(1): 65–87.

Macfarlane, A. (1977), 'History, Anthropology, and the Study of Communities', *Social History* 5: 631–52.

Maffesoli, M. (1996), *The Time of the Tribes*, London: Sage.

Manço, A. (1999), *Intégration et identiés*, Paris: DeBoeck Université.

Mandel, R. (1996), 'A Place of Their Own: Contesting Spaces and Defining Places in Berlin's Migrant Community' in B. D. Metcalf (ed.), *Making Muslim Space in Northern America and Europe*, Berkeley: California University Press, pp. 147–66; available at http://ark.cdlib.org/ark:/13030/ft2s2004p0.

Manirujjamana, M. (1999), *The Islamic Theory of Jihad and the International System*, Dhaka: Bangladesh Institute of Islamic Thought.

Markus, H. R. and Kitayama, S. (1991), 'Culture and the Self: Implications for Cognition, Emotion, and Motivation', *Psychological Review* 98: 224–253.

Marranci, G. (2000a), 'La Musique Raï: Entre Métissage et World Music Moderne', *Cahiers de musiques traditionnelles* 13: 137–150.

—— (2000b), 'A complex Identity and its Musical Representation: Beurs and Raï Music in Paris', *Music & Anthropology* no. 5, http://www.muspe.unibo.it/period/ma (accessed 21 November 2005).

—— (2003a), 'Pop-Raï: From Local Tradition to Globalisation', in G. Plastino (ed.), *Mediterranean Mosaic*, London and New York: Routledge, pp. 101–20.

—— (2003b), 'The Adhan among the Bells: Studying Muslim Identity in Northern Ireland', PhD Thesis, Belfast: The Queen's University of Belfast.

—— (2003c),'"We Speak English" Language and Identity Processes in Northern Ireland's Muslim Community', *Ethnologist* 25 (2): 59–77.

—— (2004a) 'Multiculturalism, Islam, and the Clash of Civilization Theory: Rethinking Islamophobia', *Culture and Religion* 5 (1): 107–19.

—— (2004b), 'South Asian Muslims in Northern Ireland: Their Islamic Identity, and the Aftermath of 11th of September', in A. Tahir (ed.), *South Asian Muslims in Britain, Post September 11th*, London: Zed Books, pp. 222–34.

Marty, M. E. and Scott Appleby, R. (eds) (1991), *Fundamentalisms Observed*, Chicago: University of Chicago Press.

—— (1993a), *Fundamentalisms and Society*, Chicago: University of Chicago Press.

—— (1993b), *Fundamentalisms and the State*, Chicago: University of Chicago Press.

—— (1994), *Accounting for Fundamentalisms*, Chicago: University of Chicago Press.

—— (1995), *Fundamentalisms Comprehended*, Chicago: University of Chicago Press.

McAdams, D. (1997), 'The Case for Unity in the (Post)Modern Self', in R. Ashmore and L. Jussim (eds), *Self and Identity*, New York: Cambridge University Press, pp. 46–78.

McCall, G. and Simmons, J. (1978), *Identities and Interactions*, New York: Free Press.

McRobbie, A. (1991), *Feminism and Youth Culture*, London: Macmillan.

Mead, G. H. (1934), *Mind, Self, and Society*, Chicago: University of Chicago Press.

Mernissi, F. (1975), *Beyond the Veil: Male–Female Dynamics in a Modern Muslim Society*, New York: Schenkman Publishing Company.

Metcalf, B. D. (ed.), (1996), *Making Muslim Space in Northern America and Europe*, Berkley: California University Press

Milton, K. (2002), *Loving Nature*, London: Routledge.

—— and Svasek, M. (eds) (2005), *Mixed Emotions: Anthropological Studies of Feelings*, Oxford: Berg.

Milton-Edwards, B. (2002), 'Researching the Radical. The Quest for a New Perspective' in H. Donnan (ed.), *Interpreting Islam*, London: Sage, pp. 32–50.

Mirza, K. (1989), 'The Silent Cry: Second Generation Bradford Muslim Women Speak', Research Papers: Muslim in Europe, No 43, Birmingham: CISC, Selly Oak Colleges.

Moore, N. (2002), 'Representation of Islam in the Language of Law: Some Recent

U. S. Cases', in Y. Y. Haddad (ed.), *Muslims in the West: from Sojourners to Citizens*, Oxford New York: Oxford University Press, pp. 187–205.

Mozzo-Counil, F. (1994), *Femmes maghrébines en France*, Paris: Chronique Social.

Murphy, M. (1983), 'Emotional Confrontations between Sevillano Fathers and Sons', *American Ethnologist* 10: 650–64.

Nielsen, J. S. (1985), *Muslims in Britain: An Annotated Bibliography 1960–84*, Coventry: University of Warwick, Centre for Research in Ethnic Relations.

—— (1992), *Muslims in Western Europe*, Edinburgh: Edinburgh University Press.

—— (2000), 'Muslim in Britain', in H. Coward, J. R. Hinnels and R. B. Williams (eds), *The South Asian Religious Diaspora in Britain, Canada, and the United States*, New York: State University of New York Press, pp. 109–26.

Nisbet, E. C., Nisbet, M. C. Scheufele, D. A. Shanahan, J. E. (2004), 'Public Diplomacy, Television News, and Muslim Opinion', *The Harvard International Journal of Press/Politics* 9 (2): 11–37.

Nonneman, G., Niblock, T. and Szajkowski, B. (eds) (1997), *Muslim Communities in the New Europe*, Reading: Ithaca Press.

Noorani, A. G. (2002), *Islam and Jihad: Prejudice Versus Reality*, London: Zed Books.

Obeyesekere, G. (1981), *Medusa's Hair: An Essay on Personal Symbols and Religious Experience*, Chicago: Chicago University Press.

Olwig, K. F. (2002), 'The Ethnographic Field Revisited. Towards a Study of Common and not so Common Fields of Belonging', in V. Amit (ed.), *Realizing Community*, New York: Routledge, pp. 106–24.

Patai, R. (1973), *The Arab Mind*, New York: Scribner.

Pels, T. (2000), 'Muslim Families from Morocco in the Netherlands: Gender Dynamics and Father's Roles in a Context of Change', *Current Sociology* 48 (4): 75–93.

Peristiany, J. G. (1965), *Honour and Shame: The Values of Mediterranean Societies*, London: Weindenfeld and Nicolson.

Peters, R. (1985), *The Jihad in Classical and Modern Times*, Princeton, N. J: Markus.

—— (1996), *Jihad in the Classical and Modern Islam*, Princeton: Markus Wiener Publishers.

Pipes, D. (1981), 'The Politics of Muslims Anti-Semitism', www.danielpipes.org/article/161 (accessed: 8 June 2004).

—— (1983), *In The Path of God: Islam and Political Power*, New York: Basic Books.

—— (1997), 'The New Anti-Semitism', www.danielpipes.org/article/288 (accessed: 25 November 2005).

Pirandello, L. (1927/1987), *Uno, Nessuno, Centomila*, Milan: Rizzoli.

Piscatori, J. P. (ed.) (1983), *Islam in the Political Process*, Cambridge: Cambridge University Press.

—— (ed.) (1991), *Islamic Fundamentalism and the Gulf Crisis*, Chicago: Fundamentalism Project, American Academy of Arts and Sciences.

Poliakov, L. (1993), 'L'antisémitisme est-il un racisme?' in M. Wieviorka (ed.), *Racisme et modernité*, Paris: Découverte, pp. 82–4.

Pruthi, R. K. (ed.) (2002), *Encyclopaedia of Jihad*, New Delhi: Anmol.

Qureshi, K. and Moores, S. (1999), 'Identity Remix: Tradition and Translation in the Lives of Young Pakistani Scots', *European Journal of Cultural Studies* 2 (3): 311–30.

Rapport, N. (1993), *Diverse World-Views in an English Village*, Edinburgh: Edinburgh University Press.

—— and Dawson, A. (eds) (1998), *Migrants of Identity*, London: Berg.

—— and Overing, J. (2000), *Social and Cultural Anthropology: The Key Concepts*, London: Routledge.

Rashid, H. (2002a), *Jihad: The Rise of Militant Islam in Central Asia*, London: Yale University Press.

—— (2002b), *Taliban: Islam, Oil and the New Great Game in Central Asia*, London: I. B. Tauris.

Rattu, K. K. (2002), *Jihad and Terrorism*, Jaipur, India: Book Enclave.

Reguer, S. (2000), 'Judaism in the Muslim World' in J. Neusner and A. J. Every-Peck (eds), *The Blackwell Companion to Judaism*, London: Blackwell Publishers, pp. 131–41.

Rex, J. (1998), 'The Urban Sociology of Religion and Islam in Birmingham', in T. Gerholm and Y. G. Lithman (eds.), *The New Islamic Presence in Western Europe*, London: Mansell Publishing, 78–87.

Roald, S. A. (2001), *Women in Islam: The Western Experience*, London and New York: Routledge.

—— (2002), 'From "People's Home" to "Multiculturalism": Muslims in Sweden', in Y. Y. Haddad (ed.), *Muslims in the West: From Sojourners to Citizens*, Oxford and New York: Oxford University Press, pp. 101–20.

Robison, A. (2001), *Bin Laden: Behind the Mask of the Terrorist*, Edinburgh: Mainstream.

Rosaldo, M. Z. (1984), 'Toward an Anthropology of Self and Feeling' in R. A. Shweder and R. A. LeVine (eds), *Culture Theory: Essays on Mind, Self, and Emotion*, Cambridge: Cambridge University Press, pp. 137–57.

Roy, O. (1994), *The Failure of Political Islam*, Cambridge, MA: Harvard University Press.

Sabbah, A. F. (1984), *Women in the Muslim Unconscious*, New York: Pergamon Press.

Sadowski, Y. (1993), 'The New Orientalism and the Democracy Debate', *Middle East Report* 183: 14–21.

Said, E. (1978), *Orientalism*, New York: Pantheon Books.

Salih, R. (2000), 'Shifting Boundaries of Self and Other: Moroccan Migrant Women in Italy', *The European Journal of Women's Studies* 7 (3): 321–35.

—— (2001), 'Moroccan Migrant Women: Transnationalism, Nation-States and Gender', *Journal of Ethnic and Migration Studies* 27 (4): 655–71.

Salla, M. E. (1997), 'Political Islam and the West: A New Cold War or Convergence?', *Third World Quarterly* 18(4): 729–42.

Sanchez, J. J. (2002), *Al-Qaeda and Jihadi Movements Worldwide*, Seattle: Reference Corporation.

Sayyid, B. S. (1997), *A Fundamental Fear: Eurocentrism and the Emergence of Islamism*, London and New York: Zed Books.

Schechter, D. (2003), *Media Wars: News at a Time of Terror: Dissecting Media Coverage after 9/11*, Lanham, MD: Rowman & Littlefield.

Scheler, M. (1954) *The Nature of Sympathy*, London: Routledge.

Shalinsky, A. C. (1993), 'Women's Roles in the Afghanistan Jihad', *International Journal of Middle East Studies* 25 (4): 661–75.

Shankland, D. (2003), *The Alevis in Turkey*, London and New York: Routledge Curzon.

Shaw, A. (1998), *A Pakistani Community in Britain*, Oxford: Blackwell.

Smith, N. D. (1996), 'The Social Construction of Enemies; Jews and the Representation of Evil', *Sociological Theory* 14 (3): 203–40.

Smith, R. (1999), 'Reflection on Migration, The State and the Construction, Durability and Newness of Translational Life', in L. Pries, (ed.), *Migration and Transnational Social Space*, Aldershot: Ashgate, pp. 187–219.

Sobhy as-Saleh, (1983), *Mabaheth Fi 'Ulum al-Qur'an*, Beirut: Dar al-'Ilm Lel-Malayee.

Sökefeld, M. (1999), 'Debating Self, Identity, Cultural Anthropology', *Current Anthropology*, 40(4): 417–47.

Souilimas, N. G. (2000), *Des 'beurettes' aux descendantes d'immigrants nord-africains*, Paris: Editions Grasset.

Stewart, F. H. (1994), *Honor*, Chicago: University of Chicago Press.

Strathern, M. (1982), 'The Village as an Idea: Constructs of Village-Ness in Elmond Essex', in A. P. Cohen (ed.), *Belonging: Identity and Social Organization in British Rural Cultures*, Manchester: Manchester University Press, pp. 247–77.

Straub, J. (2002), 'Personal and Collective Identity: A Conceptual Analysis', in H. Friese (ed.), *Identities: Time, Difference, and Boundaries*, Oxford and New York: Berghahn Books, pp. 57–75.

Strauss, A. (1959), *Mirrors and Masks: The Search for Identity*, Glencoe, IL: Free Press.

Stryker, S. and Serpe, T. (1994), 'Identity Salience and Psychological Centrality: Equivalent, Overlapping, or Complementary Concepts', *Social Psychological Quarterly* 51: 16–35.

Tajfel, H. (1979), 'Individuals and Groups in Social Psychology', *British Journal of Social and Clinical Psychology*, 18: 183–90.

—— and Turner, J. C. (1986), 'The Social Identity Theory of Intergroup Behaviour', in S. Worchel and W. G. Austin (eds), *The Psychology of Intergroup Relations*, Chicago: Nelson-Hall, pp. 7–24.

Taylor, P. M. (1992), *War and the Media*, Manchester: Manchester University Press.

Thoits, P. A. and Virshup, L. K. (1997), 'Me's and We's, Forms and Functions of Social Identities', in D. R. Ashmore and L. Jussim (eds), *Self and Identity*, New York and Oxford: Oxford University Press, pp. 106–36.

Thornton, S. (1995), *Club Culture*, Oxford: Polity.

Timmerman, C. (2000), 'Muslim Women and Nationalism: The Power of the Image', *Current Sociology* 48 (4): 15–27.

Tribalat, M. (1995), *Faire France*, Paris: La Découvert.

Tuastad, D. (2003), 'Neo-Orientalism and the New Barbarism Thesis: Aspects of Symbolic Violence in the Middle East Conflict(s)', *Third World Quarterly* 24 (4): 591–9.

Turner, J. C. (1999), 'Some Current Issues in Research on Social Identity and Self-Categorization Theories', in N. Ellemers, R. Spears and B. Doosje (eds.), *Social Identity*, Oxford: Blackwell Publishers, pp. 6–34.

—— and Brown, R. (1978), 'Social Status, Cognitive Alternatives and Intergroup Relations', in H. Tajfel (ed.), *Differentiation between Social Groups: Studies in the Social Psychology of Intergroup Relations*, London: Academic Press, pp. 201–34.

——, Hogg, C. M. A. Oakes, J. P. Reicher, S. D. and Blackwell, M. S. (eds) (1987), *Rediscovering the Social Group: A Self-Categorization Theory*, Oxford: Basil Blackwell.

Turner, V. W. (1967), *The Forest of Symbols: Aspects of Ndembu Ritual*, Ithaca: Cornell University Press.

—— (1969), *The Ritual Process: Structure and Anti-Structure*, Chicago: Aldine.

Varisco, M. D. (2005), *Islam Obscured: The Rhetoric of Anthropological Representation*, Basingstoke and New York: Palgrave Macmillan.

Vertovec, S. (2001), 'Transnationalism and Identity', *Journal of Ethnic and Migration Studies* 27 (4): 537–582.

—— (2002), 'Islamophobia and Muslim Recognition in Britain', in Y. Y. Haddad (ed.), *Muslims in the West: From Sojourners to Citizens*, New York: Oxford University Press, pp. 19–35.

Watt, M. (1968), *Islamic Political Thought*, Edinburgh: Edinburgh University Press.

Welsch, W. (1990), 'Identität im Übergang', in W. Welsch (ed.), *Ästhetisches Denken*, Reclam: Stuttgart, pp. 168–200.

Werbner, P. (1994), 'Diaspora and Millennium: British Pakistani Global-Local Fabulations of the Gulf War' in S. Ahmed and H. Donnan (eds), *Islam, Globalization and Postmodernity*, London and New York: Routledge, pp. 213–36.

—— (2002), *Imagined Diaspora, among Manchester Muslims*, Oxford: James Curry.

—— and Basu, H. (eds) (1998), *Embodying Charisma*, London and New York: Routledge.

Whittaker, E. (1992), 'The Birth of the Anthropological Self and its Career', *Ethos* 20: 191–219.

Wikan, U. (1984), 'Shame and Honour: A Contestable Pair', *Man* 19: 635–52.

Wistrich, R. (2002), *Muslim Anti-Semitism: Clear and Present Danger*, New York: The American Jewish Committee. (Also available from www.ajc.org)

Ye'or, B. (1978), *Dhimmi People: Oppressed Nations*, Genève: World Organization of Jews from Arab Countries.

—— (1984), *The Dhimmi: Jews and Christians Under Islam*, London: Associated University Presses.

—— (1991), *The Decline of Eastern Christianity Under Islam: From Jihad to Dhimmitude*, Paris: Cerf.

—— (2002), *Islam and Dhimmitude: Where Civilizations Collide*, Madison, NJ: Fairleigh Dickinson University Press.

—— (2004), 'Eurabia and Euro-Arab Antisemitism', http://www.frontpagemag.com/Articles/ReadArticle.asp?ID=12857 (accessed 25 November 2005).

Yusuf, A. A. (1983), *The Holy Qur'an, Text, Translation and Commentary*, Brentwood: Amana.

Index

Interviewees